THE PICTURE BOOK OF KNOWLEDGE

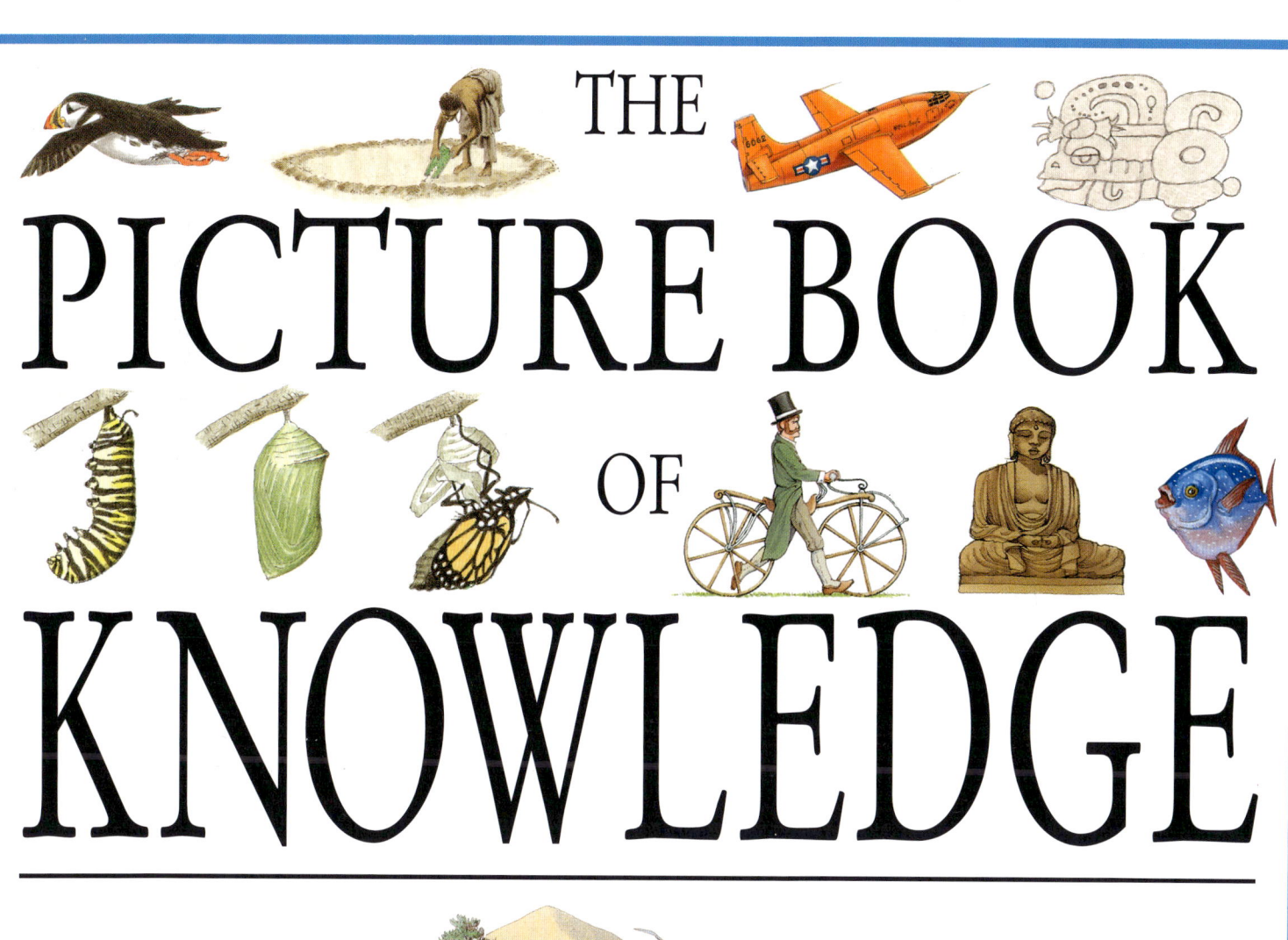

orpheus

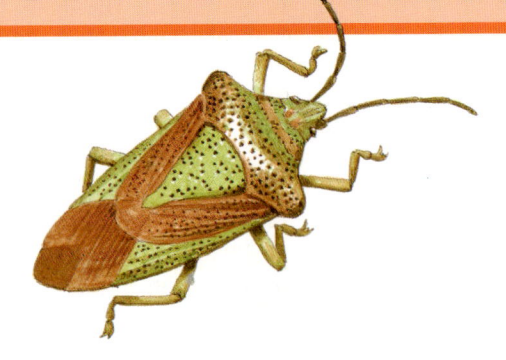

Created and produced by Nicholas Harris,
Joanna Turner and Claire Aston,
Orpheus Books Ltd

Illustrators Giuliano Fornari *(team co-ordinator)*,
Susanna Addario, Ferrucchio Cucchiarini,
Alessandro Rabatti, Claudia Saraceni, Ivan Stalio,
Thomas Trojer

Consultants Steve Parker, Andrew Sherratt

Revised edition published in 2002 by Orpheus
Books Ltd, 2 Church Green, Witney, Oxon.

Copyright © 2002 Orpheus Books Ltd

All rights reserved. No part of this book may be
reproduced, stored in a retrieval system, or
transmitted in any form or by any means,
electronic, mechanical, photocopying, recording or
otherwise, without the prior written permission of
the copyright owner.

ISBN 1 901323 02 1

A CIP record for this book is available from the
British Library.

Printed and bound in Italy

CONTENTS

YOUNG SCIENTIST

4	Stars and Galaxies
6	Solar System
8	Earth and Moon
10	Rocks and Fossils
12	Seasons and Climates
14	Weather
16	Time
18	Light and Sound
20	Forces and Matter
22	Electricity

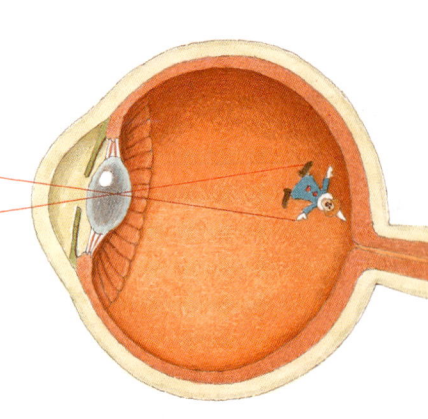

THE HUMAN BODY

24	Digestion
26	The Brain
28	The Skeleton

THE NATURAL WORLD

30	Prehistoric Life
32	Insects
34	Fish
36	Reptiles and Amphibians
38	Birds
40	Mammals (1)
42	Mammals (2)
44	Plants
46	Trees

THE WORLD ABOUT US

- 48 Polar Lands
- 50 Woodlands
- 52 Grasslands
- 54 Deserts
- 56 Rainforests
- 58 Mountains
- 60 Rivers
- 62 Seashore
- 64 Oceans

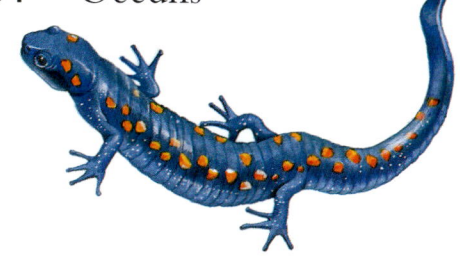

WORLD NATIONS

- 66 Europe
- 68 Asia
- 70 Oceania
- 72 North America
- 74 South America
- 76 Africa

PEOPLE

- 78 Homes around the World
- 80 Farming
- 82 Buildings and Bridges
- 84 Languages and Writing
- 86 Musical Instruments
- 88 Television
- 90 Religions
- 92 Sports

THE STORY OF TRANSPORT

- 94 Ships
- 96 Trains
- 98 Road Transport
- 100 Aircraft
- 102 Space Travel

PAST WORLDS

- 104 Early People
- 106 Ancient Egypt
- 108 Ancient Greece
- 110 The Romans
- 112 Ancient China
- 114 Ancient America
- 116 Great Empires
- 118 Middle Ages
- 120 Explorers

- 122 Index

STARS AND GALAXIES

STARS are giant, spinning balls of hot, glowing gas. They are like enormous power stations, producing vast amounts of energy as they shine for billions of years. Our local star, the Sun, is "only" 150 million kilometres from Earth. Other stars are incredibly far away. Even the next nearest is so distant it takes four years for its light to reach us. Almost certainly, many other stars will, like the Sun, have planets circling around them. On some of those there may be life.

Nearly everything we see in the night sky is part of the Milky Way Galaxy, an enormous spiral-shaped cluster of stars. There are billions of stars in the Galaxy—and billions of galaxies in the Universe. The Universe includes everything there is: space, galaxies, stars, Earth, your home and you, yourself!

The Sun and its planets, including Earth, are on one of the Galaxy's spiral arms.

◀ Some stars have been shining for millions of years. Others have only just begun to do so. New stars are born in gigantic clouds of dust and gas called nebulas. This nebula has a shape just like a horse's head. (The Horsehead Nebula is in the constellation of Orion. It can be seen only by using a telescope.) The dust and gas eventually come together to form incredibly hot, young stars.

The constellation of Orion. The three stars of his belt point downwards towards Sirius, the brightest star in the sky.

YOUNG SCIENTIST

◀ This gigantic spiral of stars, gas and dust revolving in space is our home in the Universe: the Milky Way Galaxy. Our Sun, just one of its many billions of stars, is situated about halfway out from the centre. The faint, misty band that stretches right across the night sky is our side-on view of part of the Galaxy.

STUDYING STARS

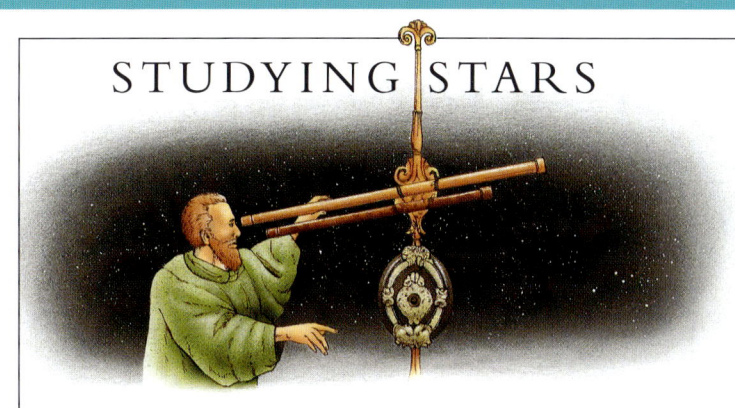

PEOPLE have been studying the night skies since earliest times. The ancient Greeks (see page 108) thought that the Sun and planets all moved around the Earth. In 1543 the Polish astronomer Copernicus suggested that, as we now know, the Earth and planets move around the Sun. In 1609 the Italian Galileo became the first astronomer to use a telescope (above). He saw craters on the Moon and discovered Jupiter's moons. Modern telescopes allow us to see enormous distances. There is even a telescope out in space itself, the Hubble Space Telescope (below). Scientists can receive clear pictures of distant stars from it.

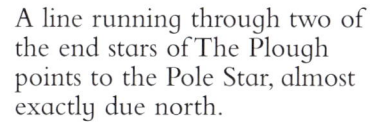

This is the Great Bear constellation. Seven of its brighter stars make up what we call The Plough.

◀▶ Looking up at the night sky, it is easy to spot certain patterns in the stars. Throughout the year, different ones appear and disappear from view. Years ago, astronomers thought that these patterns looked like people and animals from popular legends—a dog, a bull, a centaur, a scorpion and so on. The familiar shapes of these constellations, as they are called, help stargazers to find and name other stars.

A line running through two of the end stars of The Plough points to the Pole Star, almost exactly due north.

SEE ALSO: PAGE 6 SOLAR SYSTEM, PAGE 8 EARTH AND MOON, PAGE 18 LIGHT AND SOUND

SOLAR SYSTEM

OUR SUN is a star. It appears much bigger and brighter than other stars only because it is nearer to us. Circling around, or orbiting, the Sun is its family of nine planets. In order of distance from the Sun, they are: Mercury, Venus, our planet Earth, Mars, Jupiter, Saturn, Uranus, Neptune and Pluto. The Earth takes one year to complete an orbit, but some of the outer planets take many years to do so.

Besides the planets, thousands of small pieces of rock, called asteroids, orbit the Sun. Most lie in a belt between Mars and Jupiter. The Sun, the planets and their moons, asteroids, comets and meteors are all members of the Solar System.

▲ Venus is always covered by thick clouds of sulphuric acid. It has volcanoes, vast plains and deep gorges, but no signs of life.

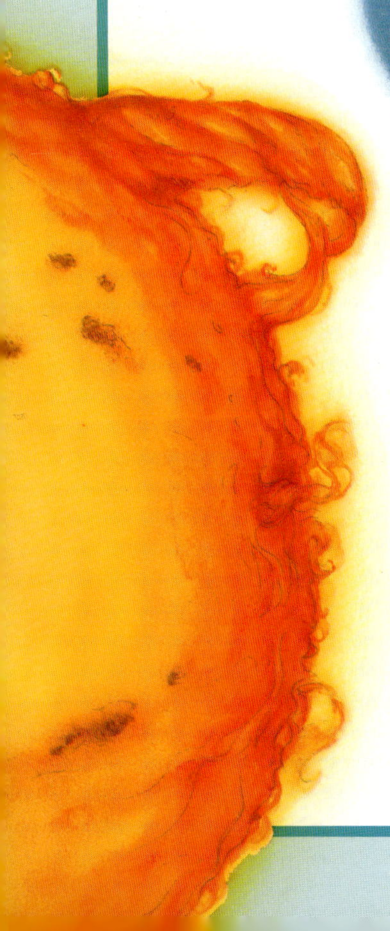

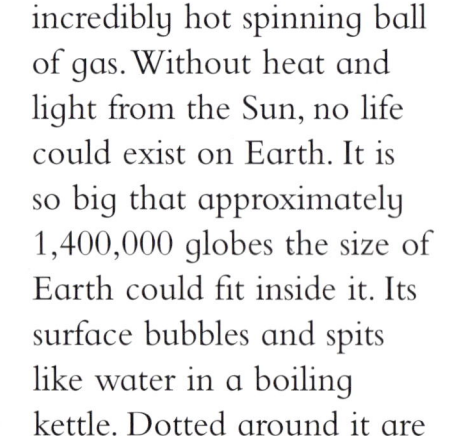

◀ The Sun is a huge, incredibly hot spinning ball of gas. Without heat and light from the Sun, no life could exist on Earth. It is so big that approximately 1,400,000 globes the size of Earth could fit inside it. Its surface bubbles and spits like water in a boiling kettle. Dotted around it are dark patches, called sunspots, that come and go.

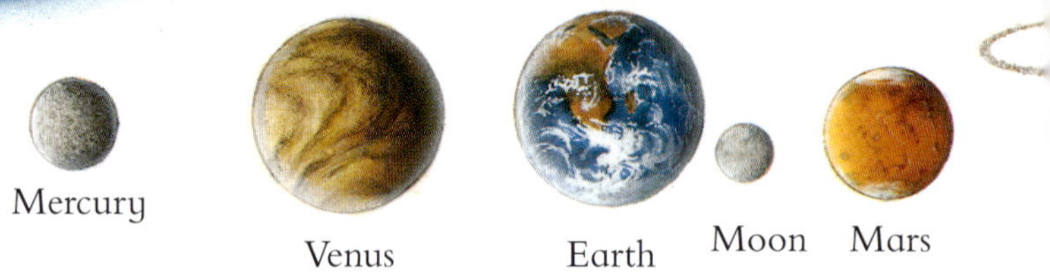

Mercury is very hot where it faces the Sun, but very cold where it faces away. **Diameter:** 4,880 km **Day:** 58.6 days **Year:** 88 days **Average distance from Sun:** 58 million km

The temperature on **Venus** is hotter than molten lead. **Diameter:** 12,109 km **Day:** 243 days **Year:** 225 days **Average distance from Sun:** 108 million km

Earth is our home planet. **Diameter:** 12,761 km **Day:** 24 hours **Year:** 365.26 days **Average distance from Sun:** 149.7 million km **Moons:** 1

Dry riverbeds show that water once flowed on **Mars**. **Diameter:** 6,797 km **Day:** 24.6 hours **Year:** 687 days **Average distance from Sun:** 228 million km **Moons:** 2

▶ Most planets have moons. One of Saturn's moons, Mimas, has a giant crater. Jupiter's Io is covered with volcanoes. Miranda, a moon of Uranus, is scarred by grooves. Neptune's Triton is the coldest world of all.

Io   Mimas

Miranda   Triton

COMETS AND METEORS

COMETS are lumps of dust and ice that hurtle across the Solar System. Comets come from the edge of the Solar System and pass very close to the Sun. As they approach the Sun, two long tails trail behind them. If you are lucky, you may see a comet "hanging" in the night sky.

Dusty pieces sometimes break off comets. We see them as split-second streaks of light. They are called meteors, or shooting stars. Meteorites are fragments of rock that fall through our skies and crash to the ground.

When a comet nears the Sun, some of its ice melts. Gas and dust escape, forming a cloud called a coma. The coma is swept back, forming tails.

Pluto has an odd orbit. Its path is shaped like a squashed oval. For 20 years of its 248-year-long journey, it lies inside Neptune's orbit.

Jupiter

Saturn

Uranus   Neptune

Pluto

THE PLANETS
(not drawn to scale)

Jupiter is the largest planet. Its surface (including the Great Red Spot) is not solid, but consists of swirling gases. Only its core, twice the size of Earth itself, is made of solid rock. Jupiter's largest moons are bigger than Mercury and Pluto.
Diameter: 142,960 km
Day: 9.8 hours **Year:** 11.8 years **Average distance from the Sun:** 779 million km **Moons:** 16

Second in size to Jupiter, **Saturn** is also a "gas giant". It is the outermost planet visible with the naked eye. It spins very quickly and bulges in its middle. Saturn's amazing rings are made up from countless blocks of ice and rock.
Diameter: 120,514 km
Day: 10.2 hours **Year:** 29.5 years **Average distance from Sun:** 1,427 million km **Moons:** 18

Uranus, also a gassy planet, has 11 faint rings. Unlike the other planets, it spins on its side.
Diameter: 51,166 km **Day:** 17.2 hours **Year:** 84 years **Average distance from Sun:** 2,869 million km **Moons:** 15

Neptune is streaked with wispy clouds.
Diameter: 49,557 km **Day:** 16.1 hours **Year:** 164.8 years **Average distance from Sun:** 4,496 million km **Moons:** 8

Pluto is the smallest and coldest planet.
Diameter: 2,300 km **Day:** 6.4 days **Year:** 248 years **Average distance from Sun:** 5,900 million km **Moons:** 1

SEE ALSO: PAGE 8 EARTH AND MOON, PAGE 20 FORCES AND MATTER, PAGE 102 SPACE TRAVEL

EARTH AND MOON

ABOUT 4,600 million years ago, our Earth was born. At first, it was a ball of very hot, liquid rock. Then volcanoes started to erupt everywhere. The gases they blasted out surrounded Earth with air and clouds. Rains fell and filled the oceans with water.

Earth has the perfect conditions for life to exist. It is neither too hot nor too cold, and there is also liquid water, which is essential for life. The blanket of air around the Earth, the atmosphere, protects us from the harmful rays of the Sun, but it also lets in warmth.

◀ Many volcanoes are mountains shaped like cones. They have circular openings, called craters, at their summits. If you were to peer over the edge of a crater, you might see a bubbling lake of red-hot melted rock, called lava. When a volcano erupts, lava, rocks, and huge clouds of ash and dust are exploded high into the air. Rivers of lava flow down the volcano's slopes.

(far left) Inside a volcano, melted rock rises up through a cone made of layers of ash and lava.

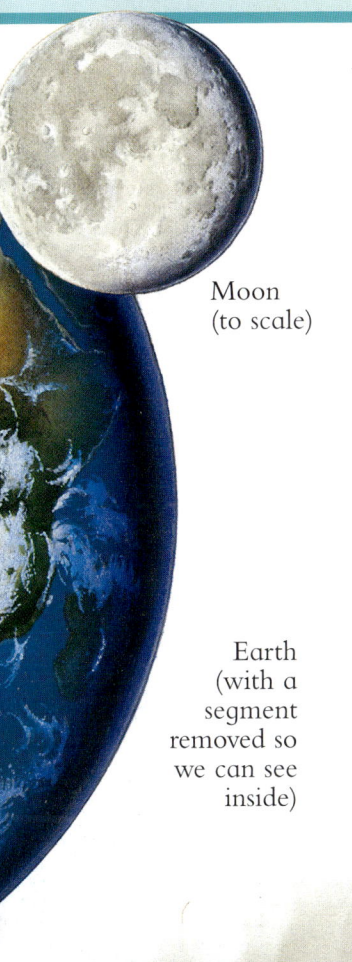

◀ The Earth has several layers inside it. The rocks that make up the continents and the ocean floors form a thin outer layer called the crust. The crust lies above a thick layer of very hot, partly melted rocks, called the mantle. The lava that erupts through volcanoes comes from here. Below the mantle is the liquid metal outer core. The solid inner core, mostly made of iron, is nearly as hot as the surface of the Sun.

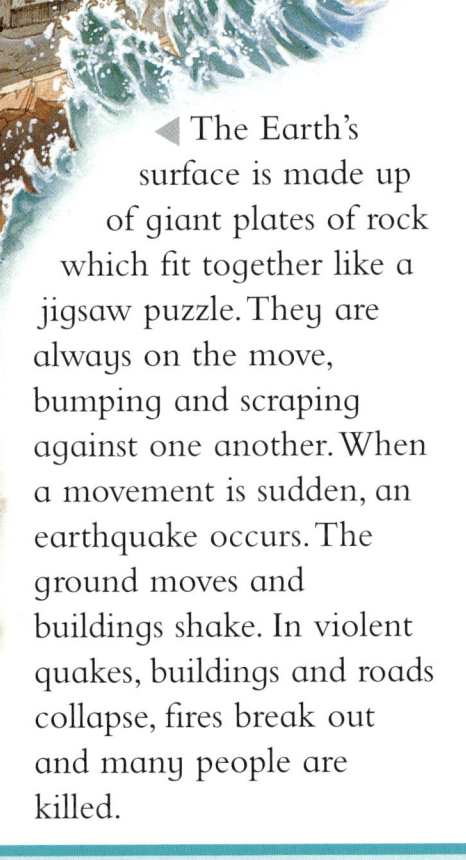

Moon (to scale)

Earth (with a segment removed so we can see inside)

A BARREN WORLD

THE MOON is a ball of rock that travels around our planet Earth. It is much smaller than our planet and, unlike ours, a barren world. No life can exist there because there is no air or water. The surface of the Moon is covered with craters. These are made by pieces of rock, called meteorites, crashing down from space. On a clear night, you can quite easily see the "splash" marks surrounding one of the Moon's craters without the need of a telescope.

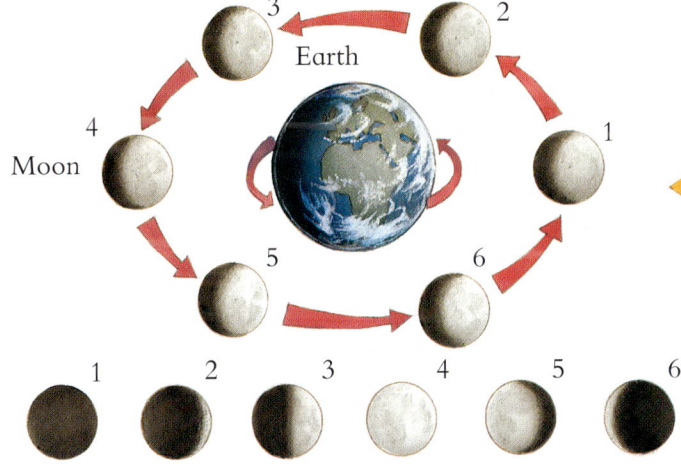

Sun's rays

This is how we see the Moon as it goes round the Earth.

◀ The Earth's surface is made up of giant plates of rock which fit together like a jigsaw puzzle. They are always on the move, bumping and scraping against one another. When a movement is sudden, an earthquake occurs. The ground moves and buildings shake. In violent quakes, buildings and roads collapse, fires break out and many people are killed.

CHANGING SHAPE

THE MOON seems to change shape from one night to the next. This happens because, as it travels around the Earth (taking about 27 days to complete the circle), the same side of it faces us all the time. It is our view of the sunlight on it that changes. When the side facing us is completely turned away from the Sun, we cannot see the Moon at all (1). When it is turned fully towards the Sun, we can see a Full Moon (4).

SEE ALSO: PAGE 6 SOLAR SYSTEM, PAGE 10 ROCKS AND FOSSILS, PAGE 12 SEASONS AND CLIMATES

ROCKS AND FOSSILS

DIG DOWN beneath the soil and in the end you will reach solid rock. Rocks are made of chemical substances called minerals. Minerals are, themselves, made up from combinations of elements *(see page 21)* such as silicon, oxygen, sodium or magnesium, found naturally in the Earth.

There are many different kinds of rock and they can be divided into three groups. Igneous rocks, the first group, result from the cooling of very hot, melted rock that comes from the mantle, deep inside the Earth. Sedimentary rocks, the second group, are made up from fragments of sand, mud or the remains of living creatures compacted together. The third group, the metamorphic rocks, are formed when rocks are changed in some way by great heat or pressure underground.

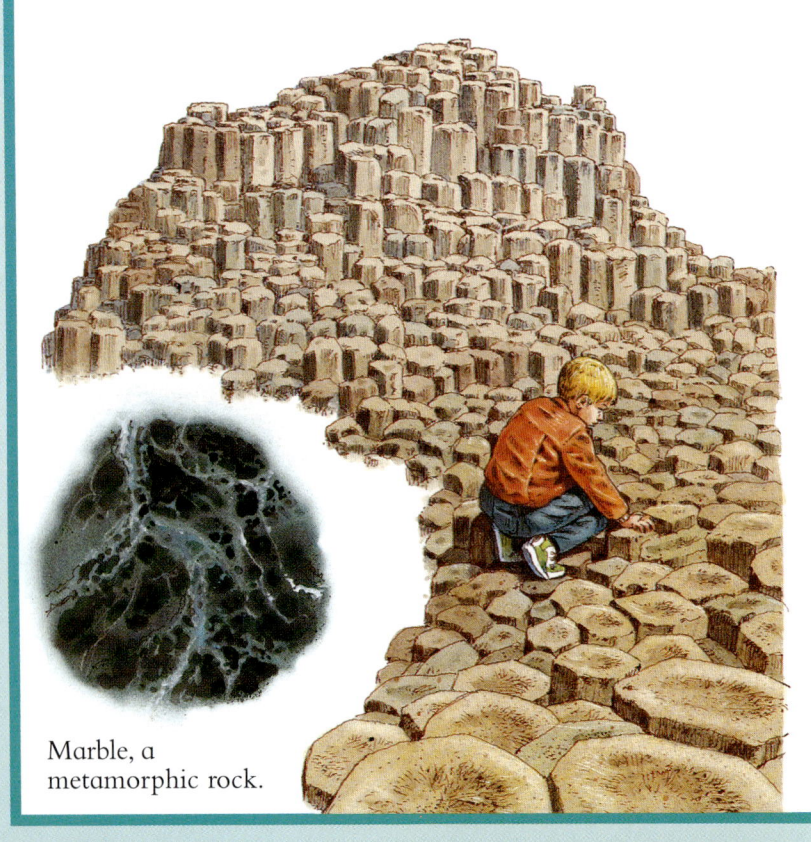

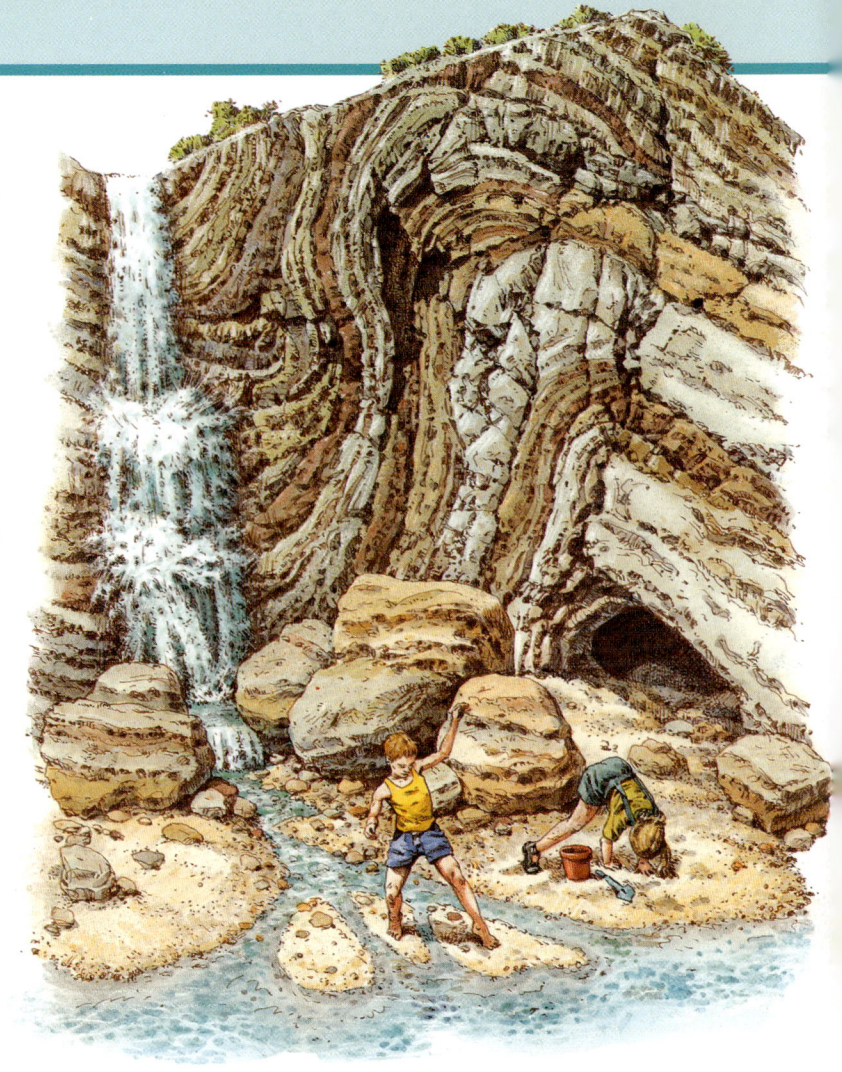

▲ One of the best places to look at rocks is at the seashore. This cliff shows layers of rock all following the same curved shape, known as folds. It takes millions of years for rocks to fold. It happens when the giant plates of rock that make up the Earth's crust *(see page 9)* push against one another. The layers of rock buckle and fold like creases in a blanket on a bed.

◀ Igneous rocks sometimes take on amazing shapes. Here, the melted rock that formed these basalt rocks cooled very slowly and cracked into regular shapes known as crystals.

Marble, a metamorphic rock.

Millions of years ago, swampy forests covered the tropics. As the trees decayed, they formed a thick black soil called peat that later hardened to coal.

SEE ALSO: PAGE 8 EARTH AND MOON, PAGE 20 FORCES AND MATTER, PAGE 30 PREHISTORIC LIFE

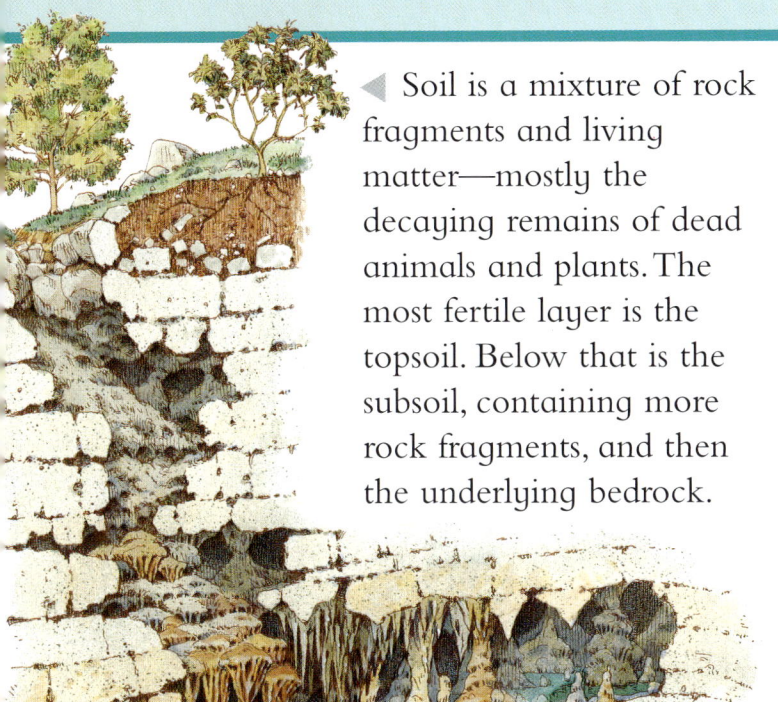

◀ Soil is a mixture of rock fragments and living matter—mostly the decaying remains of dead animals and plants. The most fertile layer is the topsoil. Below that is the subsoil, containing more rock fragments, and then the underlying bedrock.

Today, shafts (vertical tunnels) are made so people can go down to the coal layer and mine it for fuel.

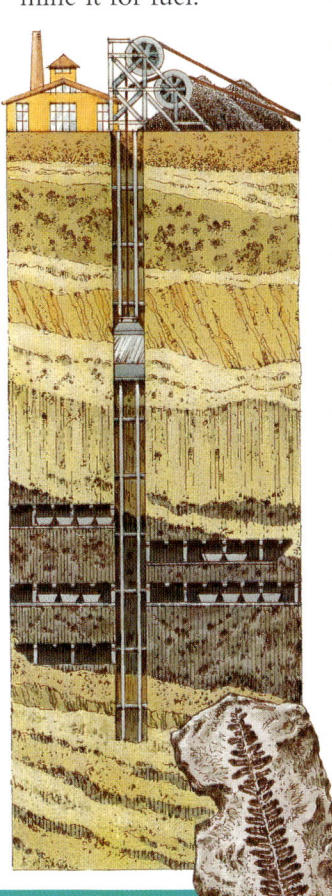

▲ Limestone is a sedimentary rock, made up of the remains of tiny sea creatures that lived millions of years ago. Water that seeps into the cracks in the limestone gradually dissolves it away, hollowing out underground caves. Dripping water containing minerals produces hanging "icicles" of rock called stalactites. Stalagmites, growing up from the cave floor, are formed by splashes from above.

A fossil leaf in coal.

LIFE TURNED TO STONE

Ammonite

Fossilized resin

FOSSILS are the remains of animals or plants that have been preserved in rocks. Sometimes, as in this example of an insect trapped in fossilized resin (a sticky substance found in tree trunks), the whole creature is preserved, soft parts and all. But most fossils, like this ammonite, a prehistoric sea creature with a coiled shell, are of the hard parts such as shell or bone.

After the soft parts have rotted away, the remains of a creature are buried in sand or mud, usually under water. The original shell or bone is dissolved away and replaced by minerals in the water. The sand or mud turns to rock, which holds a fossil of the creature. Another kind of fossil is made when a living thing leaves a mark on its surroundings, such as a footprint, that is preserved in rock.

Fossils can tell us about the story of life millions of years ago because they formed at the same time as the rocks around them.

A fossil of a dinosaur's footprint.

The fossilized skeleton of an ichthyosaur, an ancient sea reptile.

An ichthyosaur as it looked 200 million years ago.

YOUNG SCIENTIST

YOUNG SCIENTIST

SEASONS AND CLIMATES

THE EARTH takes just over 365 days to complete a full circuit, or orbit, around the Sun. It also spins on its own axis (an imaginary line running through it from the North to the South Pole) once every 24 hours. As the Earth spins, it is not perfectly upright, but slightly tilted. This tilt, always in the same direction, gives us the seasons of the year.

When the northern half of the Earth (the northern hemisphere) leans nearer the Sun, it is warmer and the days are longer there: summer has arrived. At the same time, in the southern hemisphere, which is tilted away from the Sun, it is winter. When the northern hemisphere leans away from the Sun, it is winter, while it is summer in the southern hemisphere.

On 21st March it is the equinox. The Sun shines directly overhead at the Equator and everywhere on Earth there are 12 hours of daylight and 12 hours of darkness. In the northern hemisphere, spring begins; in the southern hemisphere, autumn begins.

21ST MARCH

Equator

The Equator is an imaginary line round the widest part of the Earth. It divides the Earth into two halves: the northern and southern hemispheres.

Sun

21ST JUNE
Tropic of Cancer

Earth orbits the Sun at more than 100,000 km/h.

By 21st June the Sun now shines directly overhead at the Tropic of Cancer. In the northern hemisphere, it is the summer solstice. It is winter in the southern hemisphere.

These illustrations show how the changing seasons affect the countryside in countries with a temperate climate (see opposite). Winter brings snow and ice. Deciduous trees have lost their leaves. To survive the cold, some animals sleep through the winter. This is called hibernation.

When spring comes, plants and flowers start to grow again. Leaves on deciduous trees burst into bud. The weather is warmer, and many animals and birds make nests, give birth to their young and search for food for them. Crops sown in the fields are now growing.

SEE ALSO: PAGE 6 SOLAR SYSTEM, PAGE 14 WEATHER, PAGE 16 TIME, PAGE 46 TREES, PAGE 80 FARMING

22ND DECEMBER

The summer solstice arrives in the southern hemisphere on 22nd December when the Sun is overhead at the Tropic of Capricorn. In Australia, people can celebrate Christmas on the beach, while the northern hemisphere is in the grip of winter.

Earth

Tropic of Capricorn

23RD SEPTEMBER

North Pole

Equator

South Pole

On 23rd September, it is the equinox once more as the Sun again shines directly overhead at the Equator. In the northern hemisphere, autumn begins, while the southern hemisphere enjoys the onset of spring.

WORLD CLIMATES

DIFFERENT regions of the world have different patterns of weather: for example, dry summers, mild winters, and so on. These patterns are called climates. Regions with tropical climates lie close to the Equator. They have hot, wet weather all year round. Deserts have hardly any rain. Temperate regions have warm summers and cold (but not too severe) winters. Polar lands and some high mountainous areas are always extremely cold.

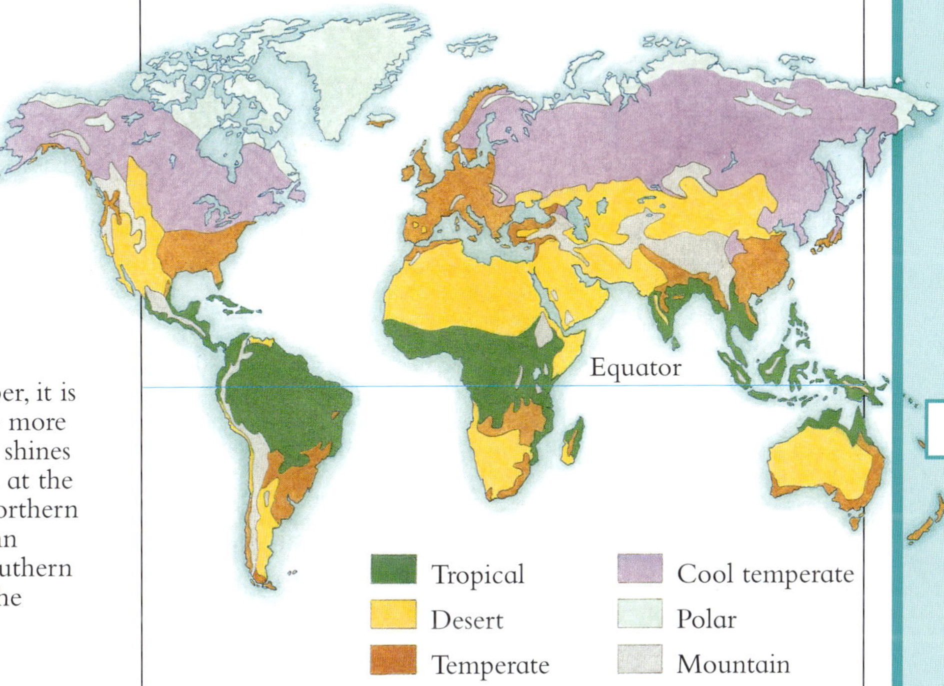

Equator

- ■ Tropical
- ■ Desert
- ■ Temperate
- ■ Cool temperate
- ■ Polar
- ■ Mountain

Summer days are long, sunny and warm. Tree leaves are fully open and their fruits ripen. Farmers work hard to bring in the harvest of crops. Birds that migrated to warmer lands for winter have returned. They feed on the rich variety of insects and fruits.

In the autumn, the leaves on the trees turn brown, yellow or red and fall to the ground. Migrating birds fly off to warmer countries for the winter. Some animals store food and find a warm, dry place to sleep. Farmers plough their fields to prepare the soil for next year's crops.

YOUNG SCIENTIST

Weather

WEATHER is the word we use to describe the conditions of the air in a certain place at a certain time: for example, whether it is raining or snowing, windy or still, hot or cold. The air around the Earth is always on the move. It also contains water vapour, which, when the air is cooled, turns to ice or liquid water and falls to the ground as rain, snow or hail (frozen raindrops).

Weather plays an important part in our lives. For example, without rain, our crops would die, but too much rain can cause floods. It is very useful to be able to predict what the weather has in store for us. To do this, weather forecasters gather together information from satellites *(see page 88)* in space and weather stations.

Moist air may be forced to rise as it crosses high land. The water vapour may then turn to liquid water or ice.

This diagram shows how water is carried from sea to land and back again. It is called the water cycle. Of course, a great deal of rain also falls from the clouds directly back into the sea.

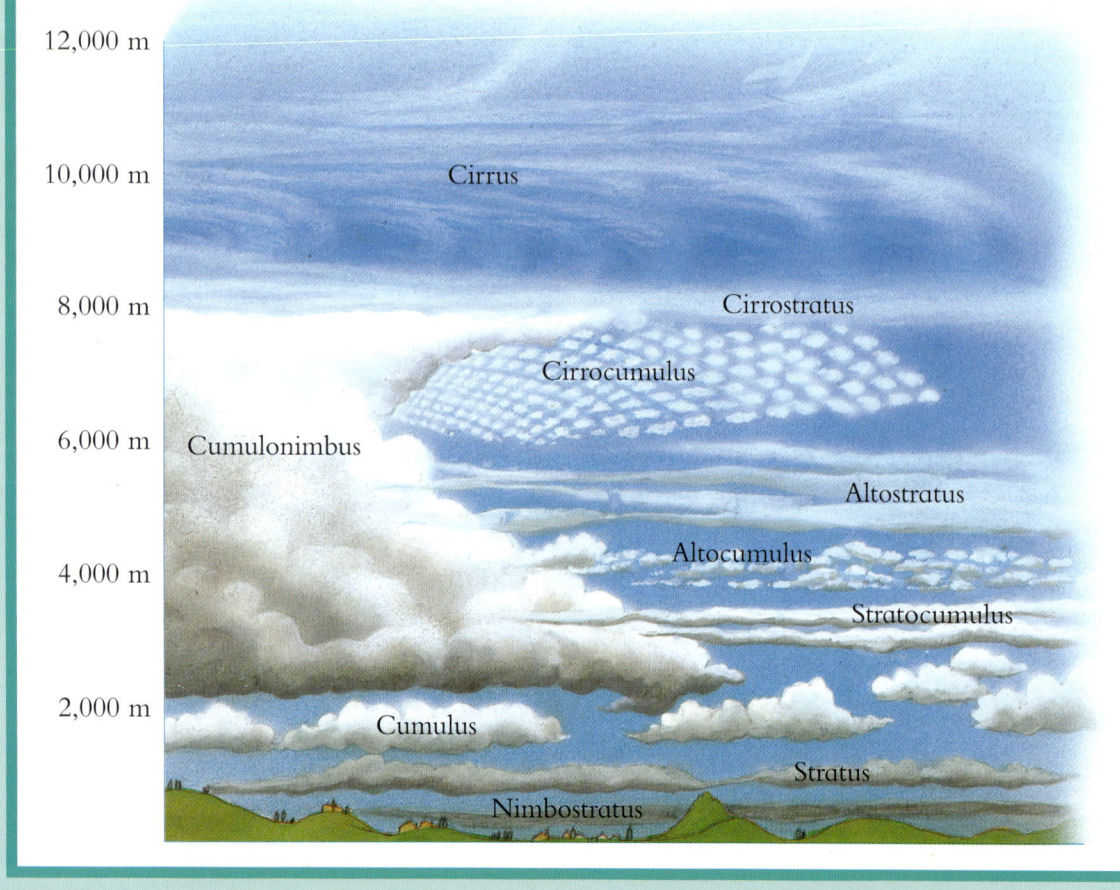

◀ Very high clouds, such as cirrus and cirrostratus, are thin and wispy and contain ice particles. Cirrocumulus clouds form a "mackerel sky", so called because they look like fish scales. Altostratus and altocumulus may signal rain is on the way. Cumulus are the fluffy white clouds we see on a summer's day. Huge, anvil-shaped cumulonimbus clouds threaten storms. Stratus are low clouds that can cover the whole sky, while dark nimbostratus clouds bring rain or snow.

SEE ALSO: PAGE 8 EARTH AND MOON, PAGE 12 SEASONS AND CLIMATES, PAGE 22 ELECTRICITY, PAGE 60 RIVERS

◀ The Sun's heat causes water from the sea, lakes, rivers or the ground itself to evaporate (turn into vapour). Winds carry the moist air to other regions. As the air rises it cools. The water vapour in the air begins to condense (turn back into liquid) around tiny particles in the air, such as sea salt or dust. Millions of these tiny water droplets gather together to form clouds (or fog when close to the ground). In the highest clouds, the water freezes into ice. When the ice or water droplets become too heavy to stay up, they fall as rain, or snow if the air is below freezing. Rivers carry the water that has collected on land back to the sea and the cycle begins again.

At night, the ground cools down faster than the air. Water vapour in the air condenses and soaks everything, even spider's webs, with dew.

If the air is below freezing, the condensed water vapour forms ice crystals. These cover everything in a layer of frost.

STORMS

Tornadoes can suck up cars, buildings and animals, dropping them kilometres away.

TORNADOES are twisting columns of air stretching up from the ground. Winds of up to 500 km/h destroy everything in their path. Hurricanes begin when warm, moist air from the oceans is stirred up into a huge, spinning mass. Strong winds and rain swirl around a calm centre, the "eye" of the storm. Hurricanes can cause serious damage, often ripping up trees and overturning cars.

◀ When warm, moist air rises into the sky and cools very quickly, thunderclouds form. Electricity can be produced inside the cloud as ice and water droplets bump together. This electricity is released as flashes of lightning. The lightning is so hot that it makes the air around it expand quickly, making a sound we call thunder.

Seen under a microscope, no two snowflakes are exactly alike, although they all have six equal sides.

YOUNG SCIENTIST

15

TIME

WHAT is the time? You probably want the answer to this question many times each day. In the modern world it is very important to know what the time is: a great number of everyday events depend on it. Television, trains, air flights, schools and sporting contests must all run on time.

People who lived in Egypt and the Middle East in ancient times also wanted to record time accurately but had no clocks with which to do so. Nevertheless, 5,000 years ago, astronomers from the ancient city of Babylon divided a day (the period from sunrise to sunrise) into 24 hours, each hour into 60 minutes and each minute into 60 seconds. Today, although we have clocks that can measure time to within the tiniest fraction of a second, the ancient Babylonian units of time still survive.

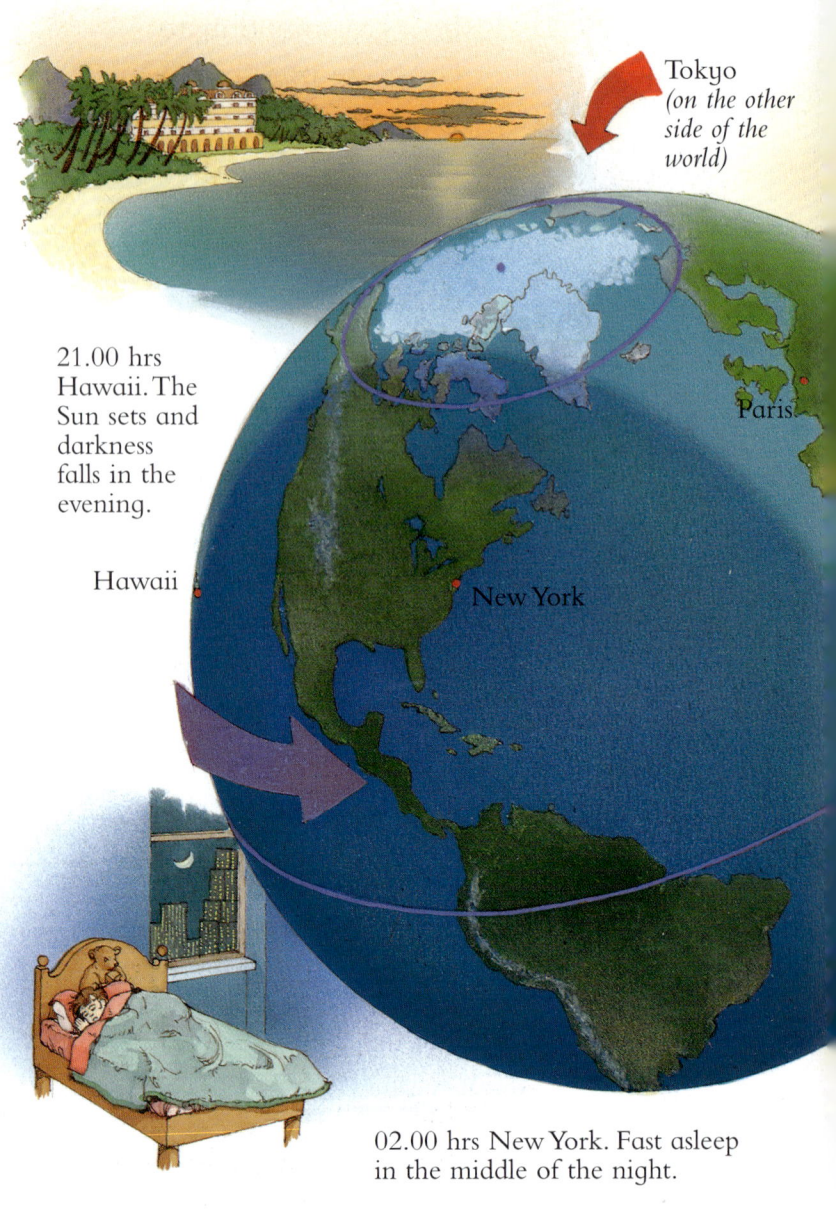

Tokyo (on the other side of the world)

21.00 hrs Hawaii. The Sun sets and darkness falls in the evening.

Hawaii

Paris

New York

02.00 hrs New York. Fast asleep in the middle of the night.

12.00 hrs   18.00 hrs   24.00 hrs   06.00 hrs

◀ We have day when our part of the world faces the Sun and night when it is turned away. Because the Earth is slightly tilted, lands near the Poles face towards the Sun for most of the summer and away from it for much of the winter. Summer days are very long, winter days very short. In northern Scandinavia, the "Land of the Midnight Sun", there is one day, shown here, when the Sun never sets.

SEE ALSO: PAGE 6 SOLAR SYSTEM, PAGE 12 SEASONS, PAGE 20 FORCES AND MATTER, PAGE 106 ANCIENT EGYPT,

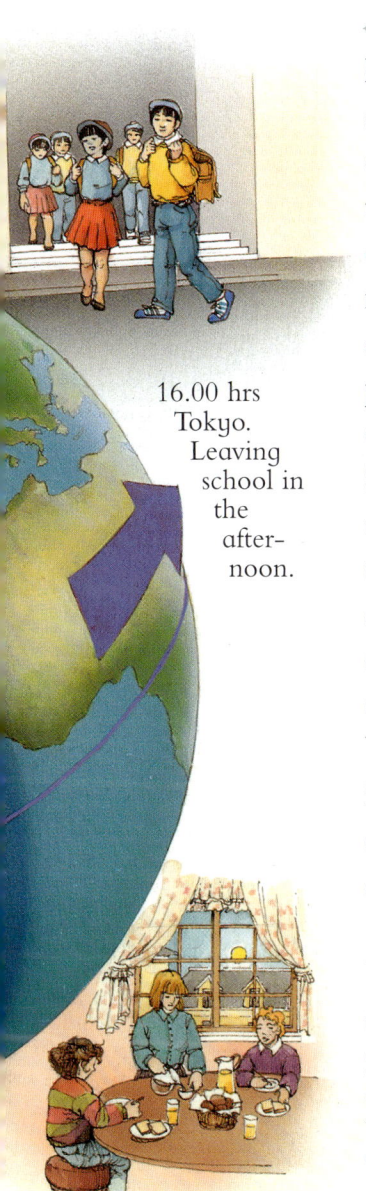

YOUNG SCIENTIST

◀ The Earth takes 24 hours, or one day, to complete one spin. While one half of the Earth is lit up by the Sun, where it is daytime, the other half remains in night-time darkness. Clocks in any part of the world are set to a time according to the Sun's position. This is different from one part of the world to the next. So, at any one moment, clocks around the world tell completely different times. When it is mid-afternoon in Tokyo, Japan, it is evening on the previous day in Hawaii!

16.00 hrs Tokyo. Leaving school in the afternoon.

08.00 hrs Paris. A family has breakfast in the morning.

▼ Built in England more than 4,000 years ago, Stonehenge may have helped people to record the days of the year, like a giant calendar. The Sun always appeared above a particular stone at a certain time of the year.

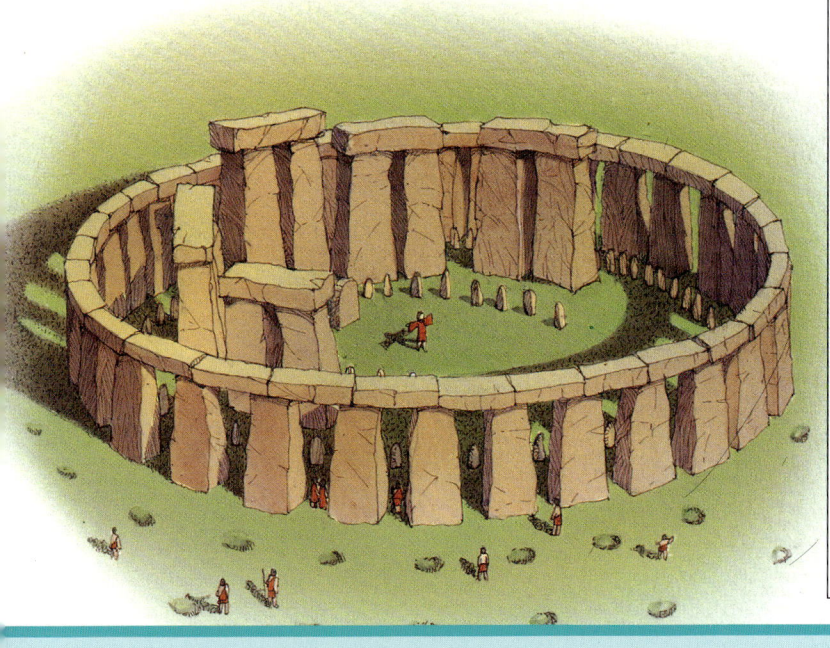

MEASURING TIME

As the Earth turns, the shadow cast by the central pointer of this sundial moves slowly across a dial marked in hours.

THOUSANDS of years ago, in order to tell the time, people simply followed the passing of days and nights and the changing seasons. The simplest clocks, to indicate the passing of hours, were sundials. They were first used in ancient Egypt.

This clock (left) was invented in China more than 1,000 years ago. A waterwheel inside had cups filled with water. It turned when the cups became too heavy, setting off levers and rods that moved the clock mechanism.

Pendulum clocks were the first accurate clocks. A pendulum, a weight hung on a long arm, swings back and forth at regular intervals. In some clocks, the pendulum takes exactly one second for each swing. It is connected by a number of cogs to a heavy weight on a string: this falls gradually, second by second. The force of the gradually falling weight drives the clock.

PAGE 112 ANCIENT CHINA

YOUNG SCIENTIST

LIGHT AND SOUND

LIGHT is a kind of energy *(see page 21)*. It allows us to see things. It travels in straight lines, so there are shadows behind things that stand in its way. Light also travels very fast: about 300,000 kilometres (seven-and-a-half times round the world) per second.

Sunlight is made up of coloured lights. We see these when a rainbow forms. In fact, only three, red, green and blue (called primary colours), are needed for our eyes to see every colour there is. Many different colours can be made by mixing together primary colours in different amounts.

Light is made by very hot things, such as the Sun, fire and the tiny wire inside a light bulb, heated by electricity.

Certain chemical reactions also make light, as in fireworks and in animals such as glow worms or deep-sea fish.

When light rays pass through raindrops, they are split into the colours of the rainbow.

▶ Light from the Sun seems to have no colour at all. In fact, as the scientist Isaac Newton *(see page 20)* once showed, sunlight, or white light, is made up of several colours. He took a prism, a piece of glass with triangular sides, and allowed a tiny chink of sunlight to shine on it. The prism split the white light into red, orange, yellow, green, blue and violet colours. These are called the colours of the spectrum. We see them whenever there is a rainbow in the sky. Raindrops act like tiny, tear-shaped prisms.

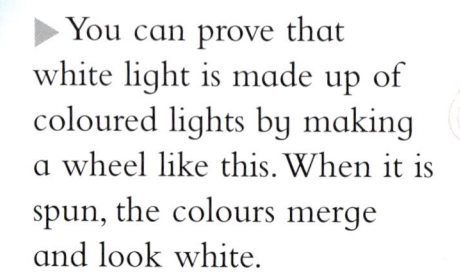

▶ You can prove that white light is made up of coloured lights by making a wheel like this. When it is spun, the colours merge and look white.

SEE ALSO: PAGE 6 SOLAR SYSTEM, PAGE 22 ELECTRICITY, PAGE 26 THE BRAIN, PAGE 86 MUSICAL INSTRUMENTS

▶ Light rays can bounce off objects. This is called reflection. In fact, for us to see any object at all, some light must be reflected from it otherwise it would appear black. A smooth, white surface reflects more light than a rough, dark one, but a flat, shiny surface reflects light best of all. Mirrors, sheets of glass with a thin layer of metal on the back, are perfect reflectors. By placing two mirrors carefully in a tube you can make a periscope, a device to see round corners. Light coming in at one end is reflected through to the viewer at the other end.

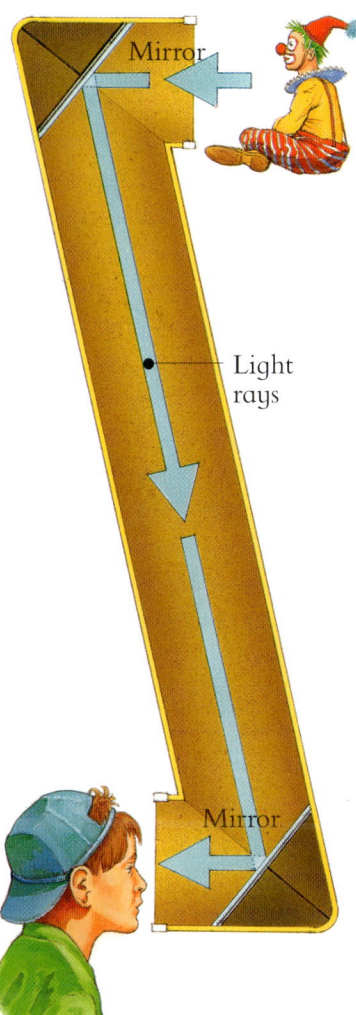

▲ A lens, a shaped piece of glass or plastic in a magnifying glass, brings light rays together to a point called a focus. It makes something we see through it appear larger. Our eyes have natural lenses in them *(see page 27)*.

SOUND

SOUND is made by vibrations: very quick movements backwards and forwards. When something vibrates, it sets the air around it vibrating, too. The effect is like ripples in a pond. When a pebble is thrown in, tiny waves spread out from that point. Sound also travels in waves. The stronger the vibrations, the greater the waves and the louder the sound.

Music is simply a series of controlled and—usually!—pleasant sounds. A trumpeter *(above)* blows into a metal tube and sets the air inside vibrating to produce musical sounds.

A high-pitched sound has faster vibrations than a lower-pitched one. A rocket taking off makes a very loud, low-pitched sound, a female opera singer can produce loud, high-pitched sounds, while falling leaves make very soft, medium-pitched sounds.

Sound travels through solids and liquids as well as air. Sound waves can also bounce off another surface and be reflected back. This is called an echo.

We can use very high-pitched sounds, called ultrasound, to echo back through the human body and find out about an unborn baby inside. The echoes can be turned into pictures on a computer screen.

YOUNG SCIENTIST

FORCES AND MATTER

WHAT makes something move? Anything that pushes or pulls an object is called a force. A breath of wind, a car engine, a magnet and an elastic band are all examples of things that can produce a force. Gravity is a very important force. You can see it at work if you let a pen drop. The pen is being pulled towards a very large object—the Earth itself.

There is also a force which tries to *stop* things moving. This is called friction. It is produced when two surfaces rub together; the rougher the surface, the greater the friction. It can be a useful force: tyres have "tread" (grooves cut in the rubber's surface) so that a car can grip the road. Sometimes it is important to reduce friction. For example, oil in an engine forms a thin, greasy layer between moving parts, allowing them to work smoothly.

◀ There is a very powerful force always pulling on you. It is called gravity, the force that attracts all objects to each other. Everything has gravity, but only really huge objects like the stars and planets have a strong pull. The Earth pulls everything on its surface towards its centre. It is said that the great English scientist Isaac Newton first realized this when he saw an apple fall from a tree.

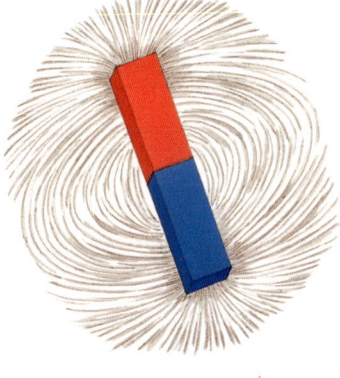

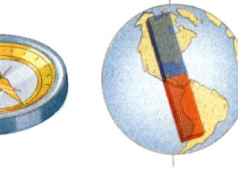

◀ An object tends to stay at rest, or keep on moving at the same speed, unless it is acted upon by a force. This tendency is called inertia. If a bus stops suddenly, everyone on it falls forward because there is nothing to stop them moving. (Seat belts would hold them in place.)

◀ Another important force is magnetism. A magnet is a piece of iron or steel that attracts other objects made of iron or steel, but has no effect on wood, plastic or most other kinds of metal. All magnets have two ends called north and south poles. North poles attract south poles but similar ("like") poles always push each other away. The area around a magnet is called a magnetic field. A sprinkling of tiny pieces of iron around a magnet shows its pattern.

The Earth itself has a magnetic field, as if it had a magnet inside it. A compass has a small magnet balanced inside it. The north pointer is attracted to the northern end of the "Earth-magnet".

SEE ALSO: PAGE 6 SOLAR SYSTEM, PAGE 8 EARTH AND MOON, PAGE 18 LIGHT AND SOUND, PAGE 22 ELECTRICITY

◀ When we sit on a fairground ride like this, we can feel a force pushing us quite strongly outwards. We have to hold tight to stay on! This force is called the centrifugal force. At the same time there is another force at work, keeping us moving in a circle around the roundabout. This force is called the centripetal force. It is these two balancing forces that keep the Earth and other planets travelling in orbit around the Sun *(see page 6)*.

MATTER

ALL matter—that is, everything around you, such as wood, plastic, glass or other people—is made up from tiny building blocks called atoms. They are so tiny you cannot see them. The tiniest speck of dust consists of a million million atoms! There are about 90 different kinds of atom, called elements. A gold bar is made of gold atoms, oxygen gas is made of oxygen atoms, coal is made of carbon atoms. Atoms often link together to make different substances. When linked, hydrogen and oxygen atoms form a very familiar substance: water. Atoms that are linked are called molecules.

Substances come in three different forms: solid, like rocks, liquid, like water, or gas, like air. In a solid, atoms or molecules are packed closely together. In a liquid, they are still close but can move slowly about. In a gas, they are widely spaced and move quickly. Water appears in nature as liquid, as a solid (ice) and as a gas (water vapour, which turns to tiny droplets to form clouds).

▲ Energy means the ability to do something: for example, walk and run, power a car, light up a room or cook a meal. There are several different kinds of energy. This illustration shows them at work. We receive light and heat energy from the Sun. Light bulbs, microwave ovens and toasters can also supply this energy, of course: they work by using electrical energy *(see page 22)*. For our bodies to work, they need the chemical energy that is stored inside food. Mechanical energy is used for activity and movement, such as lifting a box or riding a bicycle.

▶ Why does a heavy ship float? Some objects are denser than others: their atoms are more tightly packed together. Anything that is less dense than water (like wood) will float, while a denser object (such as a pebble) will sink. A ship contains lots of air, so its overall density is less than water.

YOUNG SCIENTIST

ELECTRICITY

ELECTRICITY is a kind of energy. It is invisible and stored inside atoms, the minute building blocks of which all things are made *(see page 21)*. Atoms themselves are made up of even tinier pieces, called particles. They include electrons, which have a negative electric charge, and protons, which have a positive electric charge. In normal atoms, there are the same number of electrons and protons, and so the charges cancel each other out. To make electricity, we must make the atoms lose or gain electrons.

Things that run on electricity are connected to the source of electrical power by metal wires. When the current is switched on, or a battery is connected, the electrons in the wire all move in the same direction. This is called current electricity. We can use electricity in all sorts of ways: to light our homes, switch on a television, power a train, and so on.

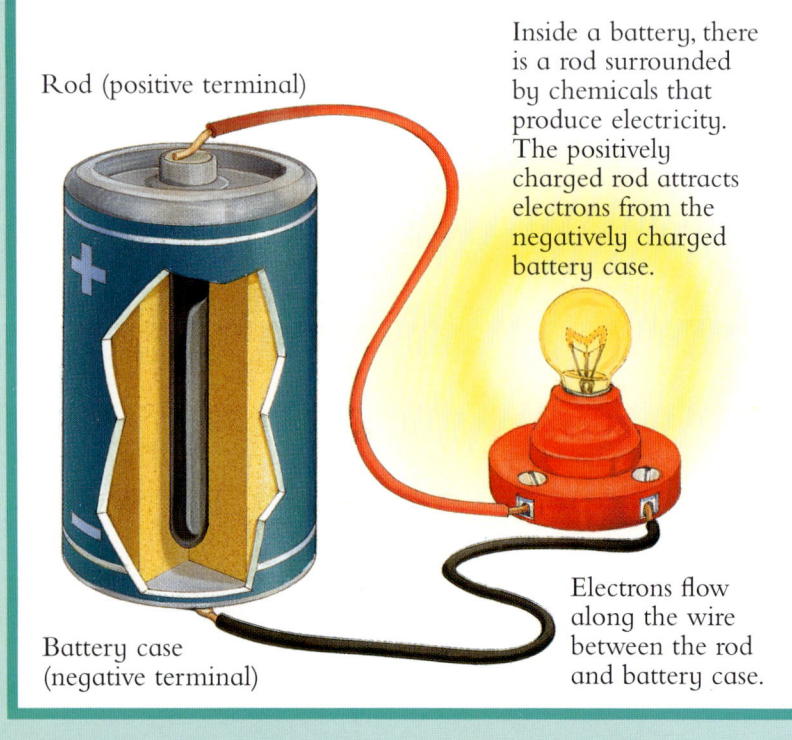

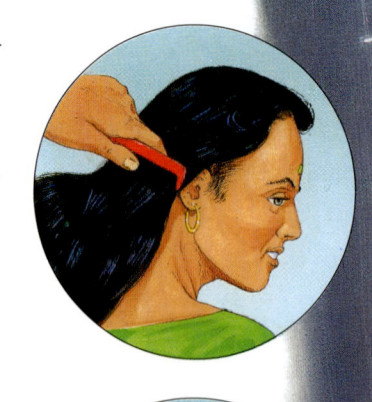

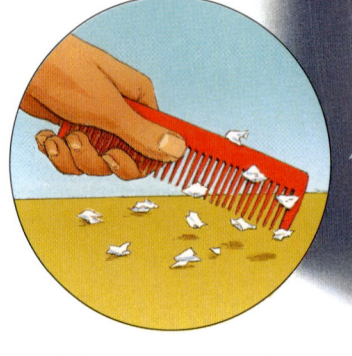

▲▶ In static electricity, the electrons do not move. You can make static electricity by running a comb through your hair. The comb leaves a few of its electrons behind in the hair, so the comb now has a small positive charge. It can pick up small pieces of paper because it attracts the electrons in the paper's atoms. If you comb your hair in a dark room then hold the comb close to your thumb, you will see a tiny spark. The electric charge heats the air atoms between comb and thumb, producing a flash of light. This is exactly what happens—but on a much grander scale—when lightning strikes during a thunderstorm *(see page 15)*. Thunder is the noise of the air expanding rapidly in the intense heat.

Rod (positive terminal)

Inside a battery, there is a rod surrounded by chemicals that produce electricity. The positively charged rod attracts electrons from the negatively charged battery case.

Battery case (negative terminal)

Electrons flow along the wire between the rod and battery case.

SEE ALSO: PAGE 20 FORCES AND MATTER, PAGE 88 TELEVISION, PAGE 96 TRAINS

YOUNG SCIENTIST

▶ We need electricity for all kinds of things in our homes. Most homes are connected to mains electricity. A power station makes electricity in the first place. Boosted by transformers, electricity travels along cables (thick wires) supported high above the ground by pylons, to a sub-station. From here, the wires run to our homes. When we plug an electrical appliance into a socket, it connects up to mains electricity.

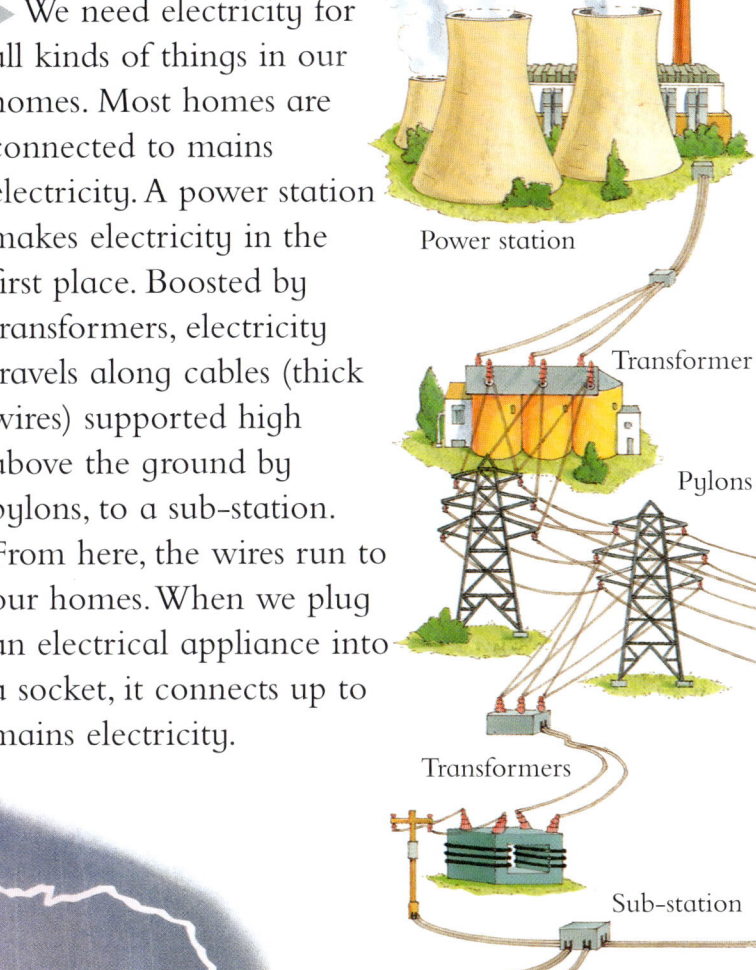

Power station

Transformer

Pylons

Transformers

Sub-station

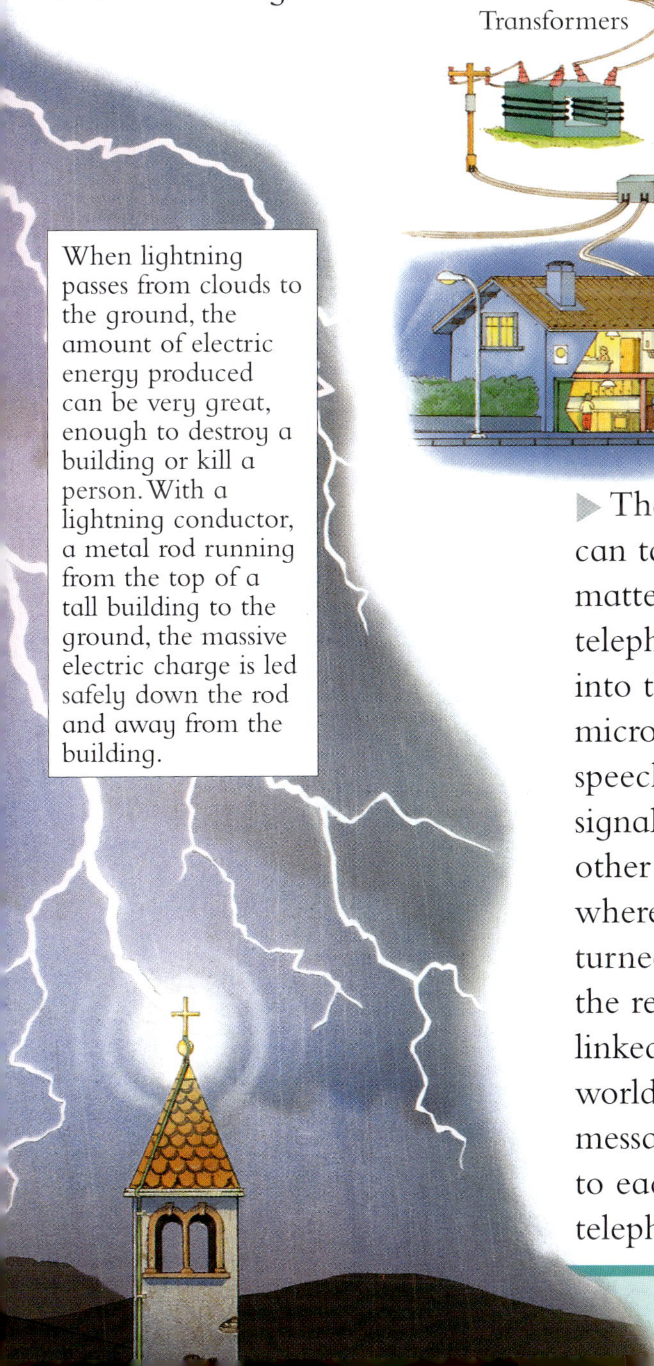

When lightning passes from clouds to the ground, the amount of electric energy produced can be very great, enough to destroy a building or kill a person. With a lightning conductor, a metal rod running from the top of a tall building to the ground, the massive electric charge is led safely down the rod and away from the building.

ELECTRONICS

Calculator

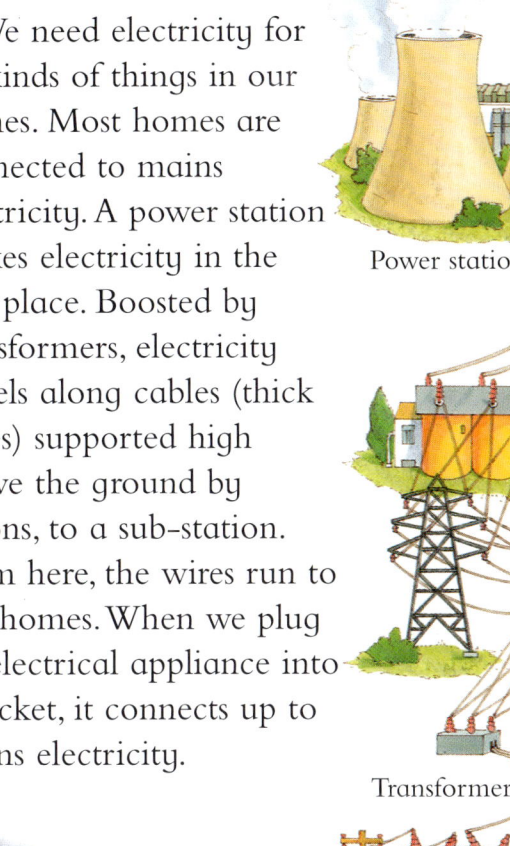

Personal computer

Hi-fi system

BESIDES metal wires, electricity can also flow through empty space and other materials such as silicon. Devices that make use of this are called electronic components. These are essential parts of machines that enable us to hear sounds from a radio or a hi-fi stereo system, and use a calculator or computer. Modern electronic components can all be fitted on to a miniature integrated circuit, or silicon chip *(below)*. A computer uses them to store information and make calculations. Like a person, a computer has a memory and a "brain" or central processing unit.

This silcon chip is even smaller than an ant!

▶ Thanks to electricity, we can talk to anyone—no matter how far away—by telephone. When you speak into the telephone, a microphone turns your speech into electrical signals. These travel to the other end of the line, where the signals are turned back into sounds in the receiver. Computers linked to the Internet the world over also send messages and information to each other along telephone lines.

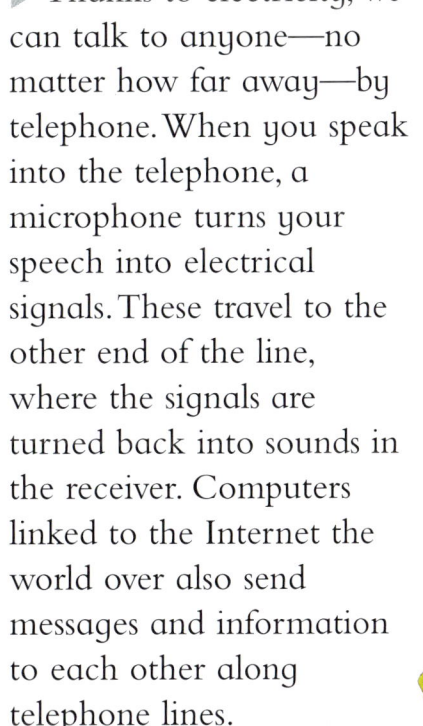

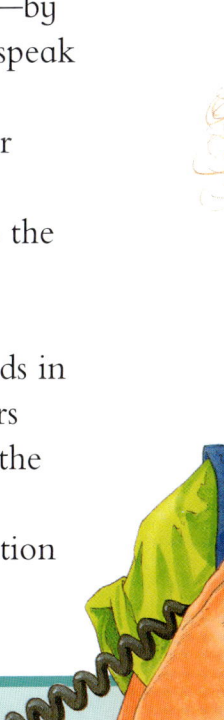

THE HUMAN BODY

DIGESTION

THE HUMAN BODY needs food and drink to survive. The things we eat and drink must first be turned into substances the body can use. This process is called digestion.

Digestion begins in the mouth where food is mashed up by the teeth and tongue. Saliva softens the food, ready for swallowing. The food travels down the oesophagus into the stomach, where powerful acids change it into a mush. This then squeezes into the small intestine, where it mixes with juices from the pancreas and gall bladder. Any useful substances pass through the walls of the small intestine and are taken by the blood to the liver. The liver stores these useful substances. Waste products are pushed out of the body through the large intestine and the rectum.

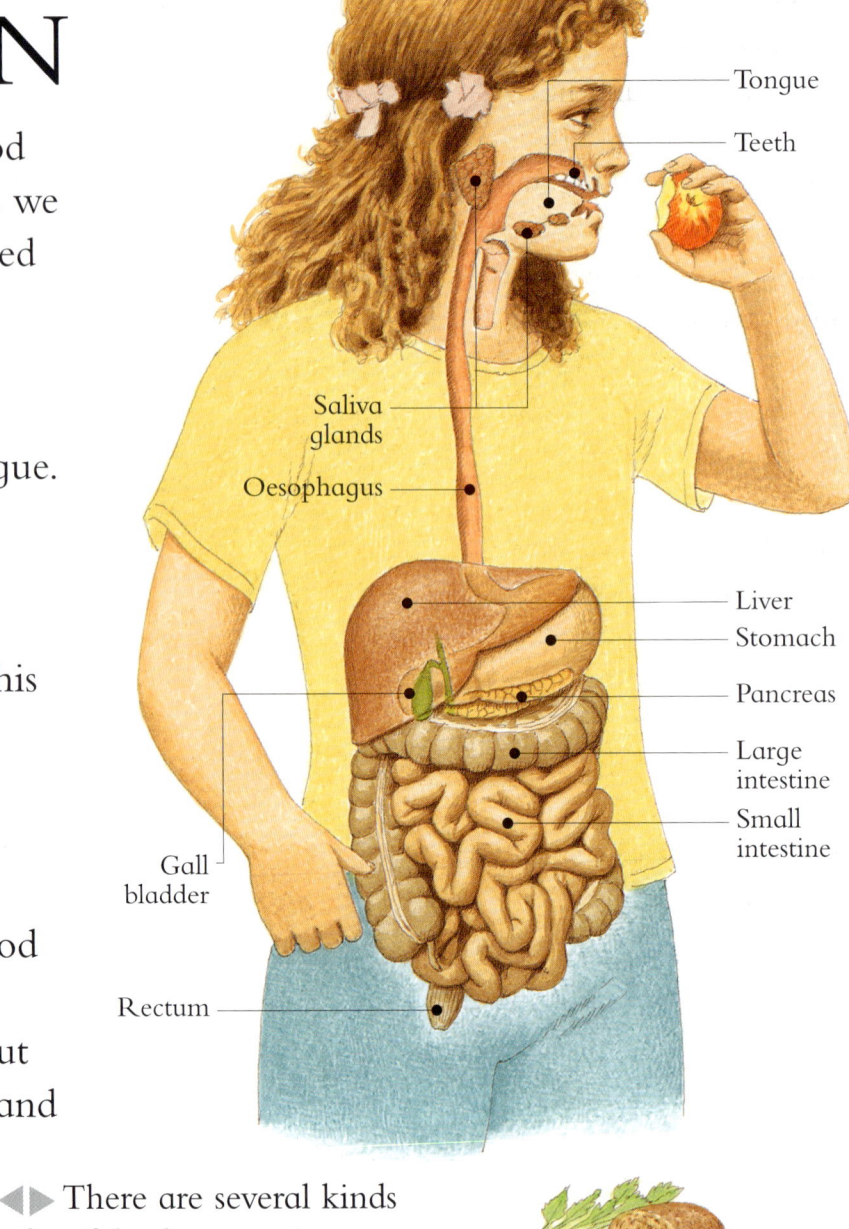

Tongue
Teeth
Saliva glands
Oesophagus
Liver
Stomach
Pancreas
Large intestine
Small intestine
Gall bladder
Rectum

Proteins are found in foods such as meat, poultry and fish, greens, beans and milk.

Fats are found in meat and dairy products, as well as pies and avocados.

Carbohydrates are found in foods such as bread, potatoes, cereals, pasta and mushrooms.

◀▶ There are several kinds of useful substances in food, called nutrients, that our bodies must have to survive and stay healthy. They are: proteins, fats, carbohydrates, fibre, minerals and vitamins. Proteins are used to build and repair muscles and body parts. Fats and carbohydrates provide energy, while fibre helps us to pass waste out of the body. Vitamins and minerals are chemicals that are essential to keep us healthy and help us grow.

Fibre is found in wholemeal bread, fruit and vegetables.

Iron, a mineral, is found in meat, green vegetables, eggs and nuts.

Vitamin A is found in cheese, carrots, fish, tomatoes and liver.

SEE ALSO: PAGE 20 FORCES AND MATTER

THE HUMAN BODY

▶ The kidneys work with the liver to clean our blood by removing any harmful substances. They also make sure that we have the right amount of salt and water. Waste from all over the body travels in the blood to the kidneys. Any useful substances are sorted out and returned to the blood. Waste chemicals and any salt and water we do not need are sent down to the bladder to be passed out of the body as urine.

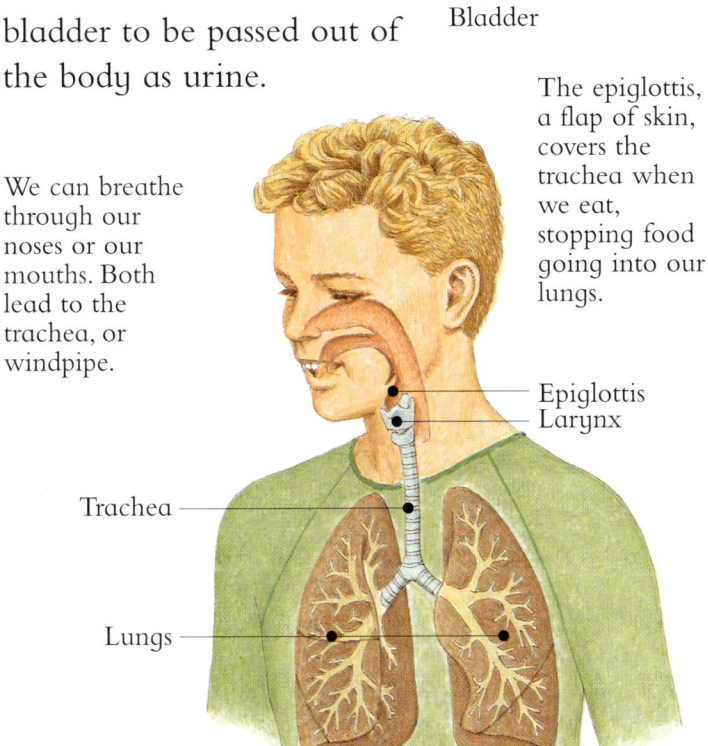

Kidneys

Bladder

The epiglottis, a flap of skin, covers the trachea when we eat, stopping food going into our lungs.

We can breathe through our noses or our mouths. Both lead to the trachea, or windpipe.

Epiglottis
Larynx
Trachea
Lungs

Two tiny cords in the larynx vibrate as air is pushed between them. This creates sounds, which our mouths make into words.

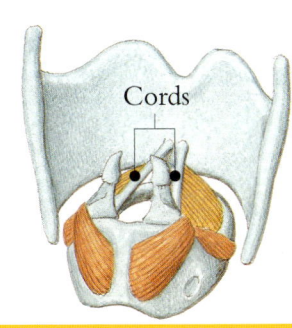

Cords

▲ By breathing in, we take oxygen from the air into our lungs. Blood vessels then carry the oxygen around our bodies. As the oxygen and the nutrients from our food are used up, we make carbon dioxide. The blood brings this back to the lungs, from where we breathe it out into the air.

HEART AND BLOOD

BLOOD carries food and oxygen all around the body and takes away waste products. The blood system is made up of a complicated network of blood vessels at the centre of which lies the heart.

The heart pumps oxygen-filled blood from the lungs around the body through blood vessels called arteries. Other vessels, called veins, bring used-up blood containing carbon dioxide back through the body. The heart sends this blood to the lungs to get rid of the carbon dioxide and take in fresh oxygen.

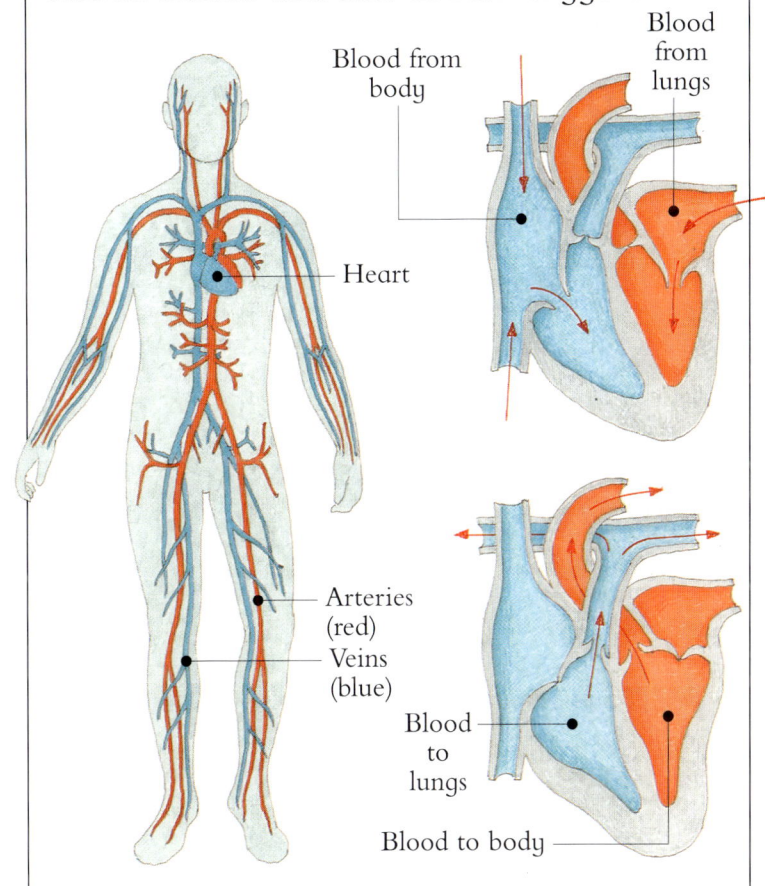

Blood from body
Blood from lungs
Heart
Arteries (red)
Veins (blue)
Blood to lungs
Blood to body

The heart is a powerful pump. As the muscles of the heart relax, blood enters its various "chambers": oxygen-filled blood from the lungs (red chambers in the diagram *above, right*), and carbon-dioxide-filled blood from the rest of the body (blue chambers). Flaps called valves stop any blood leaking backwards. The heart then squeezes and pumps the blood out. The oxygen-filled blood goes to the rest of the body, the other blood to the lungs.

25

THE HUMAN BODY

THE BRAIN

TOGETHER with the spinal cord, the brain controls everything we do, and every thought we have. The brain works all the time, even when we are asleep. The spinal cord is a thick bunch of nerves running from the brain down the spine. Branching off from it, is a complex network of nerves that runs to every part of the body.

Nerves are like telephone wires, carrying commands from the brain to the rest of the body. They also bring information back to the brain about the outside world. This information is gathered by our five senses: sight, hearing, smell, taste and touch. The nerves also tell the brain what is happening inside the body. The brain can then make sure that our body temperature or breathing, for example, is at exactly the right level.

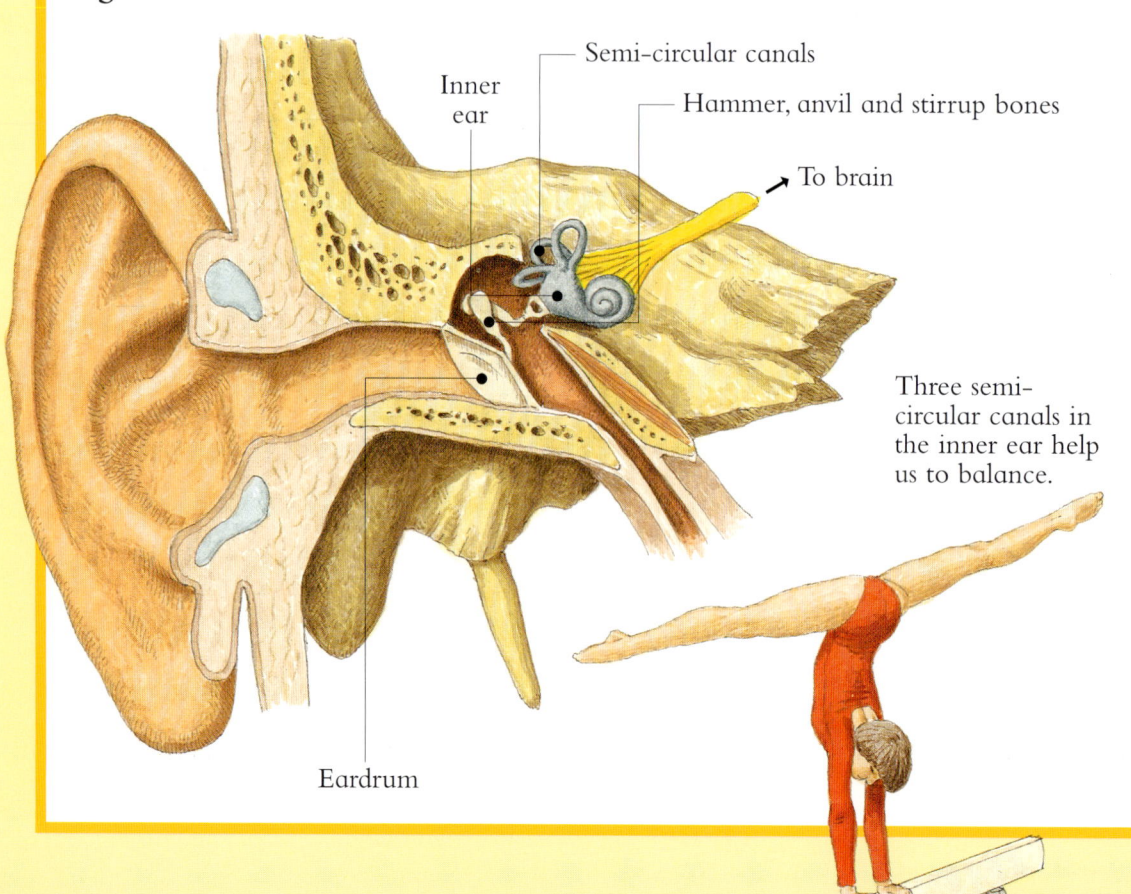

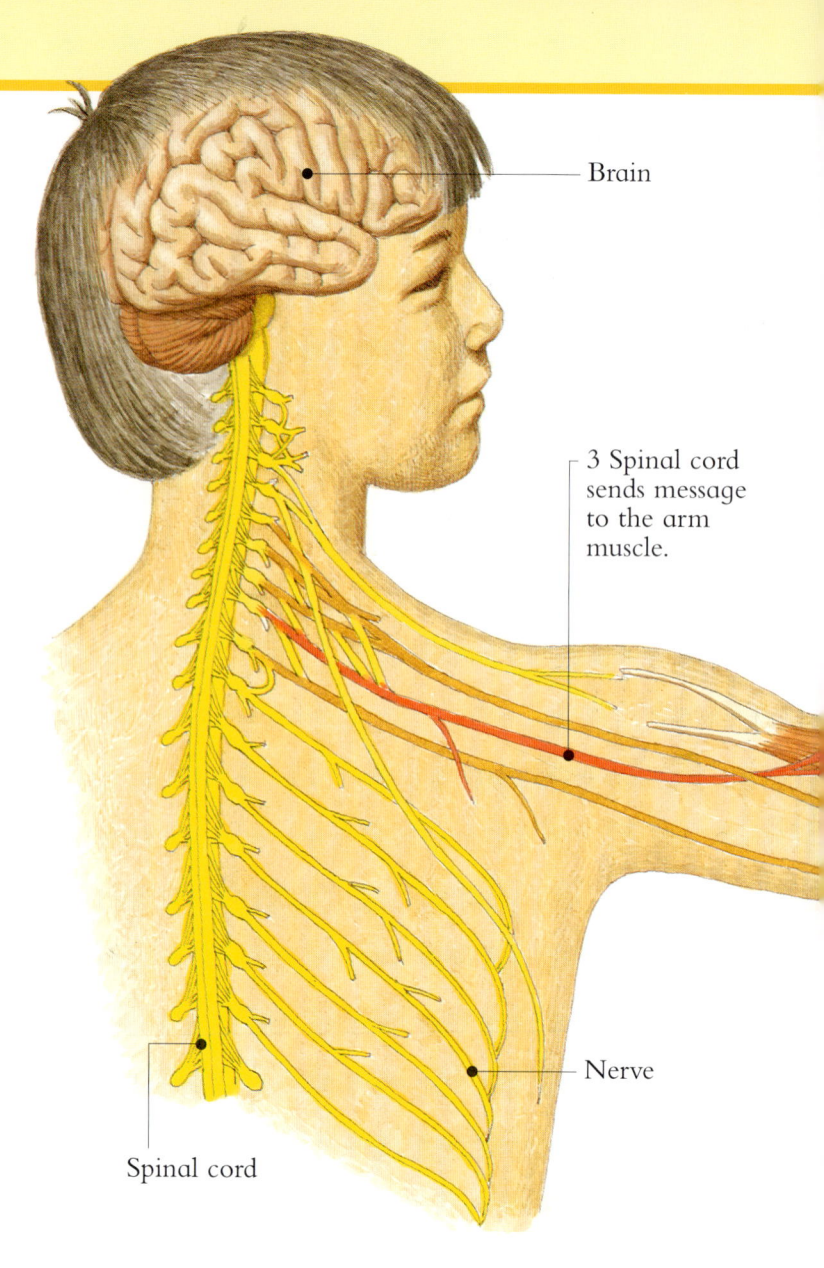

Brain

3 Spinal cord sends message to the arm muscle.

Nerve

Spinal cord

Inner ear
Semi-circular canals
Hammer, anvil and stirrup bones
To brain
Eardrum

Three semi-circular canals in the inner ear help us to balance.

◀ All sounds are really vibrations in the air. As the vibrations travel into the ear, they are picked up by the eardrum. Tiny bones, called the hammer, anvil and stirrup, send the vibrations to the inner ear. There they are changed to signals and sent along a nerve to the brain.

▶ The surface of our tongue is covered with tiny taste buds which tell us whether something we are eating is sweet, salty, sour or bitter.

THE HUMAN BODY

▼ To move a part of our body, the brain usually sends commands to certain muscles. If we touch something hot or sharp however, the nerves alert the spinal cord. It immediately tells the arm muscle to pull the hand away quickly! This is called a reflex.

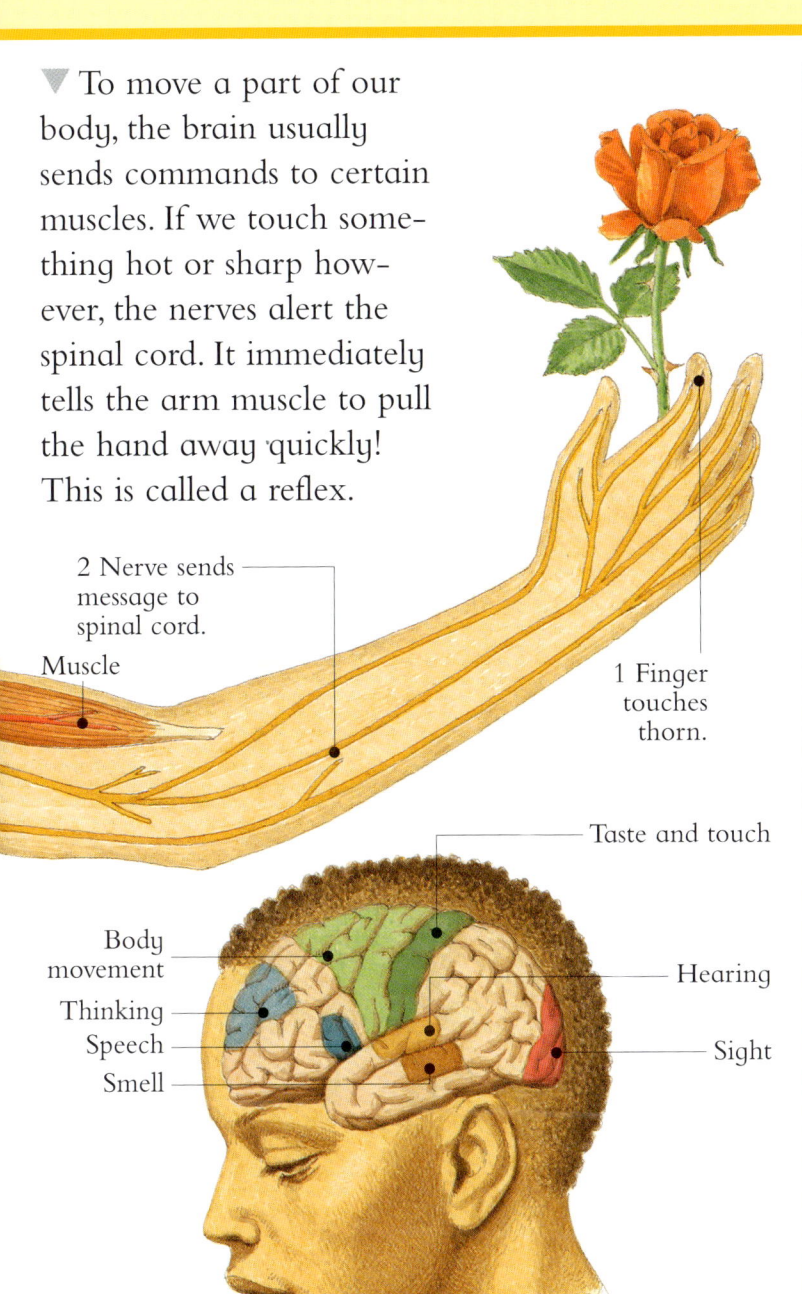

2 Nerve sends message to spinal cord.
Muscle
1 Finger touches thorn.

Taste and touch
Body movement
Thinking
Speech
Smell
Hearing
Sight

Different parts of the tongue recognize different tastes.

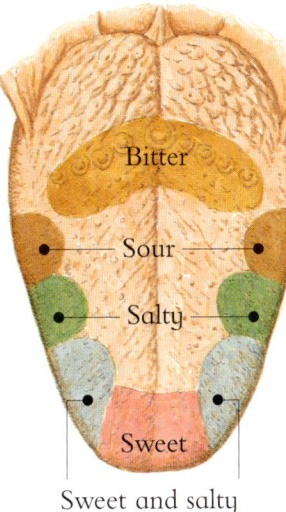

Bitter
Sour
Salty
Sweet
Sweet and salty

▲ The brain is divided into different areas. Each area controls a certain function of the body, such as speech, movement or thinking.

▶ The skin is the organ we use to sense touch. It is protective, waterproof, and keeps us at an even temperature. When we are hot, sweat is produced to lose heat into the air.

EYESIGHT

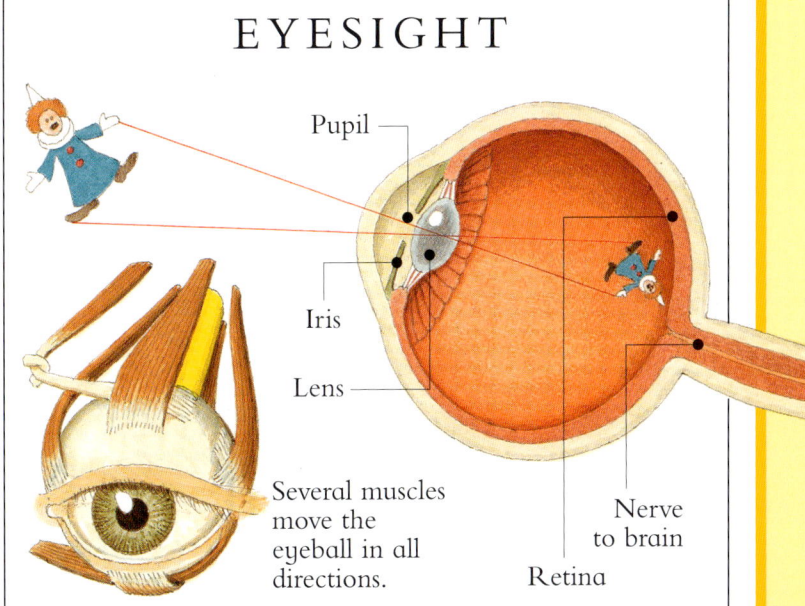

Pupil
Iris
Lens
Several muscles move the eyeball in all directions.
Nerve to brain
Retina

THE EYE is like a tiny camera, constantly taking pictures of the world around us. When we look at an object, light rays enter the eye through the pupil. The amount of light is controlled by the iris (the eye's coloured part). In dim light, the pupil must be opened wide to let in as much light as possible.

Behind the pupil is the lens. This focuses the light rays *(see page 19)* and forms a picture on the retina at the back of the eye. Because the light rays cross over in the eye, the image is upside down. The brain tells us how the world really looks.

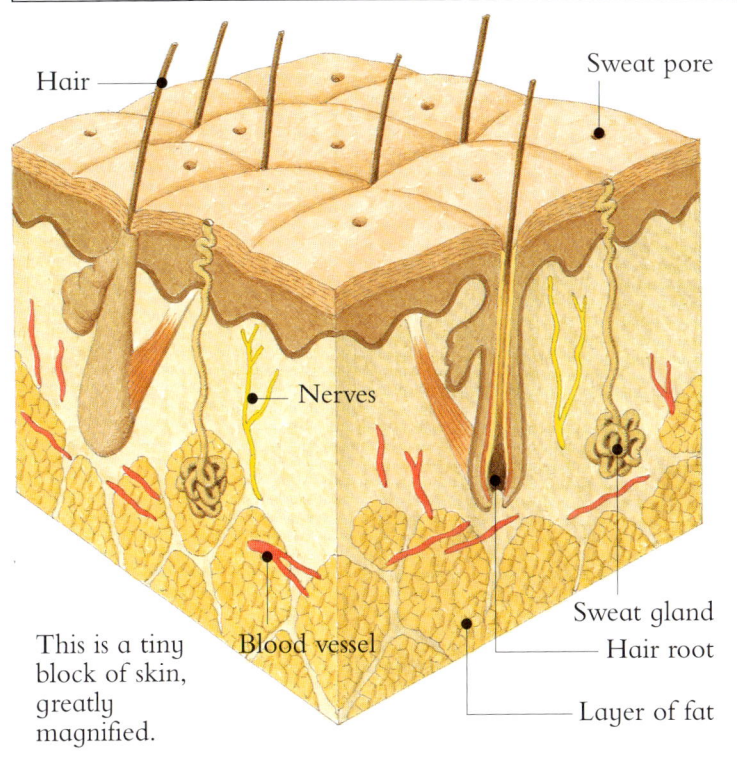

Hair
Sweat pore
Nerves
This is a tiny block of skin, greatly magnified.
Blood vessel
Sweat gland
Hair root
Layer of fat

SEE ALSO: PAGE 18 LIGHT AND SOUND, PAGE 22 ELECTRICITY, PAGE 40 MAMMALS

THE HUMAN BODY

THE SKELETON

INSIDE OUR BODIES there is a strong framework of bones, called the skeleton. The skeleton gives the body its shape, allows it to move and protects the soft organs inside against injury. Without it, we would just be like piles of jelly! There are about 206 bones in the adult human body, but a child has more. When a baby is born, it has many tiny bones, some of which (for example, those in its skull) join together as it grows.

Bones are very strong, but they are also lightweight and spongy inside. This helps us to be as agile as possible. Many bones are connected by joints that allow movement. These joints are held in place by straps called ligaments.

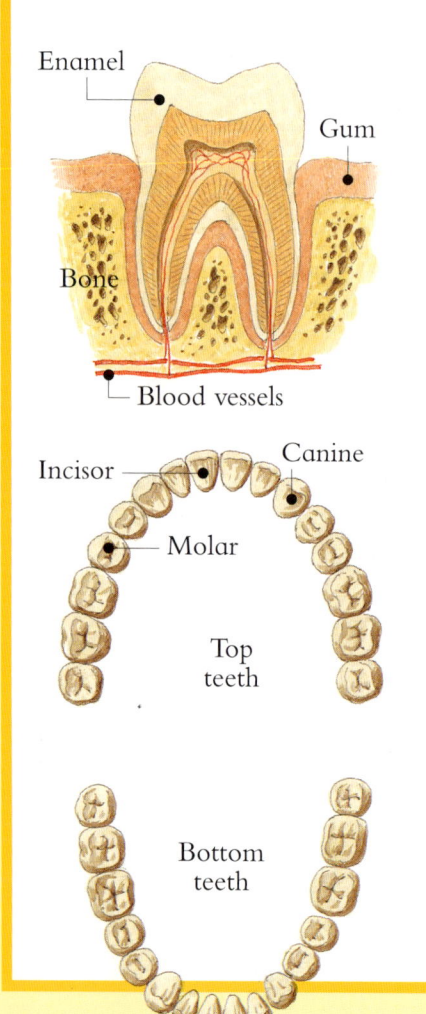

◀ Only a small part of a tooth shows above the surface of the gum. As this diagram shows, deep roots anchor the tooth to the jawbone. A tooth is covered with a protective layer of enamel which is even harder than bone. At the centre are blood vessels and nerve endings.

We have several different kinds of teeth. They each have different jobs. Incisors, at the front of the mouth, bite off pieces of food. The pointed canine teeth tear the food into smaller pieces while the wide, flat molars grind them up.

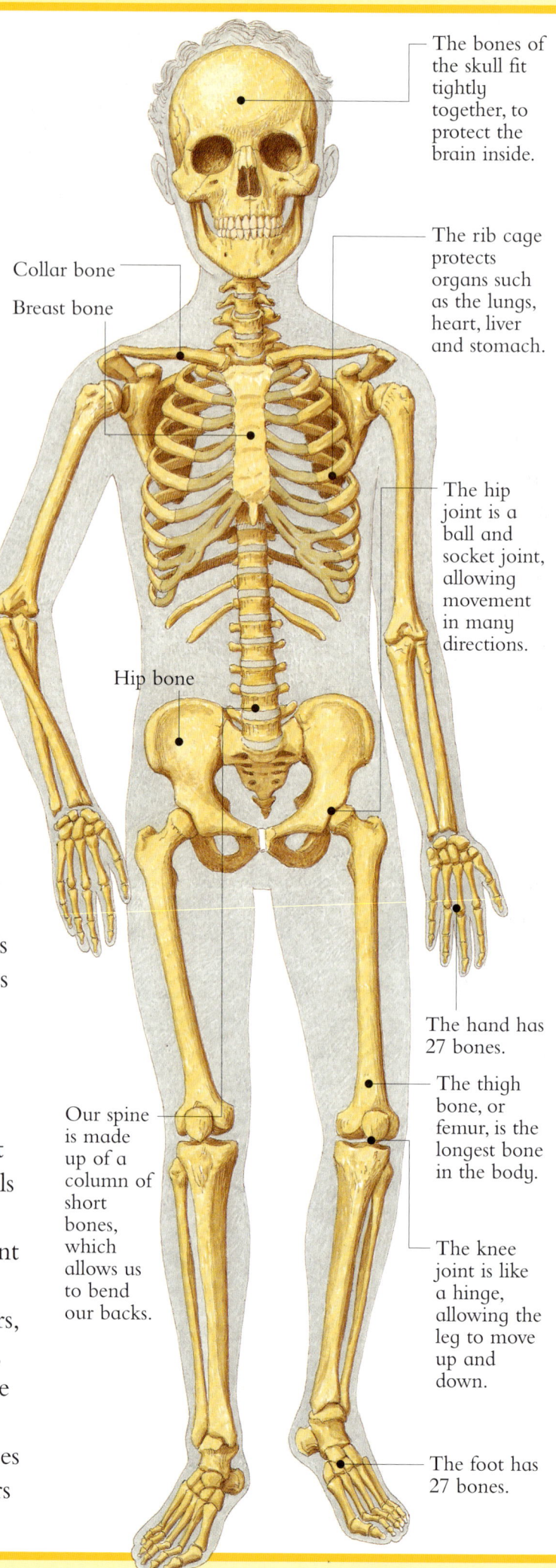

- The bones of the skull fit tightly together, to protect the brain inside.
- Collar bone
- Breast bone
- The rib cage protects organs such as the lungs, heart, liver and stomach.
- The hip joint is a ball and socket joint, allowing movement in many directions.
- Hip bone
- Our spine is made up of a column of short bones, which allows us to bend our backs.
- The hand has 27 bones.
- The thigh bone, or femur, is the longest bone in the body.
- The knee joint is like a hinge, allowing the leg to move up and down.
- The foot has 27 bones.

Enamel · Gum · Bone · Blood vessels

Incisor · Canine · Molar · Top teeth · Bottom teeth

28

THE HUMAN BODY

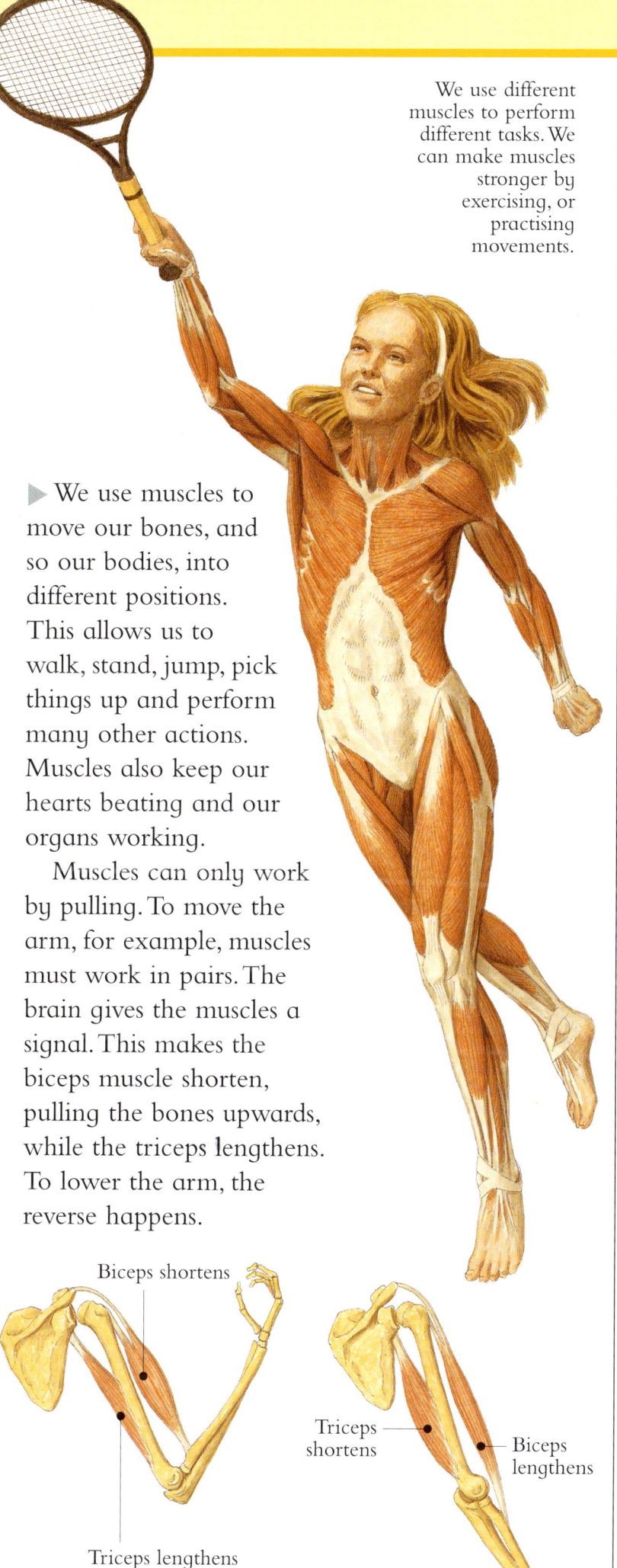

We use different muscles to perform different tasks. We can make muscles stronger by exercising, or practising movements.

▶ We use muscles to move our bones, and so our bodies, into different positions. This allows us to walk, stand, jump, pick things up and perform many other actions. Muscles also keep our hearts beating and our organs working.

Muscles can only work by pulling. To move the arm, for example, muscles must work in pairs. The brain gives the muscles a signal. This makes the biceps muscle shorten, pulling the bones upwards, while the triceps lengthens. To lower the arm, the reverse happens.

Biceps shortens

Triceps lengthens

Triceps shortens

Biceps lengthens

A BABY IS BORN

A BABY begins life when a sperm from a man and an egg from a woman join together inside the woman's body. Both the sperm and the egg are cells, tiny "building blocks" which contain all that is needed to create a new life. The two cells combine to form a new one about the size of a full stop. As the fertilized egg grows, it divides into two. Then it divides again and again, until it is a small ball of cells called an embryo. It moves to the woman's womb, where its cells carry on growing and dividing. After eight weeks, it is called a foetus. Food and oxygen are passed from the mother's blood to the foetus through the umbilical cord. (This is cut when the baby is born, leaving a scar or "belly button".)

The growth of an embryo (actual size)

24 days   5 weeks   6 weeks   7 weeks

It takes nine months before a baby is ready to be born. In the first few weeks, the heart, brain and spine form. By the 12th week, the foetus has nearly all its organs and its legs and arms have grown. After about 24 weeks, it is almost completely formed. It then steadily grows in size. When the baby is ready to be born, it usually turns round inside the womb so that its head is pointing downwards. Then, strong muscles in the womb push the baby along the birth canal and into the outside world.

29

SEE ALSO: PAGE 40 MAMMALS,   PAGE 104 EARLY PEOPLE

THE NATURAL WORLD

Prehistoric life

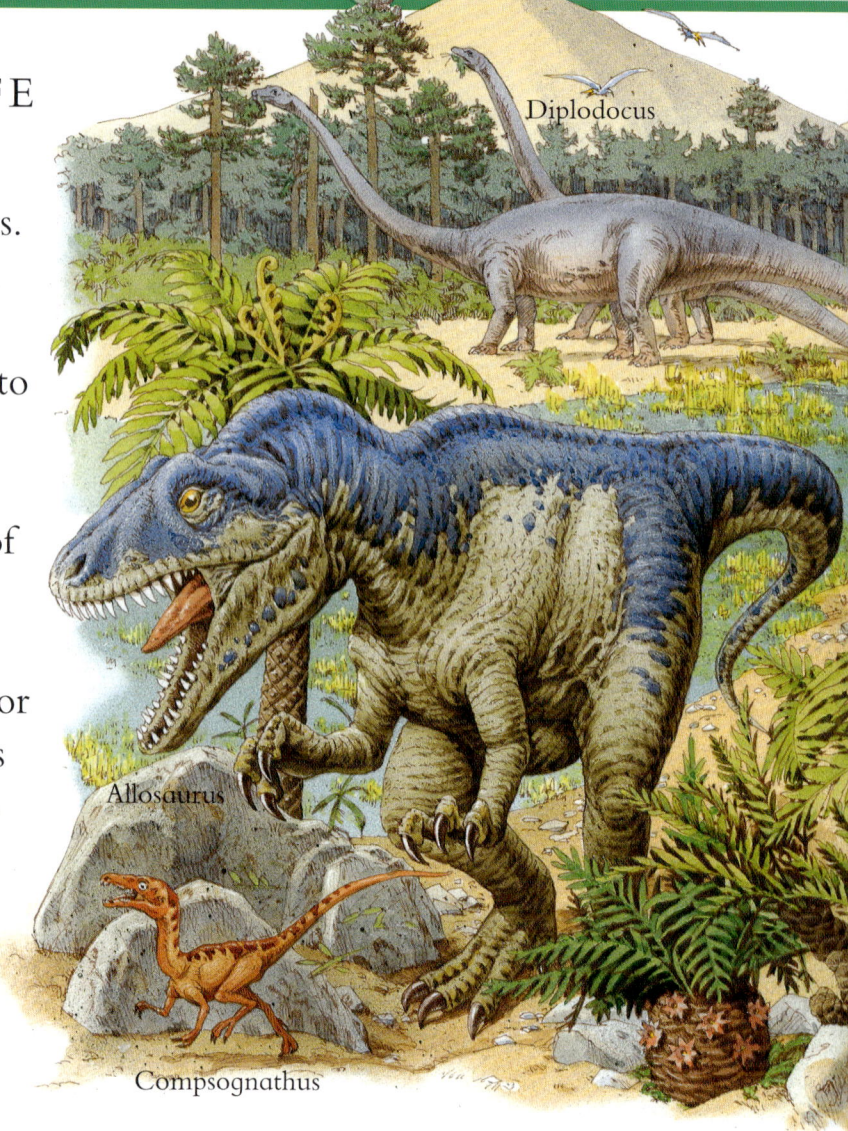

LIFE ON EARTH has existed for many hundreds of millions of years. The particular kinds of plants and animals alive today have not, however, been around for all that time. If we were to travel back millions of years, we would discover some completely different kinds, called prehistoric life. Over long periods of time, some living things have gradually changed, either becoming better able to survive in the environment around them, or becoming extinct (dying out). This process is called evolution. Some fish evolved into amphibians, some amphibians to reptiles, and some reptiles to mammals and birds. Some ape-like animals have evolved into humans.

Diplodocus

Allosaurus

Compsognathus

◀ About 300 million years ago, some parts of the world were covered with dense, hot, swampy jungle. The air was thick with insects, including giant dragonflies many centimetres long. Huge centipedes scuttled about. Over millions of years, some fish had evolved into animals capable of living out of the water. These amphibians still had fish-like heads and fishy tails, but they had legs and feet. Some later amphibians succeeded in laying their eggs out of water, and so became the first reptiles.

SEE ALSO: PAGE 10 ROCKS AND FOSSILS, PAGE 104 EARLY PEOPLE

THE NATURAL WORLD

Pterosaur (a flying reptile)

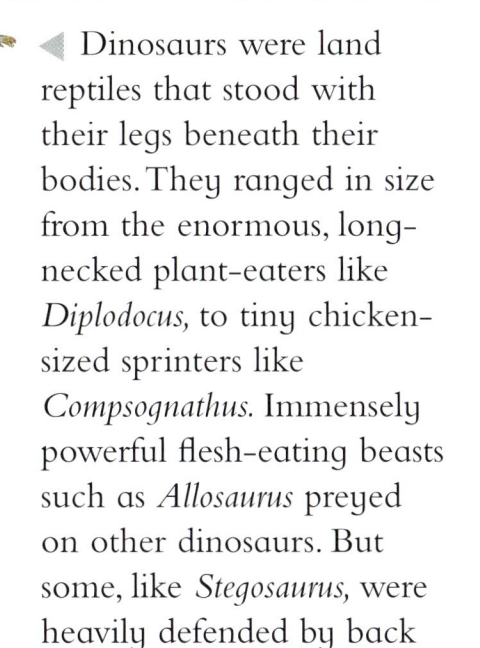

Stegosaurus

◀ Dinosaurs were land reptiles that stood with their legs beneath their bodies. They ranged in size from the enormous, long-necked plant-eaters like *Diplodocus,* to tiny chicken-sized sprinters like *Compsognathus.* Immensely powerful flesh-eating beasts such as *Allosaurus* preyed on other dinosaurs. But some, like *Stegosaurus,* were heavily defended by back plates and spiky tails. All the dinosaurs died out 65 million years ago.

Archaeopteryx was one of the first birds. It was a tiny dinosaur that developed feathery wings.

Archaeopteryx

FIRST LIFE

THE FIRST living things appeared at least 3,500 million years ago. Microscopic beings, they were similar to bacteria that exist today, the "bugs" that sometimes cause diseases. It took millions of years for them to evolve into larger creatures. But, in warm seas 550 million years ago, an amazing variety of life could be found.

For millions of years there was no life on land at all. Meanwhile, some very strange creatures lived in the sea.

◀ Mammals first appeared during the Age of the Dinosaurs. The first kinds were tiny, shrew-like animals that came out only at night for fear of attack. When the dinosaurs became extinct, an enormous variety of mammals and birds evolved. Some prehistoric mammals looked very different to modern kinds. Mammals also evolved in the oceans (whales and dolphins) while others learnt to fly (bats).

31

THE NATURAL WORLD

INSECTS

THERE ARE more different kinds of insect than of any other group of animal. They are found everywhere except in the oceans and polar ice.

Insects have three pairs of legs and three body sections: the head, the thorax and the abdomen. Most insects have wings. They do not have a skeleton inside their body but instead they have a tough outer layer of "armour". They breathe through tiny holes in their sides.

Insects are born and develop in two different ways. Some insects hatch out from eggs looking like miniature adults. These are known as nymphs. Others hatch out as larvae and then later on change completely to become adults.

There are more than 20,000 kinds of grasshopper.

The praying mantis is a predator of other insects. There are about 1,000 kinds of mantis.

Pollen • Larva • Queen • Worker • Cell containing honey • Drone

◀ Ants, termites (see page 53) and some wasps and bees live in groups called colonies. In a honeybee colony, the queen bee is the only one who lays eggs. All the other females are called workers. They build the nest and collect food. Male bees, or drones, do no work, but one will mate with the queen. The nest consists of wax combs with tiny six-sided holes, or cells. Here, the eggs hatch into larvae that later become adult bees. Also stored in the cells is the bees' winter food, honey made from flower nectar, and pollen.

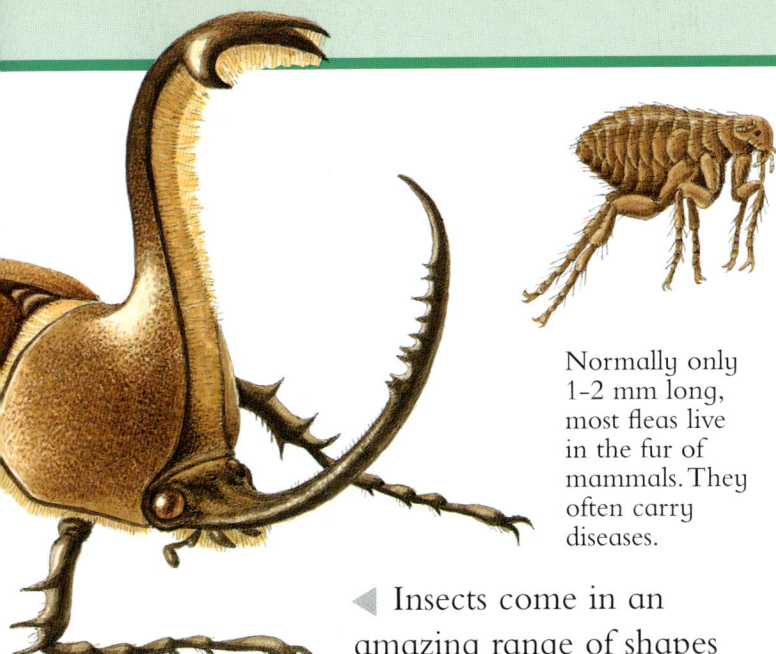

THE NATURAL WORLD

BUTTERFLIES AND MOTHS

Swallowtail butterfly

Hawkmoth

BUTTERFLIES and moths are flying insects with scaly wings and stalk-like feelers on their heads, called antennae. Butterflies usually fly during the daytime, moths at night. Moths' antennae sometimes have feathery branches. Butterflies and moths begin life as larvae, called caterpillars (below, 1). They feed constantly until fully grown. Then they spin a hard case (a chrysalis, 2) around themselves and their bodies change inside it. Finally, after a few weeks, an adult breaks out of the chrysalis (3).

1   2   3

A male rhinoceros beetle uses its horns to fight other males.

Normally only 1-2 mm long, most fleas live in the fur of mammals. They often carry diseases.

◀ Insects come in an amazing range of shapes and sizes. The gigantic rhinoceros beetle can lift more than 800 times its own weight. The tiny flea can jump more than 100 times its own length. Some insects are killers. With its huge eyes and razor-sharp front legs, the praying mantis is a ferocious predator. To defend itself, the shield bug squirts out a terrible-smelling fluid. Grasshoppers and locusts use their powerful back legs to leap to safety.

There are more than 5,000 different kinds of shield bug, so called because of their shape.

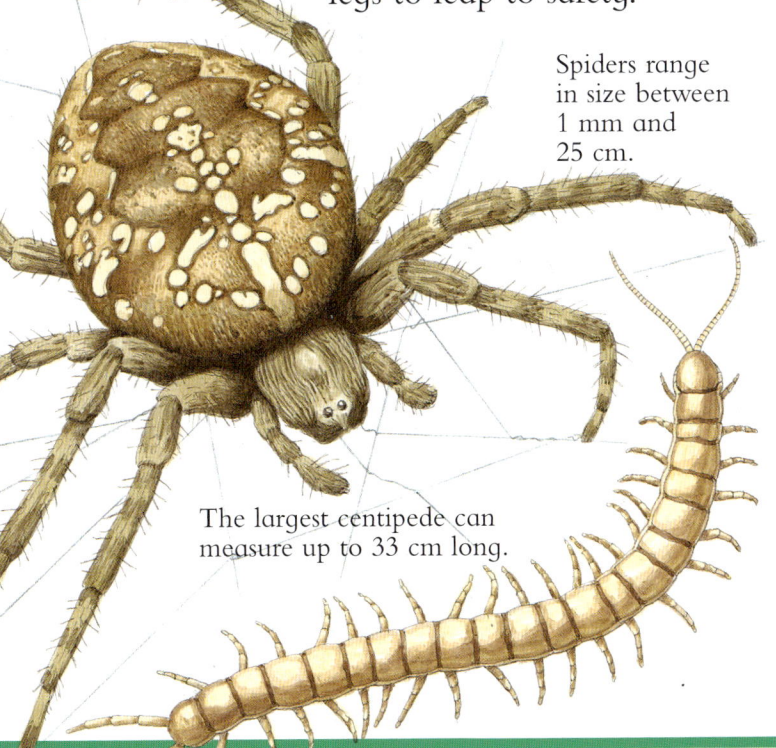

Spiders range in size between 1 mm and 25 cm.

◀ Not all creepy-crawlies are insects. Spiders and scorpions belong to a group called arachnids. All arachnids have four pairs of legs and only two body sections. Many spiders spin sticky webs to trap flying insects. They use a very strong substance called spider silk that they make inside their bodies.

Centipedes and millipedes are not insects, either. Their many pairs of legs are useful for burrowing into the soil.

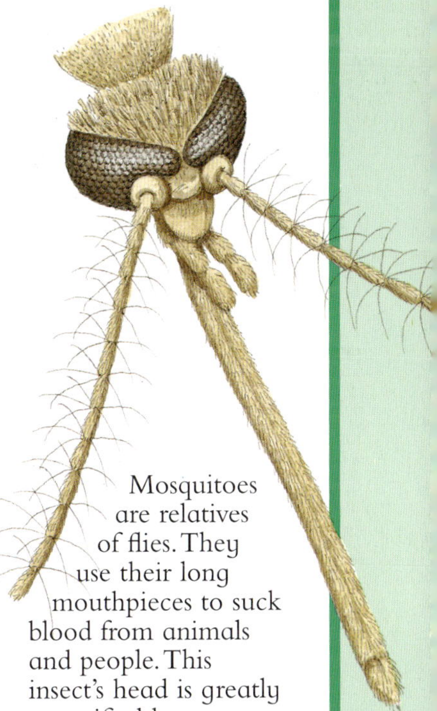

The largest centipede can measure up to 33 cm long.

Mosquitoes are relatives of flies. They use their long mouthpieces to suck blood from animals and people. This insect's head is greatly magnified here.

33

SEE ALSO: PAGE 44 PLANTS, PAGES 48–65 THE WORLD ABOUT US

THE NATURAL WORLD

FISH

FISH live in water, but unlike other water-dwellers—mammals such as whales, or reptiles such as turtles—they do not breathe air. Instead, they use their gills to take in oxygen from the water around them. Fish have fins and tails, and many are covered with scales. Most fish lay eggs but some, like sharks, give birth to live young. There are some kinds of fish that live in fresh water—rivers and lakes—and others that live in the oceans.

There are two main groups of fishes. Bony fish have skeletons made of bone. Sharks and rays have softer skeletons made of cartilage.

Salmon are born in rivers, then swim out to sea. They return to the rivers of their birth to lay their eggs, swimming against the current and leaping up waterfalls.

▼ Fish can be extremely dangerous creatures. Some are poisonous while others have a deadly bite. Moray eels hide in holes between rocks and shoot out to grab their prey with their sharp teeth. Stingrays have long, thin tails that they whip round to drive a venomous, sharp spike into their attackers. The stonefish is the most poisonous fish in the world. The venom in its spines can kill humans. Tiger sharks are one of the few species of shark that actually kill and eat humans. They are large, powerful fish with huge jaws and teeth.

A moray eel. The largest kinds can grow up to three metres long.

◀ Seahorses are very strange-looking fish. They swim slowly through shallow waters in an upright position. In fast-moving water, they hang on to vegetation with their long tails. Seahorses, which are thought to mate for life, have an unusual way of giving birth. The female puts her eggs into a pouch on the male's body. There they develop until one day the male "gives birth" to 50 or more baby seahorses!

Stingrays flap their large side fins to "fly" through the water.

THE NATURAL WORLD

◀ Flying fish leap into the air to avoid predators. They use their large, wing-like fins to glide over the surface of the water. A flying fish can cover up to 90 metres in one "flight".

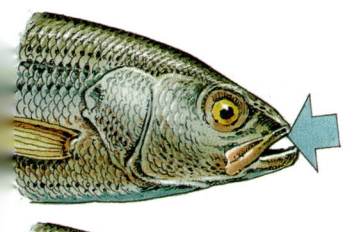

◀ Just like other animals, a fish needs to breathe in oxygen. It has a special way of taking the oxygen from the water. It allows water into its mouth. Then slits in either side of its head, called gills, strain out the oxygen as the water passes through them.

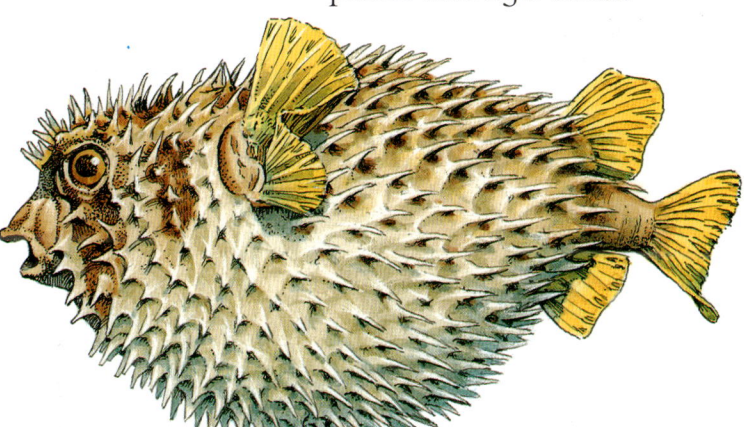

▲ When threatened, the porcupine fish puffs itself up into a balloon shape. Its sharp spines stick out in all directions.

MARINE LIFE

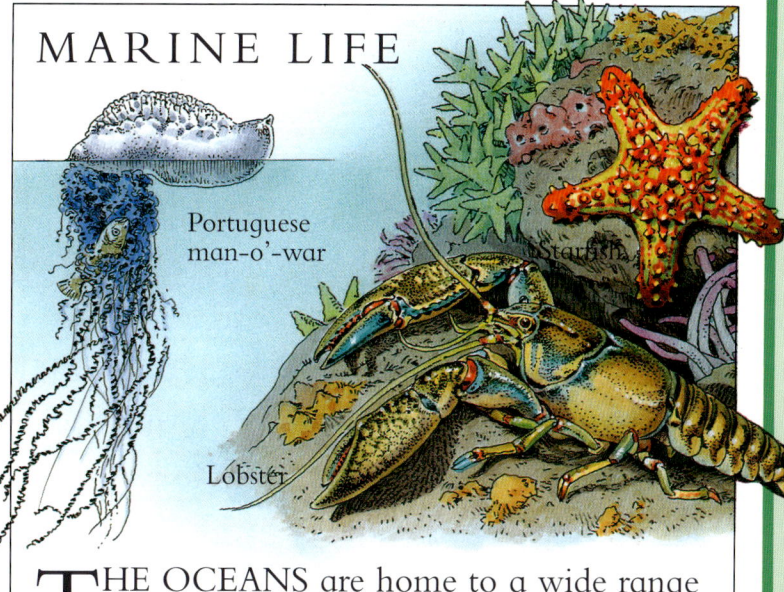

Portuguese man-o'-war

Lobster

Starfish

THE OCEANS are home to a wide range of animals called invertebrates, from a word meaning "without a backbone". There are crustaceans, such as crabs, lobsters and shrimps, which have hard outer parts for protection. Jellyfish, such as the Portuguese man-o'-war, have long, stinging tentacles to kill fish. Starfish use their five suckered "arms" to prise shellfish apart. The eight-legged octopus, a mollusc, can change colour to blend in with its surroundings. To confuse both attackers and prey, it squirts out a jet of ink.

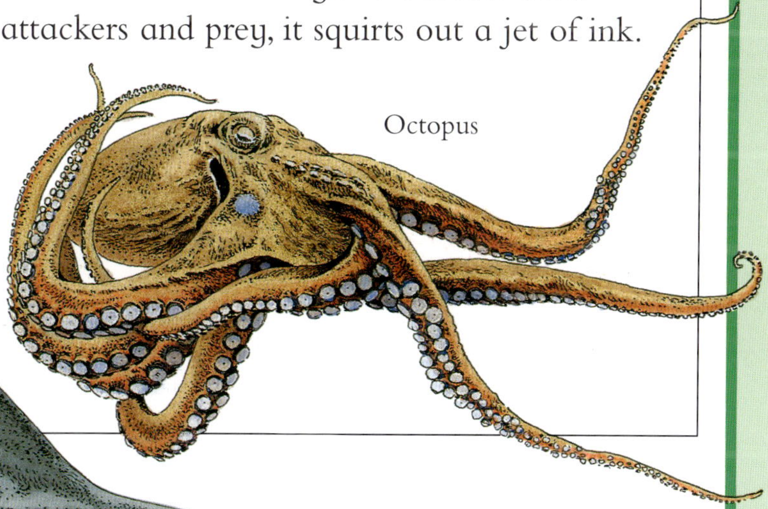

Octopus

Tiger sharks are so called because of the faint stripes on their backs.

Camouflaged on the sea bed, stonefish lie in shallow water around coral reefs.

SEE ALSO: PAGE 60 RIVERS, PAGE 62 SEASHORE, PAGE 64 OCEANS

35

THE NATURAL WORLD

REPTILES AND AMPHIBIANS

MILLIONS of years ago, reptiles dominated the land, seas and skies. Some modern kinds have hardly changed since the days of the dinosaurs. There are four main groups of reptile: snakes, lizards, crocodiles and alligators, and turtles and tortoises.

Because they are cold-blooded animals, reptiles need to warm up in the sun before they have enough energy to move around. Reptiles have hard, scaly skins. They usually lay eggs, although some snakes and lizards give birth to live young.

Flap-necked chameleon from Africa.

Common gecko from south-east Asia.

▲◄ Chameleons are slow-moving lizards that usually live in trees. They can camouflage themselves by changing colour. They shoot out their long, sticky tongues to capture insects. Other lizards, such as geckos, can break off their tails to escape from animals that attack them. A new tail will even grow in its place. The largest lizard of all, the three-metre-long Komodo dragon, has no need of such protection. It preys on deer and wild boar.

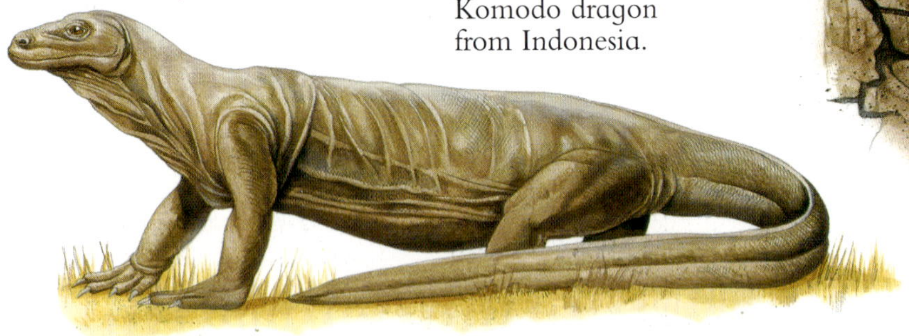

Komodo dragon from Indonesia.

▶ Crocodiles and alligators lurk in tropical rivers and swamps and feed on animals that come down to the water's edge to drink. Their eyes, ears and nostrils are on the tops of their heads so that they can lie in wait almost completely under the water. (You can tell an alligator from a crocodile as an alligator's lower teeth are not visible when its mouth is closed.)

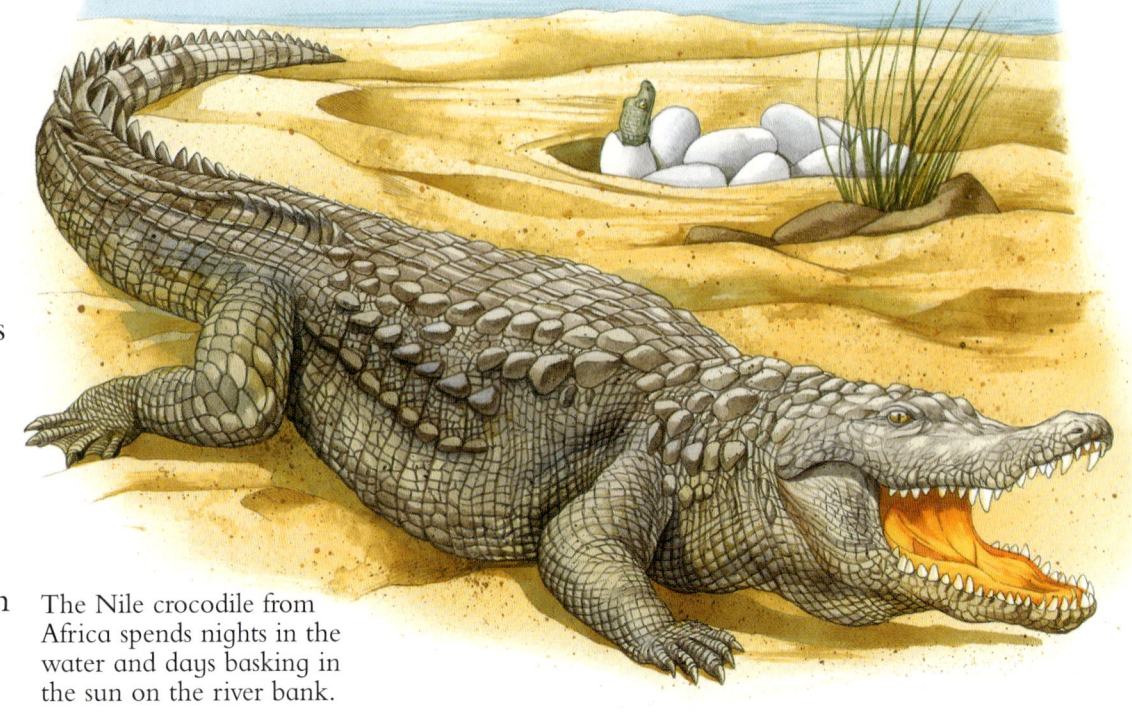

The Nile crocodile from Africa spends nights in the water and days basking in the sun on the river bank.

SEE ALSO: PAGE 30 PREHISTORIC LIFE, PAGES 48-65 THE WORLD ABOUT US

THE NATURAL WORLD

AMPHIBIANS

Blue salamander

Fire-bellied toad

The Galapagos giant tortoise, from the Galapagos Islands off South America.

The king cobra, from south-east Asia, feeds mainly on other snakes. Up to 5.5 metres long, it is the biggest poisonous snake in the world.

▲ Turtles and tortoises are a group of reptiles with strong, bony shells. Instead of teeth, they have horny beaks. Their shells protect them against predators. Turtles spend most of their time in or near water, while tortoises are land animals. They can pull their heads and legs into their shells when danger threatens. Both tortoises and turtles can live for a very long time, sometimes more than 100 years.

FROGS, toads, salamanders and newts are all amphibians. Like reptiles, they are cold-blooded animals. Most have smooth, moist skin and live in or close to water. Amphibians hatch from eggs laid in water. They breathe and feed under water until they become adults. Their bodies change and they develop lungs, allowing them to live out of the water and breathe air. Frogs and toads lose their tails and grow legs when they become adults but newts and salamanders simply grow larger.

Jelly-like frog spawn (frogs' eggs) is laid in water.

The eggs hatch into fish-like tadpoles.

The tadpole loses its tail and grows legs.

The tadpole leaves the water as a tiny frog.

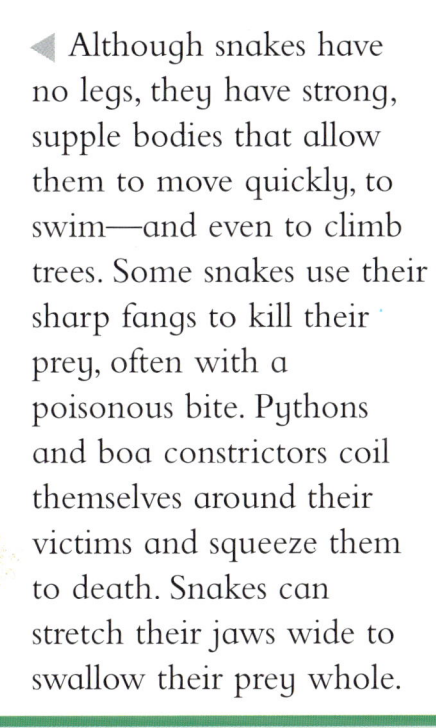

37

◀ Although snakes have no legs, they have strong, supple bodies that allow them to move quickly, to swim—and even to climb trees. Some snakes use their sharp fangs to kill their prey, often with a poisonous bite. Pythons and boa constrictors coil themselves around their victims and squeeze them to death. Snakes can stretch their jaws wide to swallow their prey whole.

The Indian python, from south-east Asia, hunts at night. It preys on rodents and even small deer.

THE NATURAL WORLD

BIRDS

BIRDS are the only animals that have feathers. They have an inner layer of short, soft feathers called down covered by long, smooth feathers that also make up their wings. Feathers keep the birds warm and dry in the coldest and wettest conditions. All birds have a pair of wings, two legs, a beak and claws. Most birds can fly, but a few, such as the ostrich and the penguin, cannot.

There are about 9,000 different kinds of bird in the world today. Most birds make sounds, or calls. Some birds produce patterns of notes which are like songs.

When the weather is cold, many kinds of bird travel long distances to warmer places around the world. This is called migration.

Flamingo

Scarlet ibis

Vulture

Macaw

◀ You can often tell what a bird eats from the shape of its beak. The flamingo holds its head upside down in shallow water and sieves out tiny animals from the water with its beak. The scarlet ibis has a long bill to stab down through the water, while the vulture tears meat with its strong, hooked beak. The macaw's short, powerful beak cracks open hard seeds.

The Andean condor is the largest bird of prey in the world. It lives in the Andes Mountains of South America. It can glide for 16 kilometres without moving its wings.

Swifts spend most of their time in the air. They can even sleep while they are on the wing!

The wandering albatross has the largest wingspan of any living bird. It spends most of its time gliding across the sea, scooping up fish and squid from the water.

Many birds of paradise live in the forests of New Guinea. They have long, colourful tail feathers.

▶ Birds' feet can vary enormously from one kind to another. Mallards have webbed feet to help them push their way through the water. The jacana has very long toes which allow it to walk on floating lily pads. A woodpecker uses its strong claws to hold on to tree trunks. The soles of the osprey's feet are covered with tiny spikes to help it grip on to slippery fish.

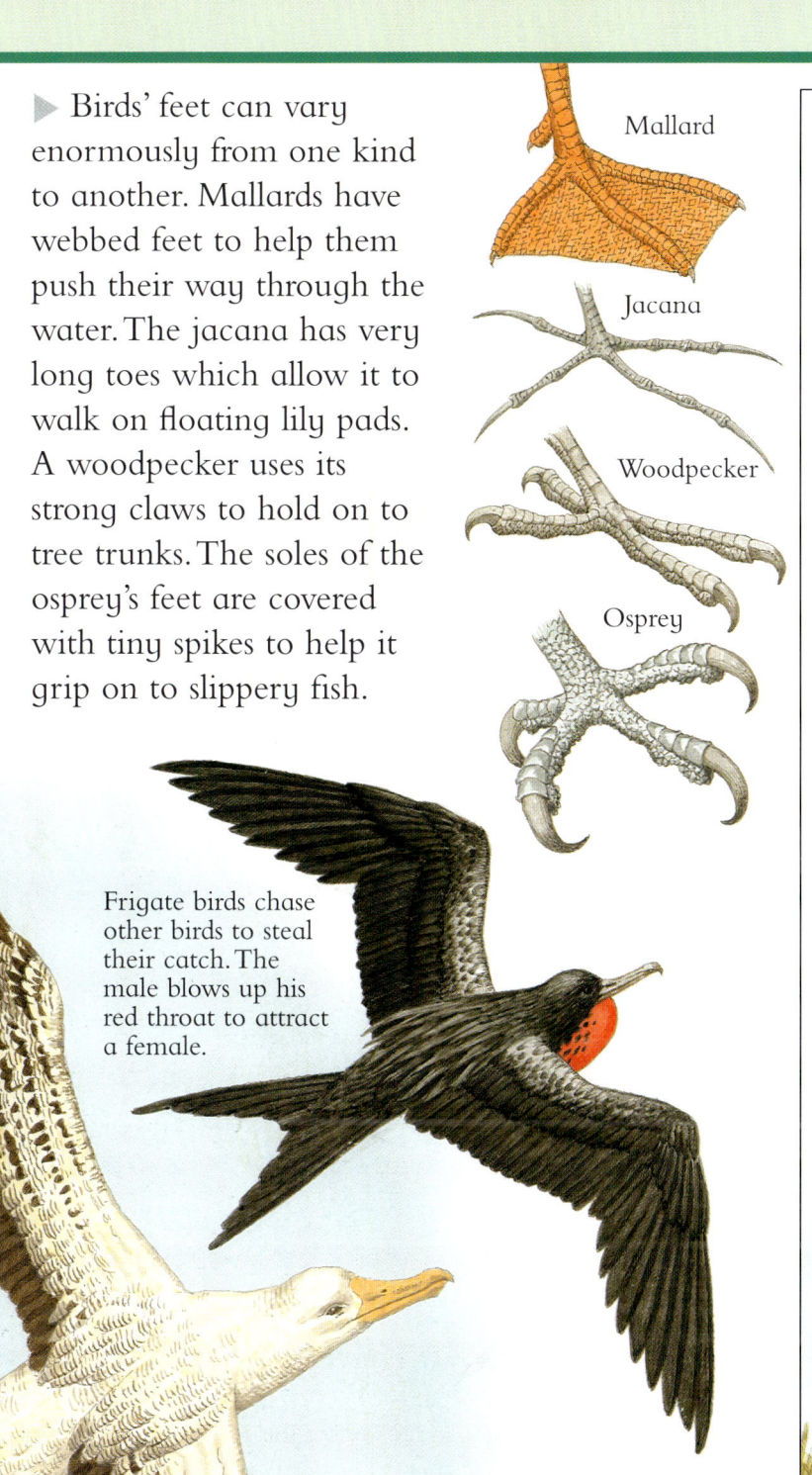

Mallard

Jacana

Woodpecker

Osprey

Frigate birds chase other birds to steal their catch. The male blows up his red throat to attract a female.

Snow buntings live in cold regions of northern Europe. They build their nests among the rocks.

▶ Some birds lay their eggs in holes, burrows, on a cliff edge, or simply on the ground. But most build nests. They collect twigs or blades of grass and weave them together. The female bird usually sits on the eggs to keep them warm until they are ready to hatch. Then the baby bird pecks open the eggshell and comes out into the world.

THE NATURAL WORLD

GREAT AND SMALL

THE OSTRICH is the largest bird in the world. It is even taller than a human! Because it is so big, it cannot fly. However, with its powerful legs and two-toed feet it can run as fast as a racehorse. Ostriches lay the biggest eggs of all birds. They weigh about the same as 40 ordinary hen's eggs. The smallest bird is the hummingbird *(right)*. The tiniest kind is no bigger than a bee. It hovers above flowers and drinks nectar from them. Its tiny wings beat so quickly that they make a humming sound.

Ostriches have long necks and very good eyesight. This helps them to watch out for danger. They spread their wings to warn off enemies.

A baby bird inside an egg feeds on yolk.

SEE ALSO: PAGE 30 PREHISTORIC LIFE, PAGES 48-65 THE WORLD ABOUT US

THE NATURAL WORLD

Mammals (1)

MAMMALS are warm-blooded animals. They feed their newborn young with milk and protect them from danger during the earliest part of their lives. Most mammals develop inside the mother, instead of hatching from eggs. Except for some sea mammals, they all have four limbs and are covered with hair or fur.

There are about 4,000 kinds of mammal living on the land, in the water or in the air. They range in size from tiny mice to giant blue whales. Mammals are the group of animals to which humans belong.

The mandrill, a kind of baboon, is from the rainforests of Africa.

Giant pandas live in the mountain forests of China.

◀ By day, the mandrill searches on the ground for fruits, seeds and insects to eat. It sleeps in the trees at night.

◀ The giant panda is one of the rarest mammals in the world. It is slow to breed and, when it does have young, only one survives. The giant panda's main food is bamboo. If there is a shortage, the pandas starve.

A three-toed sloth from the Amazon rainforest.

◀ Sloths spend much of their time hanging upside down from branches of rainforest trees. They can eat, sleep and even give birth in this position. For food they eat leaves.

A tiger from south-east Asia.

◀ Tigers are the largest members of the cat family. They usually live and hunt alone, carefully stalking their prey before leaping to make a kill. Because of hunting by man and the destruction of their habitat, tigers are in danger of extinction.

SEE ALSO: PAGES 24-29 THE HUMAN BODY, PAGE 30 PREHISTORIC LIFE, PAGE 42 MAMMALS (2).

▶ These skulls belong to four mammals that eat very different things. Rats have long, hard front teeth for gnawing. The anteater has no teeth at all, just long jaws and an incredibly long, sticky tongue for lapping up ants. The grey wolf has strong jaws and sharp teeth for tearing through meat. Zebras have sharp front teeth to cut through grass stems, while their back teeth grind and chew.

Rat

Giant anteater

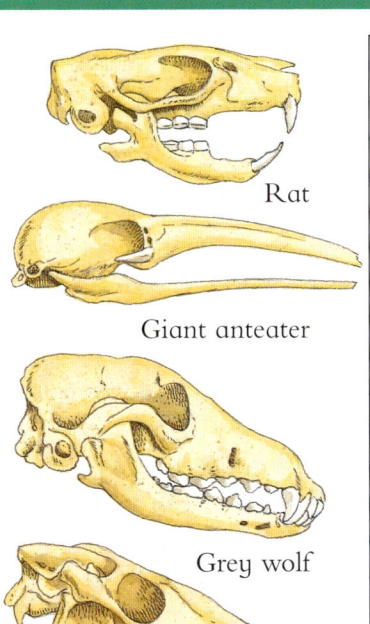

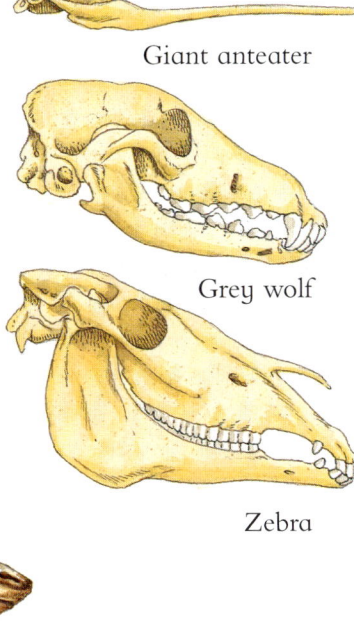

Grey wolf

Zebra

POUCHES AND EGGS

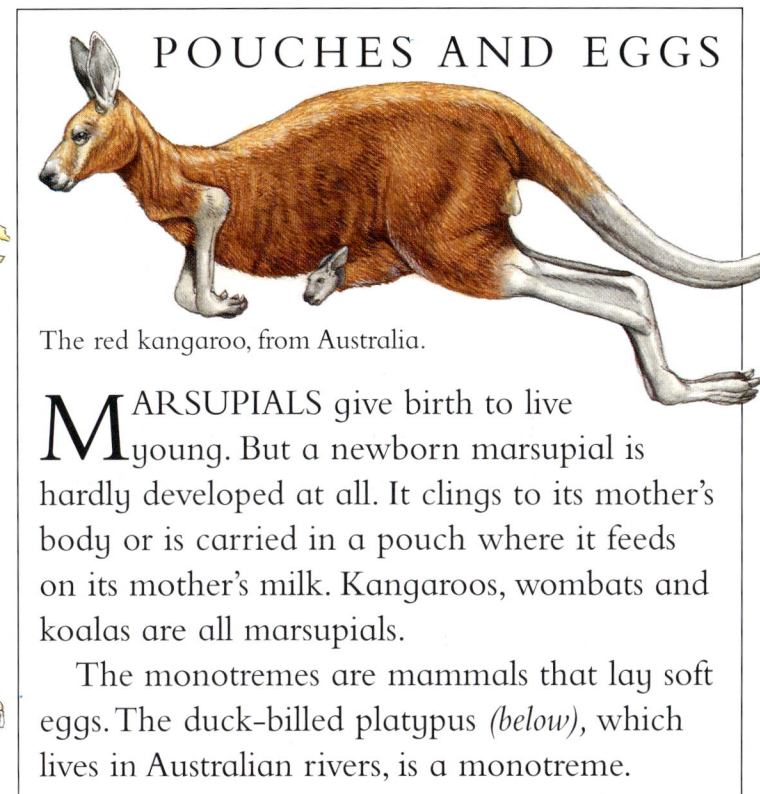

The red kangaroo, from Australia.

MARSUPIALS give birth to live young. But a newborn marsupial is hardly developed at all. It clings to its mother's body or is carried in a pouch where it feeds on its mother's milk. Kangaroos, wombats and koalas are all marsupials.

The monotremes are mammals that lay soft eggs. The duck-billed platypus *(below)*, which lives in Australian rivers, is a monotreme.

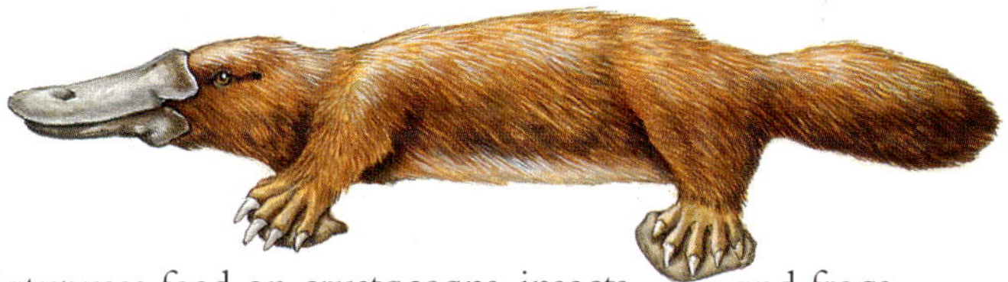

Platypuses feed on crustaceans, insects and frogs.

The giraffe from Africa is the tallest animal in the world.

The black rhinoceros is, in fact, grey. It feeds on leaves and shoots.

◀ Giraffes are well known for their long necks. They use them to stretch up into trees to eat leaves. Some kinds of rhinoceros, especially in south-east Asia, are in danger of extinction because they are hunted for their horns.

▶ Elephants, too, are hunted for their tusks, which are actually long front teeth. Elephants live in family groups, and can survive for as long as 70 years.

This African elephant has larger ears than its Asian relative. It uses its trunk for grasping and for sucking up water.

The aardvark from Africa uses its long, sticky tongue to feed on termites and ants.

PAGES 48-65 THE WORLD ABOUT US

THE NATURAL WORLD

Mammals (2)

MAMMALS live in all kinds of environments, from polar ice to steamy rainforest. Some spend most or all their lives in water, while bats can fly in the air like birds.

Whales and dolphins live in the water all the time. Some whales have sieve-like parts called baleen in their mouths, which they use to trap tiny shrimp-like animals called krill. Other whales, and all dolphins, have teeth and prey on fish and squid.

Some mammals such as seals, feed in the water but breed and rest on land. Sea lions use their strong front flippers to move easily on land. Some can run faster than humans!

▶ Every year, grey whales make an amazing journey of migration. They travel from their feeding grounds in the Arctic to the warm waters off the coast of Mexico, where their calves are born. A few months later, it is time to swim all the way back again! This incredible journey of about 20,000 kilometres can take the whales up to three months to complete.

The northern fur seal's thick coat helps to keep it warm in the freezing waters of Alaska.

The common dolphin can easily be identified by the yellow stripe on its side.

◀ Seals and sea lions spend much of their time in the water hunting for food. Most eat whatever they can find, including krill, fish, squid and even birds. The leopard seal even eats other seals. Some seals can hold their breath under water for half an hour or longer.

Manatees are large, gentle plant-eaters that live in the shallow coastal waters, lakes and rivers of the tropics. Distantly related to elephants, and sometimes known as "sea cows", they feed only on underwater vegetation such as seaweed or sea grass.

The West Indian manatee lives near the coasts of the southern USA and northern South America.

Clusters of small crustaceans (see page 35) called barnacles live on the grey whale's skin.

SEE ALSO: PAGE 40 MAMMALS (1), PAGES 48-65 THE WORLD ABOUT US

THE NATURAL WORLD

◀ Dolphins are well known for their speed and their acrobatic leaps out of the water. Sometimes hundreds of dolphins come together in large groups called schools. They can "talk" to one another using clicks and whistles.

▼ The sea otter is one of only a few kinds of animal that use tools. While lying on its back in the sea, the otter smashes open shellfish using a stone placed on its belly. It then eats the soft insides.

Sea otters live in the north Pacific Ocean. They seldom leave the water. They even sleep floating on their backs.

MAMMALS THAT FLY

The horseshoe bat takes its name from the strange shape of its nose.

BATS are the only mammals that can fly. There are hundreds of different kinds of bat. They live everywhere but the coldest parts of the world.

Bats' wings are actually flaps of skin stretched over very long fingers. Bats live in groups in caves, trees—even in roofs! They usually sleep during the day, hanging upside down with their wings wrapped around them. At night, they go hunting. A bat finds its way in the dark by using its extraordinary sense of hearing. It makes very high-pitched sounds that echo back from objects, giving the bat a picture of its surroundings.

▶ North American beavers are expert builders of dams (see page 61). They gnaw down trees with their sharp teeth, and pile up the logs across rivers or streams, filling in the gaps with sticks, weed and mud.

The beaver's webbed hind feet and flattened tail make it an excellent swimmer.

Despite eating only grass, other plants and fruit, hippos have huge, sharp teeth which they use for defence.

◀ The hippopotamus lives in the rivers and lakes of Africa. Hippos stay in the water during the heat of the day, coming out only at night to feed.

Beavers build their homes, or lodges, in lakes which they have made them-selves by damming rivers.

43

THE NATURAL WORLD

PLANTS

THERE ARE two main types of plant: flowering plants and non-flowering plants. Flowering plants have flowers which contain male and female parts. They use them to reproduce and make seeds. Non-flowering plants include ferns and algae, simple water life-forms ranging from microscopic plankton to giant seaweeds. They reproduce by making tiny bodies called spores.

All plants make food in a process called photosynthesis. In most plants, the leaves take in sunlight and carbon dioxide from the air. Water and nutrients taken up by the roots are carried up the plant through tiny tubes in its stem. In a chemical reaction, the leaves combine carbon with water to make sugars, which are food for the plant.

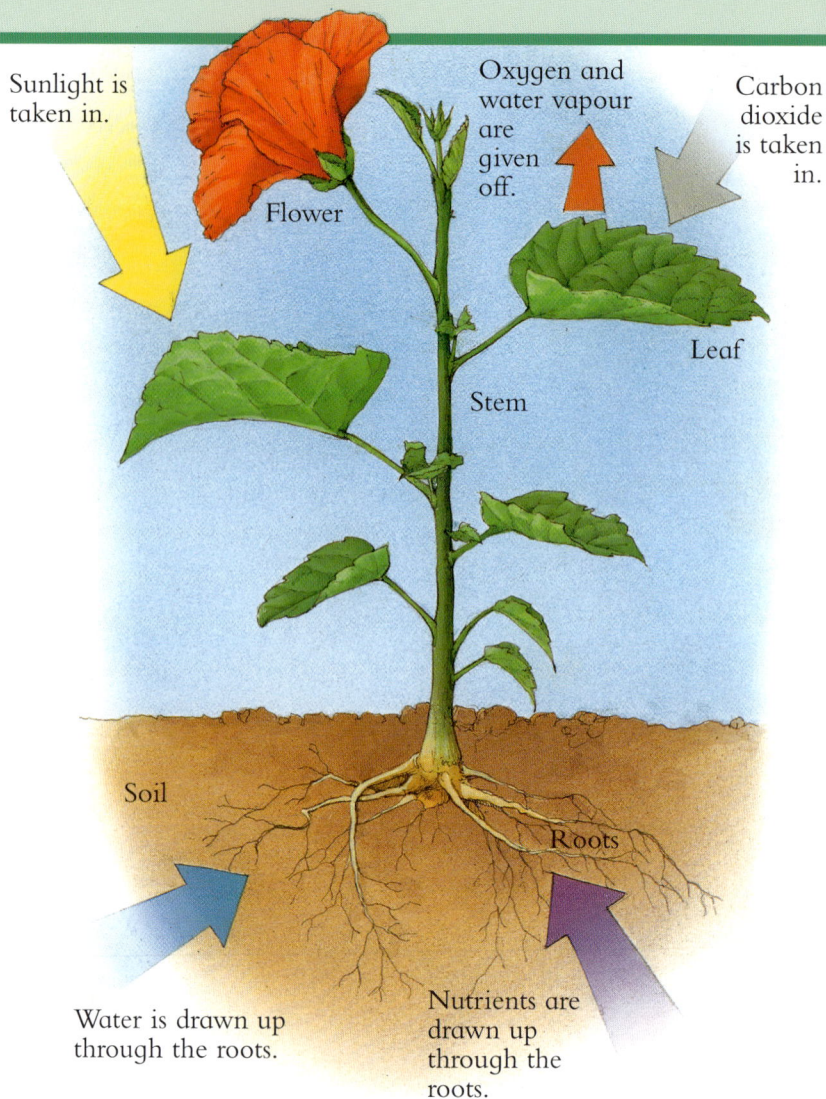

◀ Flowering plants can reproduce by a process called sexual reproduction. In some, the colour and scent of flowers attract insects. As the insects feed on nectar inside a flower, pollen from the anthers (the male parts) sticks to them. When they visit the next flower, the pollen brushes off on to the stigma (the female part). This is called pollination. The pollen joins with the female egg to make a seed. Other plants rely on the wind to spread their pollen. Some plants send out horizontal stems from which new plants grow.

THE NATURAL WORLD

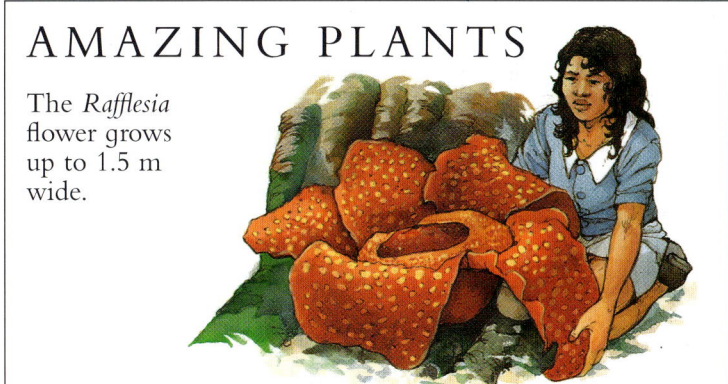

Maple

Jay, a seed-eating bird.

Hazel

◀ When plants produce seeds, they must send them away so that the seeds will have space to grow into new plants. Many seeds form inside fruits. Animals eat the tasty fruit, then drop the seeds elsewhere. Other seeds hook themselves on to feathers or fur to travel. Some tree seeds, for example the maple, have "wings" that carry them spinning through the air. Other plants, such as the hazel, throw the seeds out.

Squirrels bury oak seeds, or acorns, to eat in the winter.

▼ A fruit is the protective case enclosing the seeds of a flowering plant. Some fruits, such as nuts, have only one seed and a hard case. Others, such as apples or oranges, have soft, juicy cases containing several seeds. Pea pods are also fruits. The peas inside are the seeds.

Orange

Sunflower

Case   Seed

Pea

Sweet chestnut

Cucumber

Walnut

Cherry

AMAZING PLANTS

The *Rafflesia* flower grows up to 1.5 m wide.

THE LARGEST flower in the world is *Rafflesia*. It is a parasite, so called because it takes its food from another plant (its host), the jungle vine, to which it is attached by long, thin threads. It lives in the rainforests of south-east Asia, and smells like rotting meat.

Some plants feed on animals! When a fly settles between its jaw-like leaves, the Venus fly trap snaps shut and the unfortunate fly is slowly digested.

The Venus fly trap from south-eastern USA.

▶ Mushrooms and toadstools are not plants, but fungi. They cannot make their own food, so they take up dead plant and animal material from the soil or grow on living plants and animals. Fungi reproduce by sending spores into the air. Mushrooms and toadstools have caps raised up from the ground on stalks. The spores fall from beneath the cap and are carried away on a breeze.

A fly agaric is a colourful toadstool that is poisonous to eat.

45

SEE ALSO: PAGE 12 SEASONS AND CLIMATES, PAGE 32 INSECTS, PAGE 46 TREES, PAGE 56 RAINFORESTS

THE NATURAL WORLD

TREES

TREES are large plants that have woody stems or trunks covered with a protective layer of bark. There are two main types of tree: broad-leaved trees and conifers. All broad-leaved trees are flowering plants and produce fruits with seeds inside. Conifers produce cones which carry their seeds. Most broad-leaves are deciduous trees: their leaves fall in autumn. Nearly all conifers, and some broad-leaves, are evergreen. Their leaves also fall, but not all at the same time.

Trees are very important to us. Like all plants, they take in carbon dioxide from the air and give off oxygen for us to breathe. Their timber is used for fuel, paper, furniture and houses. Trees also give us medicines, oils, rubber and fruits. Many animals depend on trees for their homes and for food.

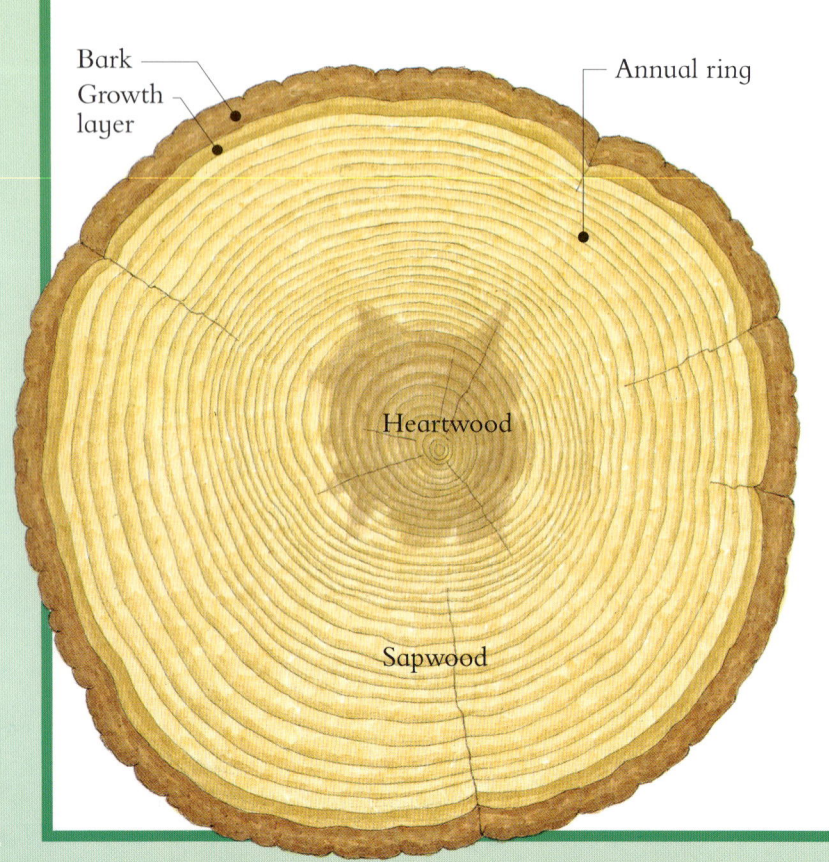

Acorns are the fruit of the oak tree.

An oak tree is home to a great variety of living creatures.

Bark
Growth layer
Annual ring
Heartwood
Sapwood

◀▲ A tree has roots below ground and a shoot (its stem) made up of a trunk, branches and twigs, which spread out the leaves so that they all receive sunlight. The central part of the trunk, the heartwood, forms the tree's strong "backbone". Water passes from the roots to the leaves through the outer layer, the sapwood. A new layer of sapwood grows each year. It appears as a single ring. We can tell how old a tree was by counting the rings in a tree stump.

THE NATURAL WORLD

◀ This giant sequoia in California is the heaviest tree in the world. More than 90 metres high and possibly more than 3,000 years old, it is 25 times heavier than the largest animal, the blue whale.

▼ Palm trees grow in hot countries and are neither coniferous nor broad-leaved trees. They have tall trunks with a few very large leaves at the top.

Coconut palm

Palms bear fruits, like this coconut.

CONIFERS

Cone

Needles

Douglas fir

THE WORD conifer means "cone-bearing". A conifer's seeds are found on the faces of each of the scales that make up the cones. In damp weather, the scales are closed. When warm weather comes, they open and the seeds flutter away in the breeze.

Most conifers have long, narrow leaves called needles. The needles are tough and can survive wind, frost and long periods of drought. This means that conifers can grow in areas where the climate is cold or dry.

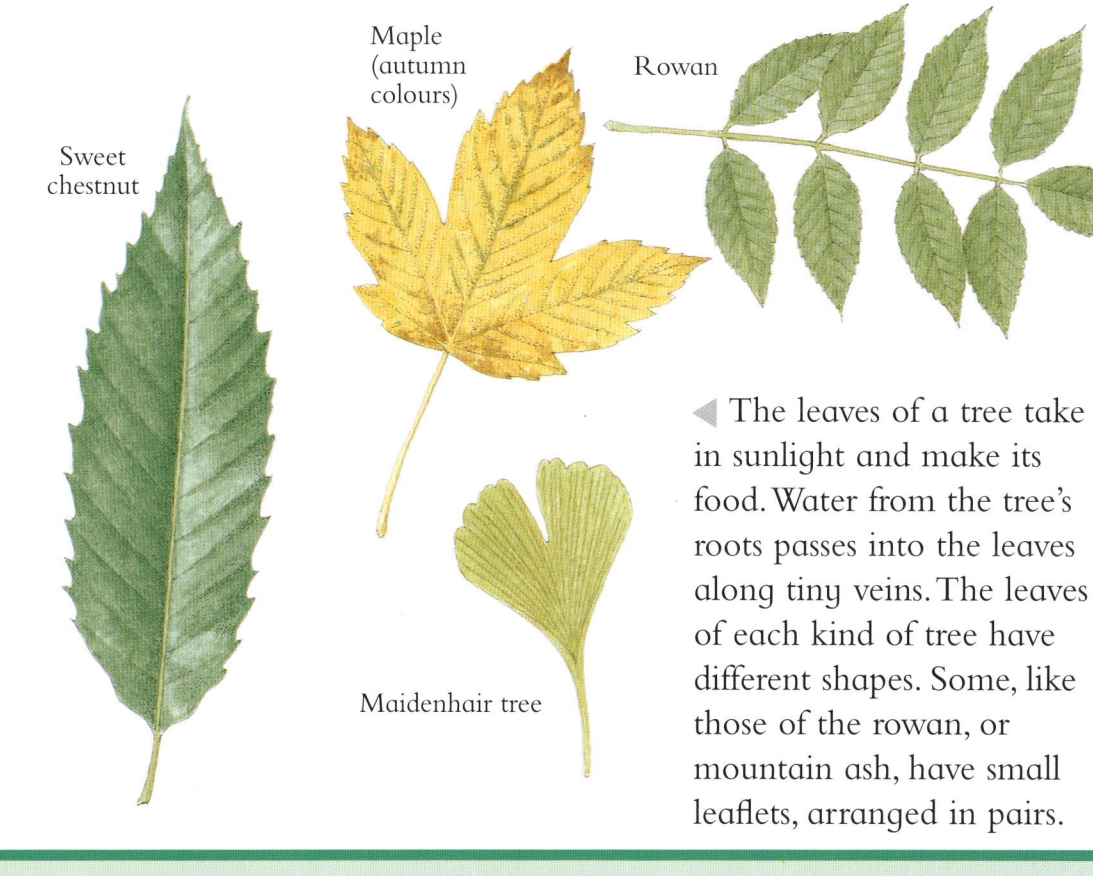

47

◀ For a new tree to grow, its seeds must find their way into the soil. When the temperature and moisture levels of the soil are right, the seed splits open. Roots probe downwards into the soil while a shoot grows upwards. New leaves grow on the shoot.

◀ Baobabs, from Africa, are weird-looking trees. They have huge trunks shaped like bottles. These store water to help them survive the dry season.

Sweet chestnut

Maple (autumn colours)

Rowan

Maidenhair tree

◀ The leaves of a tree take in sunlight and make its food. Water from the tree's roots passes into the leaves along tiny veins. The leaves of each kind of tree have different shapes. Some, like those of the rowan, or mountain ash, have small leaflets, arranged in pairs.

SEE ALSO: PAGE 44 PLANTS, PAGE 50 WOODLANDS, PAGE 56 RAINFORESTS

POLAR LANDS

THE NORTH POLE is surrounded by the permanently icy Arctic Ocean. At the opposite end of the Earth, the South Pole is on the continent of Antarctica. Because the Poles never come as close to the Sun as the rest of the Earth, they do not get as much warmth. This means that ice and snow cover the Poles all year round.

To survive in the cold, many polar animals have thick fur or layers of fat on their bodies. The only humans living on harsh Antarctica are scientists studying the environment. In contrast, different groups of people, such as the Inuit of Greenland and northern Canada, have lived in the Arctic region for thousands of years. They hunt polar animals for food and clothing.

◀ Polar lands are found at the most northerly and southerly points of the Earth. In the north, much of the Arctic Ocean is permanently covered with a mass of slowly moving ice, called pack ice. The southern continent of Antarctica is covered in a thick layer of ice called an ice cap.

Icebergs are large chunks of ice that fall into the sea from glaciers *(see page 59)* or parts of an ice cap. A small part of the iceberg floats above the water; much of its bulk lies beneath.

Iceberg

Emperor penguins

Leopard seal

Adélie penguin

◀ Antarctica is the coldest place on Earth. It has ice about two kilometres thick, high mountains and fierce blizzards. Only a very few plants and animals live on the land, although the cold waters off the coast are full of life, including fish, birds, seals and whales. Emperor penguins lay their eggs on the ice. Then the males carry the eggs, and even the newborn chicks, between their own feet and belly for warmth. The smaller Adélie penguin is the favourite meal of the ferocious leopard seal.

Walruses eat shellfish from the sea bed, which they find using their sensitive whiskers.

THE WORLD ABOUT US

When summer ends in the Arctic, the Arctic tern makes an incredible journey halfway around the world to Antarctica where summer is just beginning.

TUNDRA

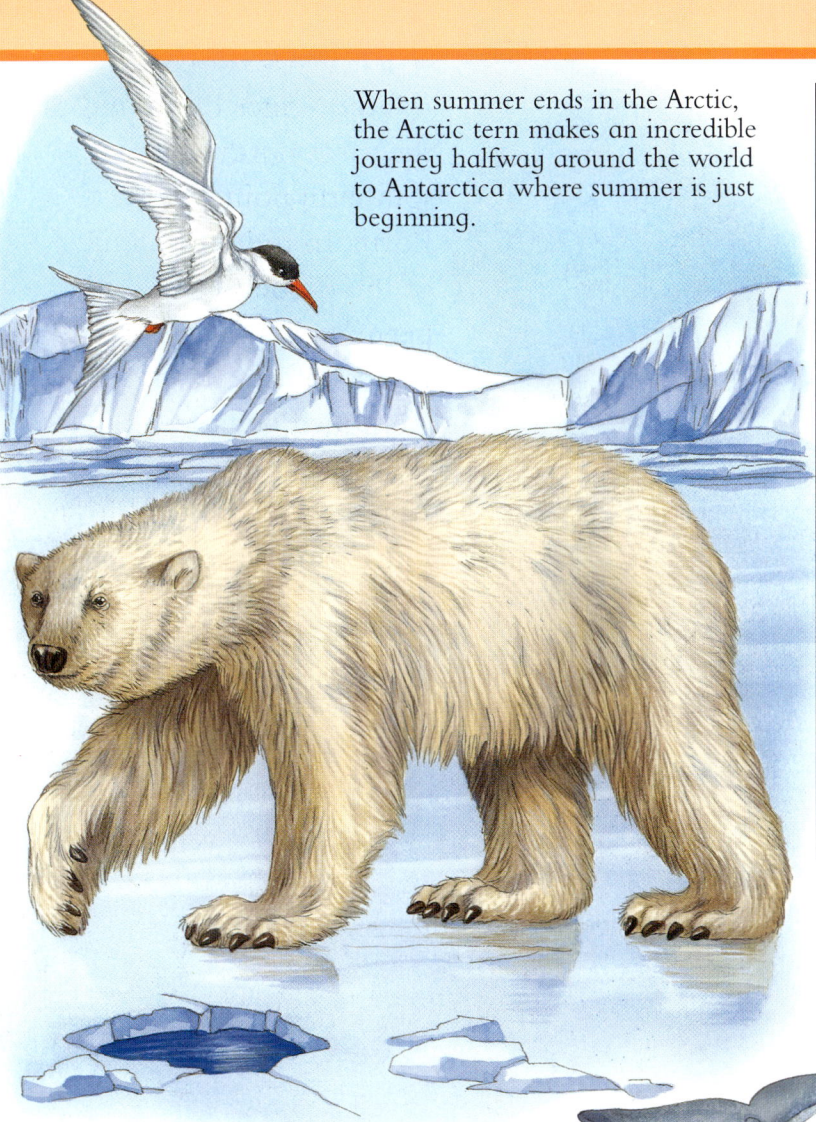

THE LANDS bordering the Arctic Ocean are bleak and treeless, with a permanent layer of ice lying beneath the soil. This is the tundra. During the short summer, small plants and mosses grow. Herds of reindeer or caribou come from the forests further south to feed on them. Musk oxen stay in the tundra all year round. If attacked by wolves, they form a circle around their young.

▲ The animals that live in the Arctic region take their food from the sea. Tiny plants and animals called plankton provide food for fish, which are then eaten by seals. They, in turn, are prey for the mighty polar bear. Polar bears lie in wait to catch seals as they come up through holes in the ice to breathe. The bear's thick white coat keeps it warm even while it is swimming in the icy waters.

Walruses *(left)* use their tusks both for fighting and defence. On warm days, large groups bask together in the sun and their skins turn pink.

The humpback whale makes underwater noises which sound like songs.

▼ Many kinds of whale visit polar waters in the summer. The giant blue and humpback whales sift through mouthfuls of water to extract tiny sea creatures, while the killer whale hunts fish and seals. The narwhal lives in the Arctic all year round.

Killer whales live in family groups called pods.

The blue whale is the largest living animal in the world.

The narwhal's long tusk is actually a tooth.

49

SEE ALSO: PAGE 12 SEASONS AND CLIMATES, PAGE 42 MAMMALS (2), PAGE 120 EXPLORERS

WOODLANDS

MANY parts of the world with a temperate climate *(see page 13)* are covered by woodlands—or would be if they had not been cleared for farmland or cities. Coniferous trees can survive in lower temperatures than deciduous trees *(see pages 46-47)*, so coniferous woodlands are often found undisturbed in northerly or mountainous regions where few people live.

The trees and plants that grow in woodlands provide food and shelter for many different kinds of animal. Many are nocturnal: they come out only at night to feed on woodland plants, or to hunt other animals.

◀ Large areas of coniferous woodland are found in North America, Scandinavia and Russia. They are called boreal forests *(shown as bright green)*. Deciduous woodland *(shown as darker green)* still covers parts of eastern North America, central and western Europe, China and, in the southern hemisphere, the hill country of Australia and New Zealand.

◀ Many small creatures live in the woodland soil. As they burrow their network of tunnels, earthworms help to spread nutrients (substances that plants and animals need in their food) through the soil. Worms are also a source of food for much larger burrowing animals: moles. Slugs and snails creep along, feeding on plant matter. Ants scurry through the tunnels and chambers that make up their nest. Ants, beetles and other small soil creatures are all prey for spiders.

THE WORLD ABOUT US

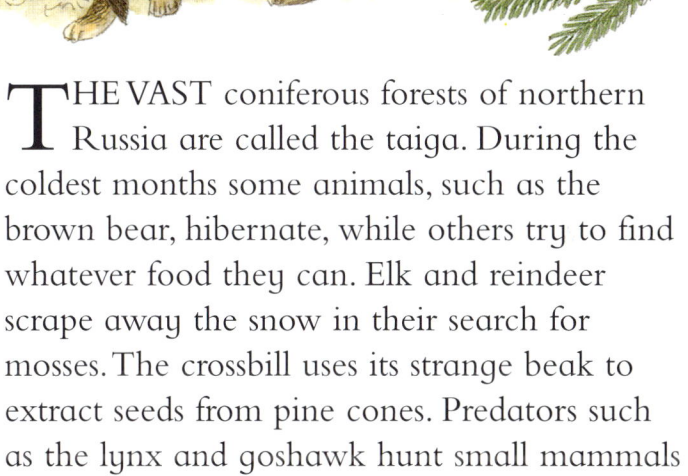

KEY
1. Red squirrel
2. Green woodpecker
3. Tawny owl
4. Dormouse
5. Roe deer
6. Grey squirrel
7. Jay
8. Badger
9. Rabbit
10. Stoat
11. Blackbird
12. Great tit
13. Song thrush
14. Fox
15. Hedgehog

TAIGA

Goshawk · Elk · Brown bear · Reindeer · Lynx · Crossbill

THE VAST coniferous forests of northern Russia are called the taiga. During the coldest months some animals, such as the brown bear, hibernate, while others try to find whatever food they can. Elk and reindeer scrape away the snow in their search for mosses. The crossbill uses its strange beak to extract seeds from pine cones. Predators such as the lynx and goshawk hunt small mammals as they search for nuts and berries.

◀ Autumn has begun in this wood in Europe. The fallen leaves start to rot and, with the help of the tiny creatures that feed on them, form a rich upper layer to the soil. Toadstools grow well in the moist ground. Squirrels and jays hide stores of nuts which will last them through the winter. Dormice prepare to hibernate during the cold months to come. Small mammals such as voles and rabbits must look out for foxes or owls in search of a meal.

51

SEE ALSO: PAGE 12 SEASONS AND CLIMATES, PAGE 38 BIRDS, PAGE 40 MAMMALS (1), PAGE 44 PLANTS, PAGE 46 TREES

GRASSLANDS

GRASSLAND is the name given to large areas of wild grass, with small plants and sometimes scattered trees. Grasslands are found in areas where there is enough rainfall to stop the land becoming a desert, but not enough to support woodland or forest.

During the wet season in Africa, grasslands are green and rich with fresh new grass and plants. These are food for the many kinds of plant-eating animals that live there. The plant-eaters are themselves prey for meat-eaters such as lions, cheetahs or hyenas. In such an open landscape there is nowhere to hide from predators, so the only means of escape for plant-eaters is to run. Many live in herds, with one member always on the lookout for approaching danger.

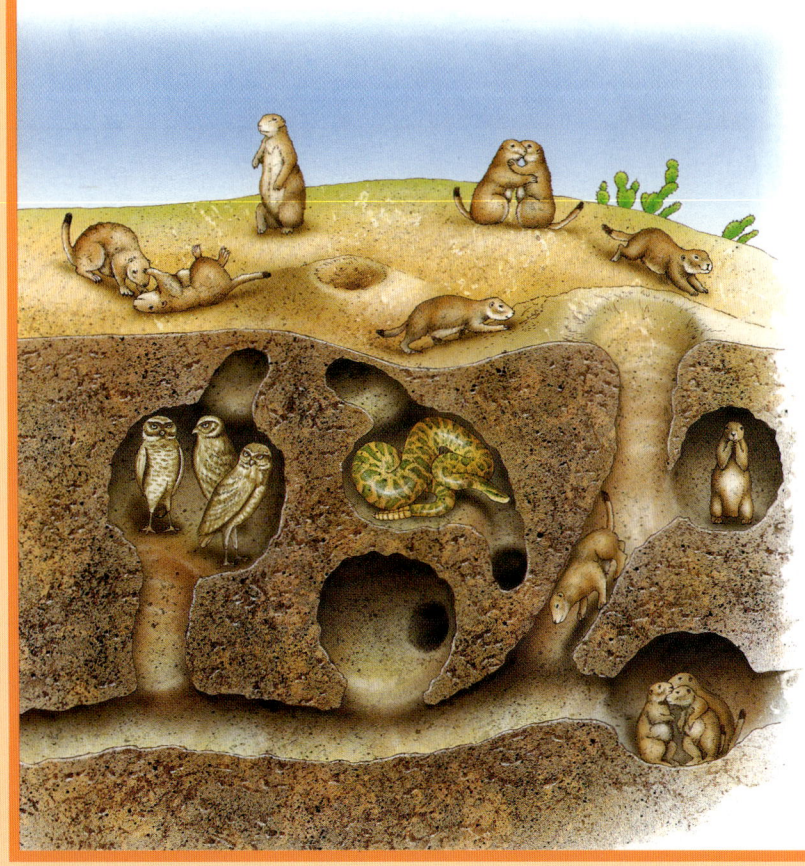

Grasslands are found the world over. They are known as prairies in North America, steppes in Asia and pampas in South America. In Africa, the savannah, a mixture of grasses and trees, is rich with wildlife. Giraffes and elephants reach up to leaves in the trees. Zebras eat tall, coarse grass, leaving shorter grass for wildebeest, antelopes and warthogs.

On the North American prairie, a kind of ground squirrel called the prairie dog lives in a vast network of burrows. Hundreds of prairie dogs may live together in one underground "city". Friendly greetings are made by touching noses. A high warning bark from one of the group will send the others rushing down into their burrows. Old prairie dog burrows are often used by other animals such as burrowing owls and rattlesnakes.

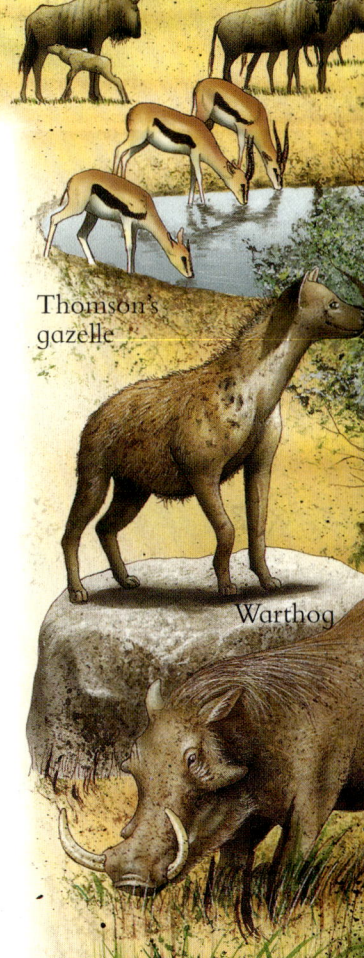

SEE ALSO: PAGE 12 SEASONS AND CLIMATES, PAGE 32 INSECTS, PAGE 40 MAMMALS (1)

THE WORLD ABOUT US

A scene of the East African savannah grasslands, beneath the slopes of Kilimanjaro, Africa's highest mountain.

Wildebeest

Giraffe

Zebra

Marabou stork

Hyena

Lion

TERMITES

DOTTED around tropical grasslands are huge towers made of rock-hard soil. These are termite nests, which can be home to millions of termites. Deep inside the nest live the king and queen. The queen's huge body is full of eggs. Other termites, called workers, look after the young and go out to find food. The workers collect dead plant material and put it into moist chambers in the nest, where "gardens" of fungus soften the plant material ready for eating. Soldier termites stand guard outside the nest.

A soldier termite

Inside each tower is a complex system of rooms and passage-ways, including storerooms, nurseries for eggs and young and even a garden! Fresh air flows about the nest.

◀ The cheetah hunts by bringing down its prey after a chase. It can sprint faster than any other land animal, reaching 100 km/h for short distances. Lions usually live and hunt in groups called prides. It is the females that stalk and kill their prey. Hyenas have powerful jaws that allow them to crunch and swallow bones. Like marabou storks, they also feed on the leftovers of animals killed by others.

53

THE WORLD ABOUT US

DESERTS

A DESERT is an area of land which has very little or no rainfall. Many deserts are hot places, bare and rocky or sometimes covered with sand. There are also cold deserts, such as the Gobi in Asia, where winters are bitterly cold.

In hot deserts, temperatures can soar to over 50°C during the day. There are no trees to give shade and very few places to find water. Even so, some kinds of plant and animal are still able to survive. Desert plants can take in water that condenses from dew or fog *(see page 14)*. The headstander beetle from Africa stands on its head on foggy mornings to drink the condensation which trickles down its body.

◀ Areas of desert are found in the west of the USA and South America, as well as in Asia, Australia and Africa. The largest and hottest desert in the world, the Sahara, is in northern Africa. Most of it is covered by rock or gravel, only one tenth by sand. At night, with no cloud cover, the ground cools very quickly and temperatures drop to below freezing.

The addax, a rare antelope from the Sahara desert, does not need to drink. It survives on the moisture that is contained in the vegetation it eats.

◀ Cacti are common plants of the American desert. They collect water from dew or rain whenever it falls, and store it in their swollen stems. The saguaro can grow up to 15 metres tall. Many desert animals, such as the kangaroo rat and sidewinder, a kind of snake named after the way it moves across the ground, avoid the scorching daytime temperatures by hiding in burrows or under rocks. Cold-blooded reptiles, such as lizards, *(see page 36)*, warm their bodies in the mornings before they can hunt.

SEE ALSO: PAGE 10 ROCKS AND FOSSILS, PAGE 12 SEASONS AND CLIMATES, PAGE 78 HOMES AROUND THE WORLD

THE WORLD ABOUT US

GRAND CANYON

THE GRAND CANYON is a deep cleft in the desert of Arizona, USA. More than 350 kilometres long and about 1.6 kilometres deep, it began to be formed millions of years ago as the land around the Colorado River gradually rose up. The river started to flow faster and cut down deeper and deeper into the surrounding rock. Today, the Grand Canyon is so deep that we can see many different layers of sedimentary rock *(see page 10)* laid down in prehistoric times.

In some places the wind can build up huge "waves" of sand called dunes.

◀ The Sahara desert is an inhospitable place, but even so, people live there. Towns and villages have grown up around oases, places where underground water comes to the surface. Desert travellers like the Tuareg people once commonly used camels to carry their belongings or goods across the desert. Camels can travel for weeks without eating or drinking. Nowadays, most people use cars and lorries to cross the desert.

"Living stones" look just like pebbles when they are not in flower. They live off water trapped between cracks in rocks.

55

THE WORLD ABOUT US

Rainforests

HALF OF all the plant and animal species in the world live in tropical rainforests. Heavy rainfall and high temperatures are ideal for many kinds of plant and animal to thrive. Tall trees reach up to form a thick roof of branches called the canopy. Many animals live there, feeding on fruits and flowers. Beneath the canopy is a layer of lower trees. The forest floor is dark, as little light can reach through the trees.

Rivers and streams, also teeming with life, run through the rainforest. They serve as forest "highways" for the native peoples of the forest. In the rainy season in South America, the rivers flood huge areas of the forest, and fish swim in between the tree trunks.

▶ High up in the canopy of the Amazon rainforest, birds feed on fruits, insects and small mammals. Monkeys swing through the trees, while sloths hang almost motionless. On lower branches, the jaguar lurks silently in wait for its prey—a shy tapir, perhaps. Coiled up on the river's edge is a massive anaconda snake. The Amazon rivers and streams are home to fierce piranhas that can reduce a large animal to a skeleton in minutes, and to electric eels that stun their victims before devouring them.

◀ Tropical rainforest is found in lands near the Equator wherever there is high rainfall. The largest area is in the Amazon basin of South America. Other rainforests are in Central America, southeast Asia, the western part of central Africa, eastern Madagascar and northern Australia. In many of these places, wide areas of forest have been cut down.

Electric eel

Pirarucu

SEE ALSO: PAGES 30–47 THE NATURAL WORLD, PAGE 74 SOUTH AMERICA

THE WORLD ABOUT US

KEY
1 Harpy eagle
2 Howler monkey
3 Spider monkey
4 Toucan
5 Squirrel monkey
6 Kinkajou
7 Tree frog
8 Tree anteater
9 Hoatzin
10 Tree snake
11 Tree iguana
12 Sloth
13 Scarlet macaw
14 Jaguar
15 Tapir
16 Anaconda
17 Armadillo
18 Anole lizard
19 Morpho butterfly
20 Io moth
21 Capybara
22 Dragonfly
23 Suriname toad
24 Jacana

LAST CHANCE TO SEE...

Golden tamarind
Javan rhinoceros
Aye-aye
Birdwing butterfly
Cayman

EVERY DAY, large areas of rainforest all over the world are being destroyed by people. Trees are cut down to make furniture and other wood products, and to clear space for mining, roads and cattle farming. As the rainforest disappears, many animals are left homeless. Some species, such as those pictured above, are in danger of dying out altogether. Breeding programmes in zoos and reserves have helped to keep some species alive. However, many rainforest animals and plants disappear even before we have the chance to discover them.

▶ Thousands of kinds of insects and spiders live in the rainforest. Some, such as the bird-eating spider, grow to a size larger than a human hand. Leafcutter ants cut out pieces of leaf which they carry back to their nest. The ants grow little "gardens" of fungus on them, which they eat. Many butterflies are brightly coloured, warning that they are poisonous. The "eyes" on the bush cricket's wings frighten away enemies.

Piranha
River turtle

Thorn bugs
Hummingbird
Bush cricket
Leafcutter ants
Bird-eating spider

57

THE WORLD ABOUT US

MOUNTAINS

WHEN THE plates of the Earth *(see page 9)* push against one another, the land "folds up", like a rug on the floor. This is how many mountain ranges are formed. It all takes millions of years to happen. Great mountain ranges of the world include the Andes in South America, the Rockies in North America, the Alps in Europe and the Himalayas in Asia.

The tops of some mountains are so high that they are covered in snow and ice all year round. There is less oxygen in the air to breathe. Nothing can live there for long. Even on the lower slopes where the snow melts in warmer months, only the toughest plants and animals can survive.

Golden eagle

◀ In the Himalayas, food is scarce and the weather very harsh. Only animals well protected against the cold and winds can live there. Two layers of thick fur keep the enormous yak warm. The snow leopard's hairy paws keep out the cold and help it to run across the snow. Small animals, such as the pika, must be on the lookout for fierce leopards if they are to escape into their burrows. The Himalayan ibex moves about the steep slopes on its nimble hooves.

Snow leopard

Yak

Himalayan ibex

Pika

Meltwater

SEE ALSO: PAGE 8 EARTH AND MOON, PAGE 10 ROCKS AND FOSSILS, PAGE 40 MAMMALS (1)

THE WORLD ABOUT US

MOUNTAINEERS

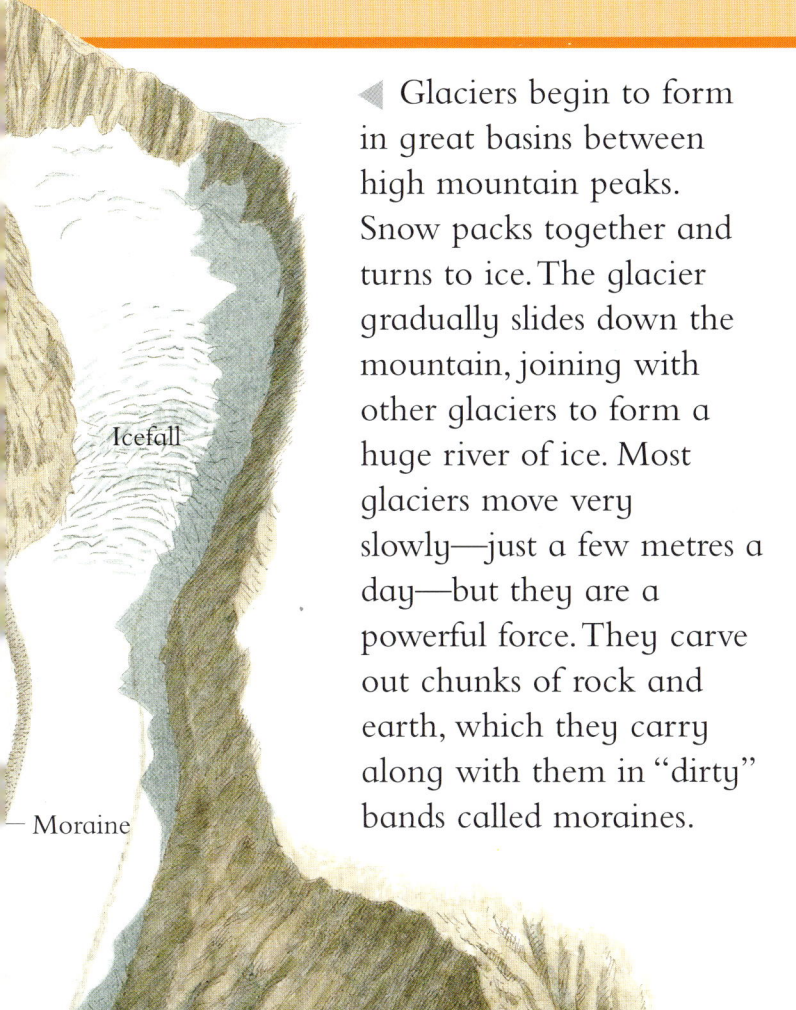

Mountaineers wear special clothes to protect themselves from the cold. They often carry supplies with them, including ice axes and ropes. Boot spikes called crampons help them climb up steep icy slopes.

◀ Glaciers begin to form in great basins between high mountain peaks. Snow packs together and turns to ice. The glacier gradually slides down the mountain, joining with other glaciers to form a huge river of ice. Most glaciers move very slowly—just a few metres a day—but they are a powerful force. They carve out chunks of rock and earth, which they carry along with them in "dirty" bands called moraines.

Icefall

Moraine

Lake

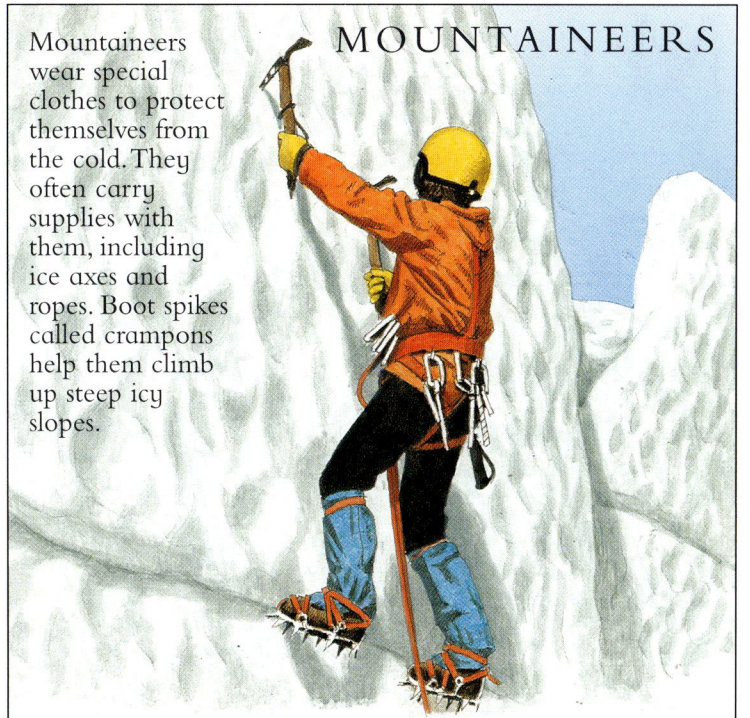

SOME PEOPLE have an ambition to climb one of the world's highest mountains. Such a difficult and dangerous journey seems worthwhile when they finally reach the top. At very high altitudes, the air is thin (lacking in oxygen). Mountaineers used to carry oxygen tanks to help them breathe. Nowadays, most prefer to do without, allowing their bodies to become used to the thin air instead.

▶ The highest mountain in the world, Mount Everest, lies in the Himalayas. In 1953 Edmund Hillary and Sherpa Tenzing Norgay became the first people to climb to the top. Both K2, the second highest mountain, and the Matterhorn in the Alps are very dangerous mountains to climb. The highest summit in Africa, Kilimanjaro, is a volcano. In AD 79 a huge eruption of the volcano Vesuvius buried the Roman city of Pompeii in ash and rock.

Everest (8,848 m)
K2 (8,611 m)

Kilimanjaro (5,896 m)

Matterhorn (4,478 m)

Vesuvius (1,277 m)

THE WORLD ABOUT US

RIVERS

RIVERS are natural channels of water that run downhill. They are an essential link in the water cycle *(see page 14)*. A river starts as a spring, meltwater from a glacier, or simply from rainwater collecting on sodden ground that has soaked up all the water it can. Near its source, the small river, often called a stream or brook, flows quickly. Streams eventually join together to form a larger river that runs to a lake or the sea.

The force of the running water and the stones it carries help the river to wear away the underlying rock, a process called erosion. The rock fragments are ground up and swept away downstream. Over millions of years, a river may carve out a wide valley.

A waterfall forms when a river crosses from hard to softer rock. It wears away the softer rock more quickly, leaving a step in its course. A river creates a gorge when the land it runs across slowly rises. The river cuts steep walls as it forces its way through.

◀ Rivers are home to many plants and animals, both above and below the water. A fast-flowing stream is too rough, but in gentler, deeper water plants can take root in a muddy river bed. They provide food, shelter and nesting sites for many animals. Worms and snails living in the mud are food for fish, which, in turn, are eaten by otters and diving birds such as the kingfisher. Mayflies and other insects living at or near the water's surface are preyed upon by other insects such as dragonflies, as well as by birds, fish and frogs.

SEE ALSO: PAGE 10 ROCKS AND FOSSILS, PAGE 14 WEATHER, PAGE 42 MAMMALS (2)

THE WORLD ABOUT US

◀ A dam is a large barrier built across a river. Some water is allowed to flow past the dam, but most builds up behind it to form a lake or reservoir. The water is used for supplying drinking water to cities, for watering cropfields or to prevent flooding further downstream. Sometimes the water gushing through the dam can be used to turn great wheels called turbines and produce electricity *(see page 22)*.

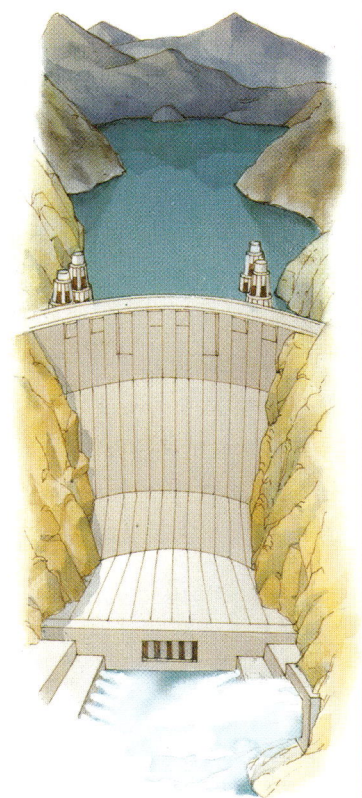

A river may divide into criss-crossing smaller channels called braids.

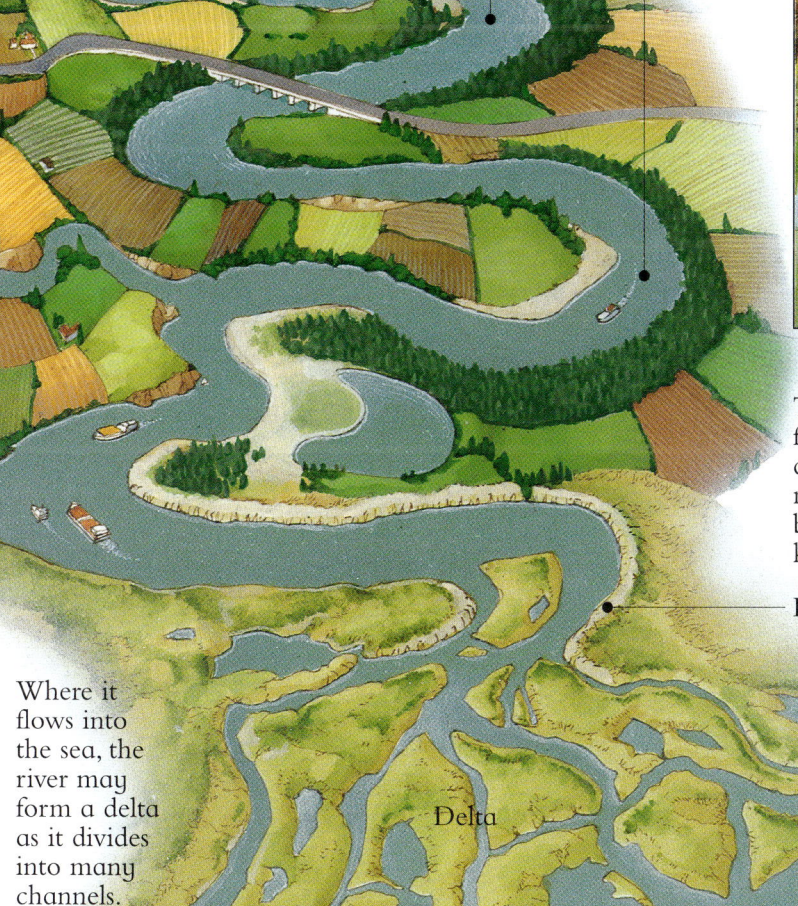

Braids

Meanders

The river water may flood its plain, dumping sediments near its banks and building up ridges known as levees.

Levees

Where it flows into the sea, the river may form a delta as it divides into many channels.

Delta

WETLANDS

WETLANDS are found on the edge of lakes, near to the seashore, or where rainwater or rivers flood the land. Many plants and animals thrive in the waterlogged conditions, although some are threatened with extinction as wetlands are frequently turned over to farming or building land.

The Everglades of Florida, USA, is an area of slow-flowing water. The swamps are a haven for many animals, including wading birds and alligators. The waters rise and fall according to the seasons.

Everglade kite
Flamingo
Alligator
Spoonbill
Swamp rabbit
Cottonmouth
Racoon
Tree frog
Tarpon (young fish)

◀ Further along its course, other streams and rivers, called tributaries, join the river. It becomes wider, deeper and more slow-moving. Some of the eroded fragments of rock it has been carrying are laid down on its bed as sediments. The river winds across a broad plain in a series of looping bends called meanders.

THE WORLD ABOUT US

SEASHORE

THE SEASHORE is the place where land meets sea. This can be rocky cliffs, sandy or pebble beaches, or marshy wetlands.

At high tide, much of a low-lying seashore is under water. The sea carries sand, pebbles and other material which it leaves on the shore. It also brings tiny particles of food for the many small creatures that live in the sand or on the rocks. These creatures are, in turn, prey for crabs, starfish and seabirds.

Seashore plants, such as seaweed, do not put down roots into the ground like other plants, but anchor themselves to rocks instead. Many kinds stay moist even after the tide has gone out, providing small animals with shelter from the sun.

◀ As powerful waves crash against the cliffs, they gradually wear away the rocks. Sometimes the waves carve a hole, or arch, right through a cliff face. If the roof of the arch later collapses, one side of the arch is left standing alone. This is called a stack. When pieces of rock fall into the sea, the waves grind them down into pebbles or sand and lay them down in sheltered places to form beaches. Seabirds nest on rocky shores. Most build them on precarious cliff faces, but puffins nest in burrows.

SEE ALSO: PAGE 20 FORCES AND MATTER, PAGE 34 FISH, PAGE 38 BIRDS, PAGE 60 RIVERS, PAGE 64 OCEANS

THE WORLD ABOUT US

◀ Wading birds, such as curlews or oystercatchers, use their long beaks to probe through the sand on a beach in search of worms and shellfish. On some seashores, pools of water are left between the rocks when the tide goes out. Crabs, starfish, prawns and even small fish live in these rock pools. Limpets and mussels cling tightly to the rocks, keeping some moisture inside their shells.

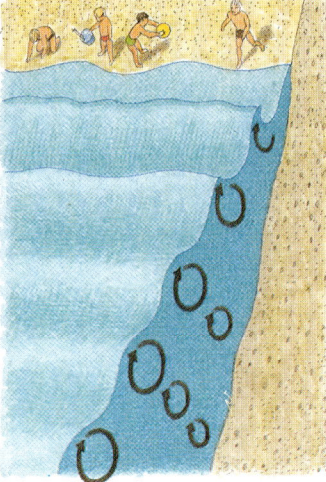

TIDES

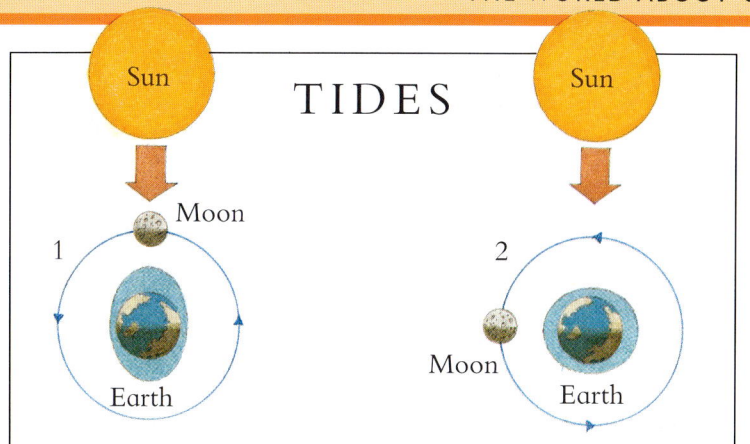

TIDES are caused by the pull of gravity *(see page 20)* by the Sun and Moon on the Earth. The ocean waters on the side of the Earth closest to the Moon (and the opposite side) bulge outwards, causing a high tide. At the same time, the rest of the Earth has a low tide. When the Sun, Moon and Earth are in line, the Sun's gravity combines with that of the Moon to increase the pull on the water. This makes high tides higher and low tides lower. These are called spring tides (1). When the Sun and Moon are not in line, the difference between high and low tides is not so great. These are called neap tides (2).

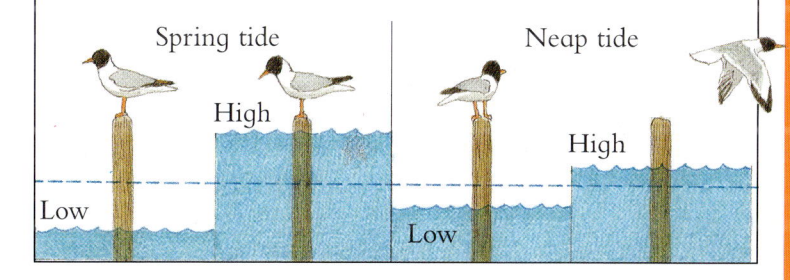

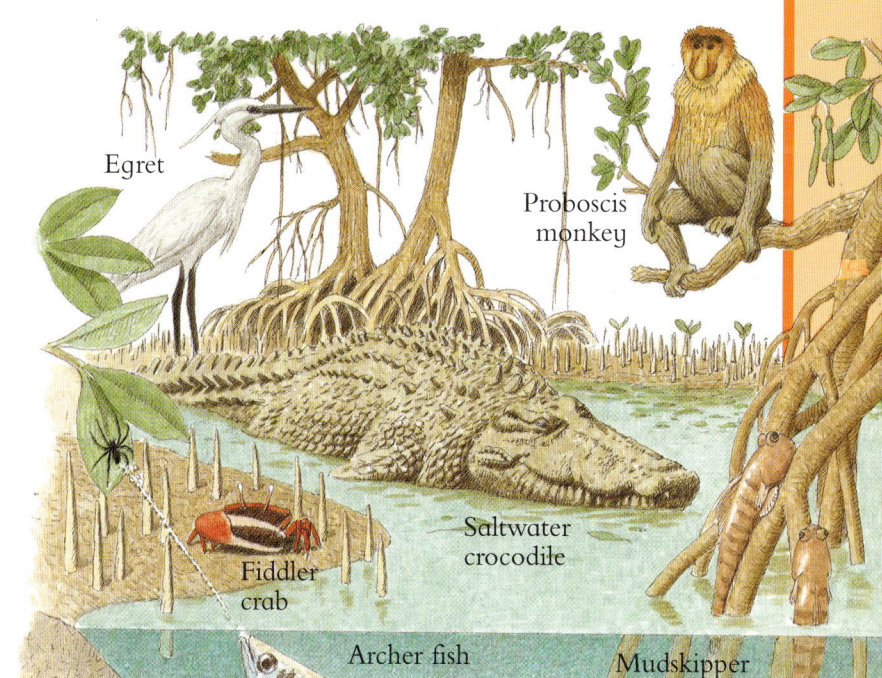

◀ When the wind moves across the sea, the water turns over and over in circles, forming waves.

The water in a wave does not actually move forward. In shallow water close to shore, the lower part of a wave drags on the sea bed, causing the upper part, or crest, to topple over and the wave to "break".

▶ Mangrove forests grow on sheltered coastlines in hot countries. South-east Asian mangroves are home to some unusual animals. When out of the water, the mudskipper fish uses its fins to "walk" across the mud and even climb trees! The archer fish "shoots down" insects with jets of water. The proboscis monkey swims across flooded areas of forest, but it is a target for hungry crocodiles.

63

THE WORLD ABOUT US

OCEANS

MORE than two-thirds of the Earth's surface is covered by vast expanses of salty water called oceans. The ocean floor lies thousands of metres under water. It is a realm of wide plains, deep trenches, high ridges and volcanoes. Some volcanoes rise above the water, forming islands.

The huge amount of water in the oceans plays a major part in creating the weather *(see page 14)*. Great movements of ocean water around the Earth are called currents. These currents, both warm and cold, affect the climates of the lands they swirl past *(see page 13)*. The oceans are also home to a wide variety of life, from microscopic plants to giant whales.

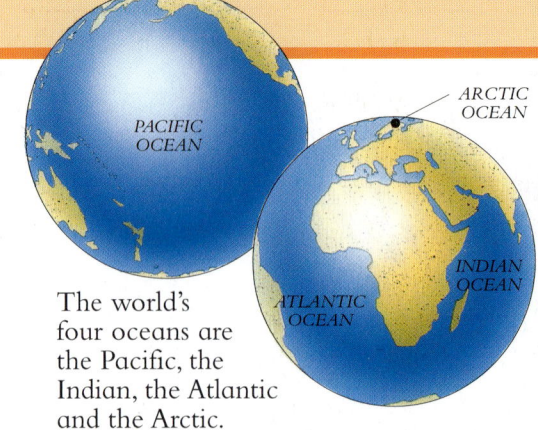

The world's four oceans are the Pacific, the Indian, the Atlantic and the Arctic.

The world's deepest trench is the Marianas Trench in the Pacific Ocean. Its deepest point is Challenger Deep (11,035 m). A long ridge snakes its way around the floors of all the oceans.

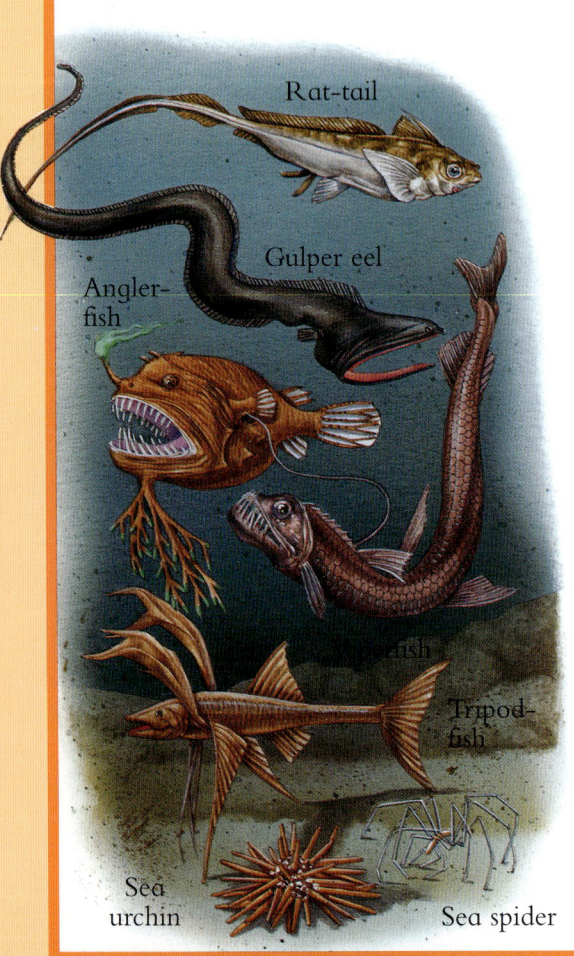

◀ Deep below the surface of the oceans, the water is dark and cold. It is the domain of some very weird creatures. The huge jaws and stretchy stomach of the gulper eel allow it to eat fish much larger than itself. The viperfish has long, sharp teeth for grabbing and holding prey. The glowing rod on the head of the anglerfish attracts small fish which it then devours. The tripod-fish stands on its stilt-like fins on the ocean bed, ready to pounce. The giant sea spider feeds on worms which live in the mud.

Rat-tail
Gulper eel
Angler-fish
Tripod-fish
Sea urchin
Sea spider

SEE ALSO: PAGE 14 WEATHER, PAGE 34 FISH, PAGE 42 MAMMALS (2), PAGE 62 SEASHORE

THE WORLD ABOUT US

▼ Coral grows in shallow, tropical seas. It is made from the outer skeletons of tiny creatures called polyps. As polyps die, new ones grow over them and huge banks, called coral reefs, are built up over the years. Many spectacular creatures live among the amazing shapes and colours. The largest coral reef is the Great Barrier Reef off the north-east coast of Australia.

FISHING

Drift net

Purse seine net

Trawl net

FOR THOUSANDS of years, people have caught fish with hooks, spears and nets. Modern fishing boats can catch huge quantities of fish with their large nets and special equipment. Fish that live near the surface are caught with purse seine nets. The net is spread around the fish and the ends pulled together, trapping the fish inside. Trawl nets are dragged along the sea bed. Drift nets hang in the sea and drift with the tide. They catch anything that swims into them, including dolphins, turtles and diving birds.

65

Ocean creatures from all over the world are shown in this illustration of a coral reef.

KEY
1 Angelfish
2 Marine turtle
3 Hammerhead shark
4 Gorgonian coral
5 Sponges
6 Kingfish
7 Butterflyfish
8 Parrotfish
9 Barracuda
10 Eagle ray
11 Moray eel
12 Crown-of-thorns starfish
13 Damselfish
14 Feather star
15 Butterflyfish
16 Sea urchin
17 Daisy coral
18 Lionfish
19 Sea anemone
20 Giant clam
21 Clownfish
22 Baler shell
23 Spiny lobster
24 Starfish
25 Seahorse
26 Sea slug
27 Red sponge
28 Angelfish

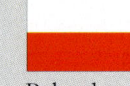

EUROPE

ABOUT the size of the USA, Europe is part of the same land mass as Asia. The two continents are separated by the Ural and Caucasus Mountains. Apart from the frozen north and mountainous regions, nearly all the land is given over to farmland or cities. Europe is home to many different peoples each with their own languages and customs. Apart from Russia, most European nations are quite small in area. Some, such as Vatican City (the smallest), Monaco and Liechtenstein, are no more than a few kilometres across.

Area: 9,700,000 sq km
Population: 727,288,655
Highest point: Elbrus (5,664 m)
Longest river: Volga (3,668 km)
Largest cities: Moscow (13,100,000), Paris (9,800,000), London (6,500,000)

★ Capital city
● Major city

LUX. LUXEMBOURG
LIECH. LEICHTENSTEIN

Just off the coast of Normandy in France, Mont-St-Michel sits atop an old hill. When the tide is in, the hill is completely surrounded by the sea.

◀ The Italian city of Venice was built on a group of islands in a shallow coastal bay called a lagoon. Instead of streets, it has canals. There are no cars, but instead you can hire boats called gondolas to take you around, or travel by a water bus, called a vaporetto. Venice was once an independent republic. Its ruler was called a doge. The Bridge of Sighs, pictured here, crossed from the Doge's Palace to the prison.

Flags

	Germany
	Austria
	Czech Republic
	Slovakia
	Russia
	Estonia
	Latvia
	Lithuania
	Belarus
	Ukraine
	Moldova
	Romania
	Yugoslavia
	Bosnia and Herzegovina
	Bulgaria
	Albania
	Greece
	Slovenia
	Croatia
	Macedonia
	Cyprus

St. Basil's Cathedral stands inside the walls of the Kremlin, a castle in the centre of Moscow, Russia.

Map Labels

Seas and Water Bodies: Barents Sea, North Sea, Baltic Sea, Black Sea, Lake Ladoga

Countries and Cities:
- NORWAY — Oslo
- SWEDEN — Stockholm
- FINLAND — Helsinki
- ESTONIA — Tallinn
- LATVIA — Riga
- LITHUANIA — Vilnius
- DENMARK — Copenhagen
- NETHERLANDS — Amsterdam, The Hague
- BELGIUM — Brussels
- LUX.
- GERMANY — Hamburg, Berlin, Bonn, Munich
- POLAND — Warsaw
- BELARUS — Minsk
- RUSSIA — St. Petersburg, Moscow, Nizhniy Novgorod, Samara, Volgograd
- (PART OF RUSSIA)
- UKRAINE — Kiev, Donetsk, Odesa
- CZECH REPUBLIC — Prague
- SLOVAKIA — Bratislava
- AUSTRIA — Vienna
- SWITZERLAND — Bern
- LIECH.
- SLOVENIA — Ljubljana
- HUNGARY — Budapest
- ROMANIA — Bucharest
- MOLDOVA — Chisinau
- CROATIA — Zagreb
- BOSNIA AND HERZEGOVINA — Sarajevo
- YUGOSLAVIA — Belgrade
- BULGARIA — Sofia
- MACEDONIA — Skopje
- ALBANIA — Tiranë
- GREECE — Athens
- ITALY — Milan, Venice, Rome
- VATICAN CITY
- SAN MARINO
- MONACO — Marseille
- TURKEY — Istanbul
- CYPRUS — Nicosia
- MALTA

Islands: Corsica, Sardinia, Sicily, Crete

Mountains and Rivers: Ural Mountains, Caucasus Mountains, Carpathian Mts., Alps, Elbrus, Rhine, Elbe, Danube, Dniester, Don, Volga

67

Turkmenistan  | Tajikistan  | Kyrgyzstan  | Mongolia  | China | North Korea  | South Korea  | Japan

Uzbekistan

Kazakhstan

Russia

Armenia

Georgia

Azerbaijan

Turkey

Syria

Lebanon

United Arab Emirates

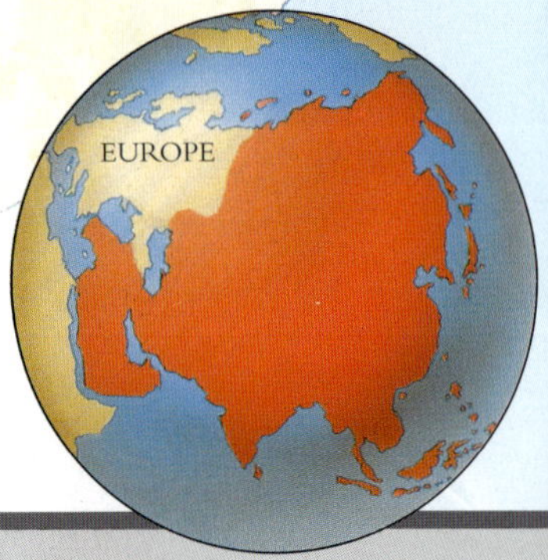

Israel | Jordan | Yemen | Saudi Arabia | Oman | Qatar | Bahrain | Kuwait

ASIA

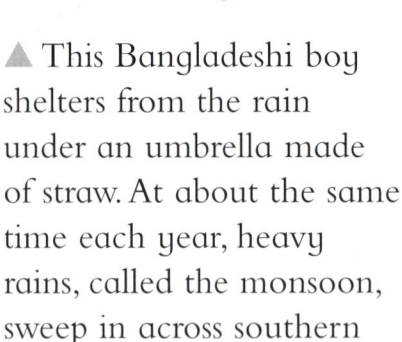

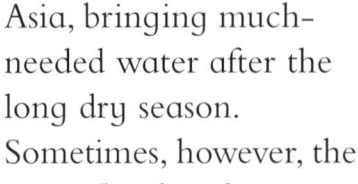

ASIA is the largest continent. It stretches from the Arctic coast of northern Siberia to the tropical rainforest islands of Indonesia, and from the Mediterranean Sea to the Pacific Ocean. Both the world's highest mountains, the Himalayas, and its lowest point on land, the shores of the Dead Sea, are in Asia. China and India have the two biggest populations in the world: together, they make up about one third of all the world's people.

◀ This Japanese girl wears traditional dress at the children's festival known as *schichi-go-san* (seven-five-three).

Area: 44,000,000 sq km
Population: 3,641,354,406
Highest point: Mt. Everest (8,863 m)
Longest river: Yangtse (6,300 km)
Largest cities: Tokyo (27,000,000), Osaka (16,450,000), Calcutta (11,100,000), Seoul (10,522,000), Jakarta (10,000,000)

▲ This Bangladeshi boy shelters from the rain under an umbrella made of straw. At about the same time each year, heavy rains, called the monsoon, sweep in across southern Asia, bringing much-needed water after the long dry season. Sometimes, however, the rivers flood and cause great damage.

◀ These tall, finely decorated buildings have stood in the city of San'a, Yemen, for many hundreds of years.

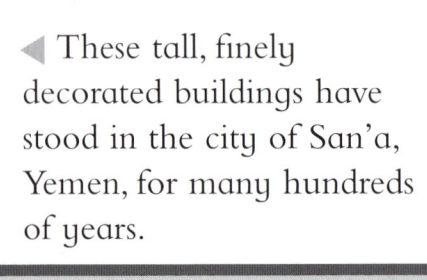

Taiwan

Philippines

Indonesia

Malaysia

Singapore

Vietnam

Cambodia

Laos

Thailand

Burma (Myanmar)

Bangladesh

Bhutan

Nepal

India

Sri Lanka

Maldives

Iraq

Iran

Afghanistan

Pakistan

Kiribati

Solomon Islands

Vanuatu

Nauru

Papua New Guinea

Australia

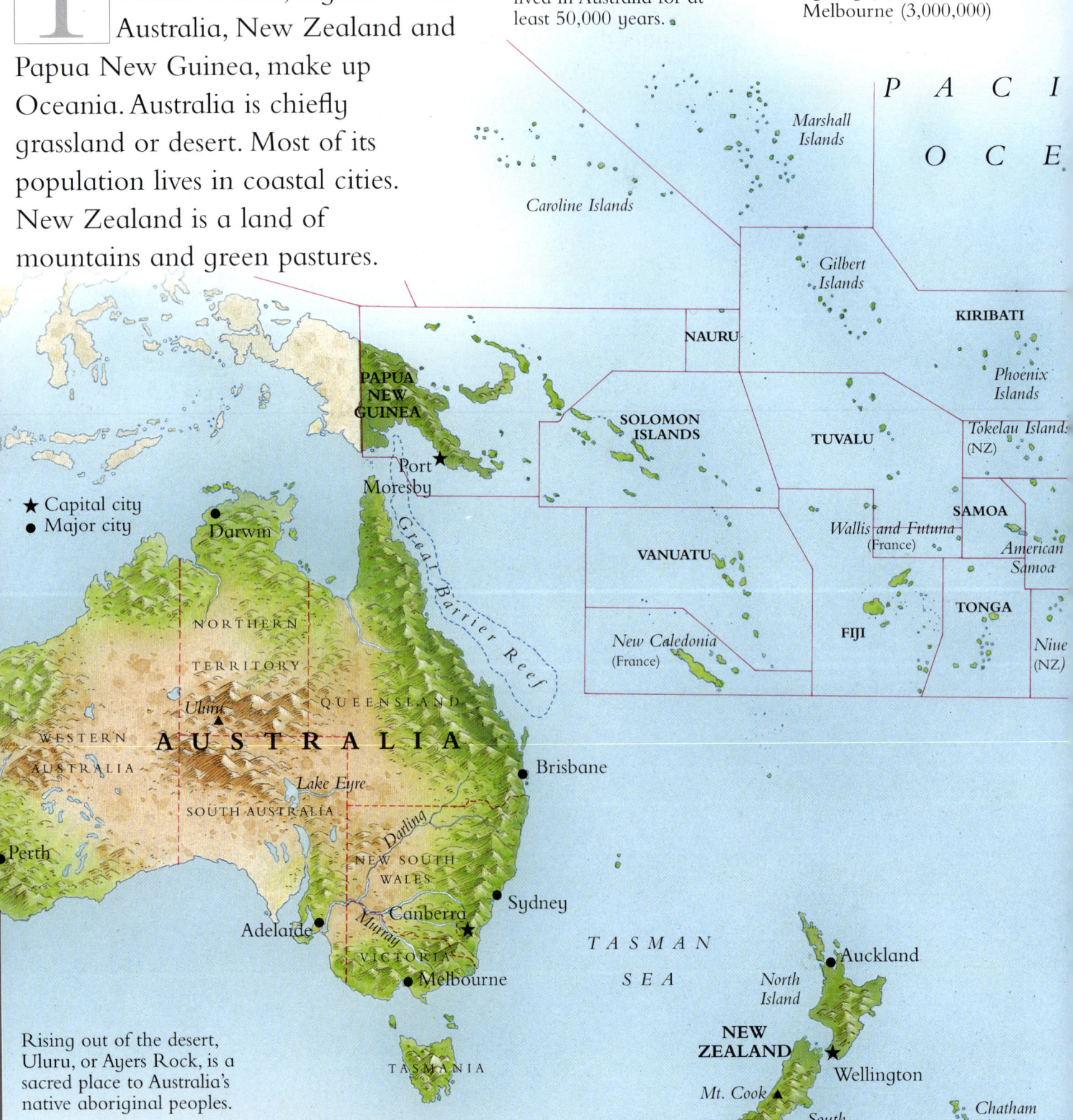

OCEANIA

THE ISLANDS of the south Pacific Ocean, together with Australia, New Zealand and Papua New Guinea, make up Oceania. Australia is chiefly grassland or desert. Most of its population lives in coastal cities. New Zealand is a land of mountains and green pastures.

Aboriginal peoples have lived in Australia for at least 50,000 years.

Area: 8,923,000 sq km
Population: 30,029,217
Highest point: Mt. Cook (3,764 m)
Longest river: Murray-Darling (3,750 km)
Largest cities: Sydney (3,600,000), Melbourne (3,000,000)

★ Capital city
● Major city

Rising out of the desert, Uluru, or Ayers Rock, is a sacred place to Australia's native aboriginal peoples.

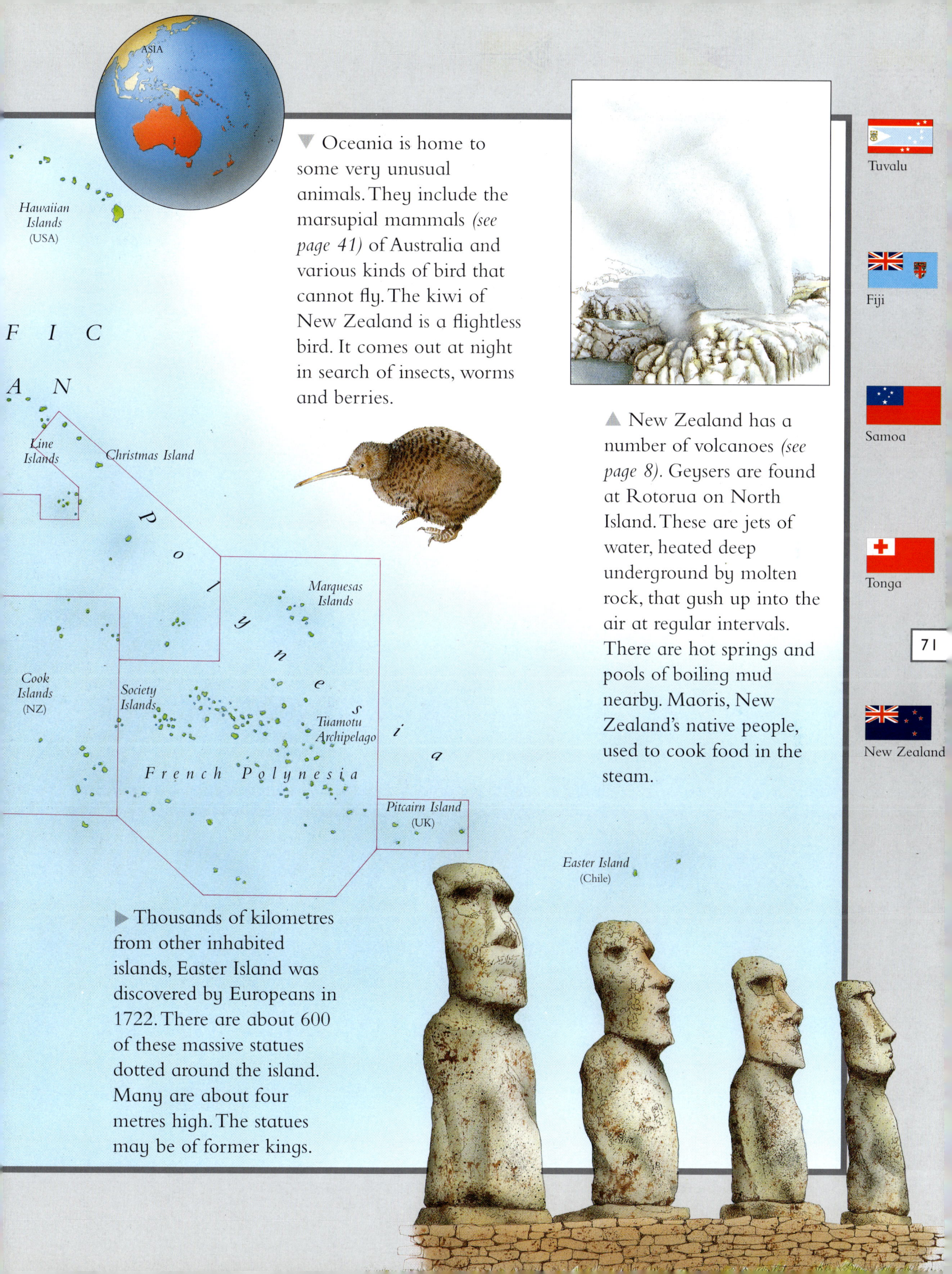

ASIA

Hawaiian Islands (USA)

P A C I F I C   O C E A N

Line Islands

Christmas Island

Cook Islands (NZ)

Society Islands

Marquesas Islands

Tuamotu Archipelago

French Polynesia

P o l y n e s i a

Pitcairn Island (UK)

Easter Island (Chile)

▼ Oceania is home to some very unusual animals. They include the marsupial mammals *(see page 41)* of Australia and various kinds of bird that cannot fly. The kiwi of New Zealand is a flightless bird. It comes out at night in search of insects, worms and berries.

▲ New Zealand has a number of volcanoes *(see page 8)*. Geysers are found at Rotorua on North Island. These are jets of water, heated deep underground by molten rock, that gush up into the air at regular intervals. There are hot springs and pools of boiling mud nearby. Maoris, New Zealand's native people, used to cook food in the steam.

▶ Thousands of kilometres from other inhabited islands, Easter Island was discovered by Europeans in 1722. There are about 600 of these massive statues dotted around the island. Many are about four metres high. The statues may be of former kings.

Tuvalu

Fiji

Samoa

Tonga

71

New Zealand

United States of America

Guatemala

Mexico

Belize

Honduras

El Salvador

Nicaragua

Costa Rica

Panama

Trinidad & Tobago

Grenada

NORTH AMERICA

NORTH AMERICA includes two of the largest countries in the world, Canada and the USA, as well as some of the smallest, the islands of the Caribbean Sea.

The northern coasts of Canada, Alaska and Greenland are icy polar lands, while the climate of the countries that border the Gulf of Mexico and the Caribbean is warm all year round. A chain of mountains runs from Alaska to Panama. Forests cover much of northern Canada, while farmland dominates most of the USA east of the Rocky Mountains.

BERING SEA

Aleutian Islands

▲ The Inuit people are one of a number of peoples that live on the Arctic shores or tundra *(see page 49)*. Many Inuit now live in modern houses and travel by snowmobile or helicopter. Some still lead a traditional life hunting walruses, seals and whales.

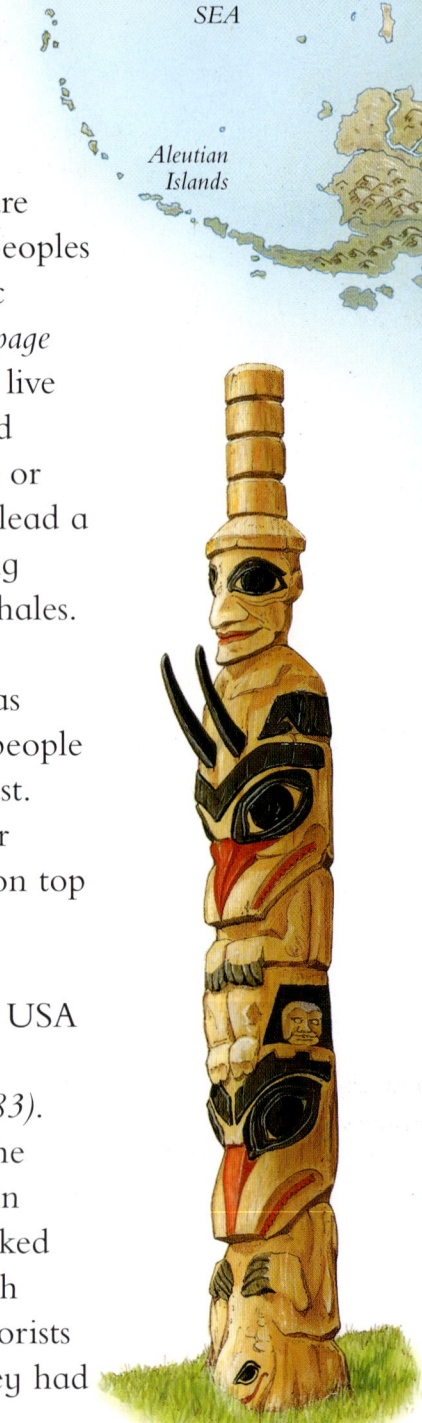

▶ This totem pole was made by the Haida people of Canada's west coast. Carvings of people or animals appear one on top of another.

◀ Many cities in the USA are famous for their skyscrapers *(see page 83)*. The twin towers of the World Trade Center in New York were attacked and destroyed on 11th September 2001. Terrorists flew airliners that they had captured into them.

This native Indian from Mexico uses "butterfly nets" for fishing, dipping them into the lake to gather the fish.

North America

Area: 24,250,000 sq km
Population: 475,814,699
Highest point: Mt. McKinley (6,194 m)
Longest river: Mississippi-Missouri (5,970 km)
Largest cities: New York (18,100,000), Mexico City (16,000,000), Los Angeles (14,500,000)

★ Capital city
● Major city

Abbreviations:
- VT. VERMONT
- N.H. NEW HAMPSHIRE
- MASS. MASSACHUSETTS
- CONN. CONNECTICUT
- R.I. RHODE ISLAND
- PENN. PENNSYLVANIA
- MD. MARYLAND

Flags

- Greenland
- Canada
- Bahamas
- Jamaica
- Cuba
- Haiti
- Dominican Republic
- St. Kitts and Nevis
- Antigua & Barbuda
- Dominica
- St. Vincent and the Grenadines
- Barbados
- St. Lucia

73

SOUTH AMERICA

SOUTH AMERICA is joined to North America by a very thin strip of land, called the Isthmus of Panama. The southern tip, called Cape Horn, is just 800 kilometres from the icy continent of Antarctica. Running down the western side of South America are the Andes Mountains. Many rivers flow east to the Atlantic Ocean. The mighty Amazon winds through a vast rainforest.

Many South Americans are descended from native Indians, settlers from Spain and other European countries, and Africans.

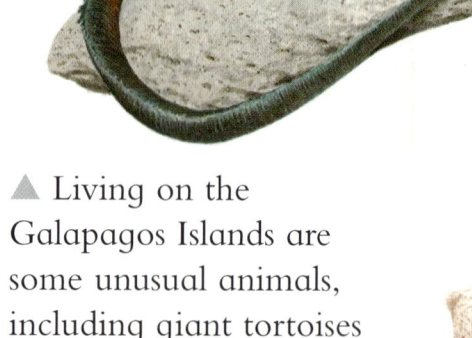

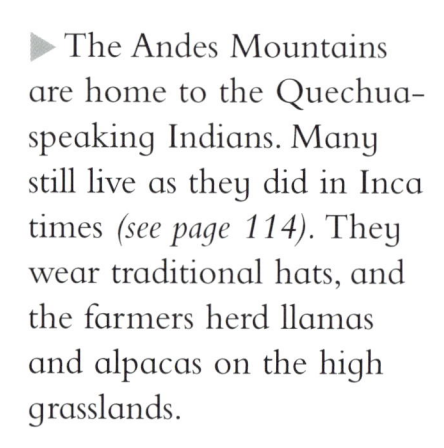

▲ Living on the Galapagos Islands are some unusual animals, including giant tortoises and these marine iguanas.

▶ The Andes Mountains are home to the Quechua-speaking Indians. Many still live as they did in Inca times (see page 114). They wear traditional hats, and the farmers herd llamas and alpacas on the high grasslands.

◀ Rio de Janeiro is Portuguese for "January River", the name given to it by explorers who came across this magnificent bay 400 years ago. They thought it was the mouth of a river. A great city has grown up by the bay, overlooked by the Sugar Loaf mountain and a statue of Jesus Christ. The city is known for its beaches and colourful festivals, but also for its shantytowns (see page 79).

South America

Area: 17,663,000 sq km
Population: 343,294,361
Highest point: Aconcagua (6,960 m)
Longest river: Amazon (6,451 km)
Largest cities:
São Paulo (15,175,000),
Buenos Aires (10,750,000),
Rio de Janeiro (10,150,000)

▼ This Kayapo Indian wears a plate stuck into his lower lip. Like many Amazon peoples, the Kayapo have had to fight to defend their rainforest home against people wanting to clear the trees and use the land for farms and quarries.

★ Capital city
• Major city

Guyana
Suriname
French Guiana
Brazil
Paraguay
Uruguay
Chile
Argentina

AFRICA

MOST OF AFRICA has a hot climate. In the northern and southwestern parts, the land is desert. Tropical rainforests cover the Congo basin and parts of west Africa. In between stretch the grasslands where animals such as the lion, giraffe and elephant still roam.

The world's longest river, the Nile, rises in the highlands of east Africa near Lake Victoria. From there it flows northwards across the dusty plains of Sudan. It has watered the farmlands of Egypt for centuries.

Hundreds of different peoples live in Africa, even in its deserts and jungle. Some countries have become wealthy from mining and farming while others have been torn by war.

▼ Most people in north Africa and many in west Africa follow the religion of Islam (see page 90). Hundreds of years ago, merchants from the Arab empire (see page 116) traded salt for gold and slaves from west Africa. Soon, local rulers took up the Arab religion and became Muslims, too. This mosque was built in Mali in the 14th century. It is made of clay. Parts of its timber frame stick out through the walls.

◀ West Africa has very fertile farmland, especially close to the Niger and Volta rivers. Some crops, such as peanuts, coffee, cocoa and many different kinds of fruit, are grown to sell abroad. Local people buy their food at markets like this. One is carrying a container called a calabash on her head. It is the dried, hollow shell of a fruit called a gourd.

◀ The Wodaabe people live in the dry grasslands of Niger. They live by herding cattle and sheep. The men wear make-up on their faces when they perform courtship dances.

Area: 29,800,000 sq km
Population: 778,434,002
Highest point: Kilimanjaro (5,894 m)
Longest river: Nile (6,670 km)
Largest cities: Cairo (9,300,000), Lagos (3,800,000), Johannesburg (3,650,000)

★ Capital city
● Major city

Niger | Tunisia | Chad
Libya
Egypt
Sudan
Djibouti
Seychelles
Eritrea
Ethiopia
Somalia
Comoros | Mauritius | Malawi | Tanzania
Burundi | Rwanda | Uganda | Kenya

77

PEOPLE

HOMES
AROUND THE WORLD

MOST PEOPLE have a home, a place that gives them shelter and safety. However, not all homes are like the one you live in. Some people live in boats on the water, others in tents in the desert. The Kombai people of Indonesia live in tree houses 50 metres above the ground! In Shanxi province, China, people live in underground houses dug out of soft, sandy soil.

Homes are often built using materials found close by. They are made to suit the places they are built in. In countries where there are many earthquakes, houses must be especially strong so that they will not fall down. In places where there are many floods, some houses are built on stilts.

◀ Nomads are people who move around from place to place. The nomads of Mongolia travel across grasslands with their herds of yak, sheep and goats. They take their homes with them wherever they go. Their homes are circular tents called yurts. They are built with a wooden framework covered with thick pads of felt made from sheep's wool. A canvas cover protects against rain. Mongolians love their comfortable yurts so much, even townspeople prefer to live in them.

In Côte d'Ivoire, west Africa, village huts have hard-baked mud walls and reed roofs.

Hong Kong is a very crowded city. Many people live in apartment blocks. Others live in the harbour, on boats called sampans.

PEOPLE

◀ The Bajau people, from the Philippines, are known as "sea gypsies" because they travel around the islands of south-east Asia, catching and selling fish, shells and coral. Their tiny boats are called lipas. Long poles fixed to either side of the boats help to steady them in the water. The Bajau people live either in the boats themselves or in houses made of wood and rushes that stand on stilts above the water.

SHANTYTOWNS

ON THE outskirts of some large cities, such as Rio de Janeiro in Brazil, lie huge, sprawling shantytowns. They are home to people who are very poor and cannot afford houses in the city. Often they have come from the countryside to look for work and money. The people build homes from corrugated iron, packing-cases or whatever they can find. Sometimes they have to search the city dumps for scraps of food or things to sell to earn a little money.

▲ The Bedouin people are nomads who travel about the desert in Arabia and North Africa. They live in tents made of wooden poles, woollen cloth and ropes. Some Bedouins travel to work in the city from the desert by car each day. Their tents have televisions and other modern appliances. In the past, Bedouins collected morning dew for their water. Today, they bring in water supplies by truck.

◀▲ The Efe pygmies of central Africa travel around the rainforest, hunting animals and collecting honey. Every time they pitch camp, they mark a circle, drive branches into the ground and weave them together. Then they cover them with large leaves to make small huts.

79

SEE ALSO: PAGES 66-77 WORLD NATIONS, PAGE 82 BUILDINGS AND BRIDGES

PEOPLE

Farming

PEOPLE first learnt how to farm about 10,000 years ago *(see page 105)*. Before that, people hunted animals and gathered fruits and plants that grew in the wild. Nowadays in rich countries, farming is an important industry that uses modern machines. In poorer countries, most people still work in the fields and depend on their animals and a small number of crops for their survival.

There are four different types of farming. First, certain types of tree or shrub are planted and the fruit, such as apples, olives and grapes, is harvested. Secondly, farmers grow food-bearing plants in the soil. This is crop cultivation, or arable farming. Thirdly, animals are put to graze on grassy land: this is livestock farming. Finally, many farms mix arable with livestock farming, often alternating field use between crops and grasses year by year.

▶ Modern cereal farmers use different machines over the year. The plough and harrow prepare the ground. When the green shoots begin to show, the crop is sprayed with chemicals to protect it from insects that feed on the crop. (Some farmers consider spraying to be harmful to the environment and prefer not to do this.) Finally, a combine harvester gathers in the crop.

The farmer uses a plough to turn over the soil. It makes narrow trenches called furrows.

A harrow is pulled over the ground to smooth it. It breaks up the clods of earth into finer soil.

A seed drill puts the seeds into the soil in tidy rows and covers them over at the same time.

SEE ALSO: PAGE 12 SEASONS AND CLIMATES, PAGE 44 PLANTS, PAGE 104 EARLY PEOPLE, PAGE 118 MIDDLE AGES

◀ Rice is the main food for millions of Asians. For the crop to grow, rice-fields, or paddies, must be flooded with water. In hilly country, flat shelves of land, or terraces, are cut into the hillside so that the floodwaters do not flow away. The rice seedlings are often planted by hand. After harvesting, the crop is threshed, to separate the grain from the stalks.

FARM ANIMALS

Pig, Sheep, Goat, Hen

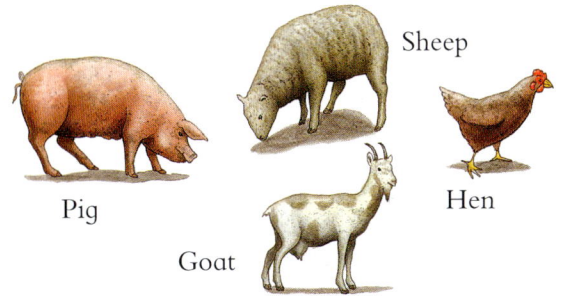

CATTLE, sheep, goats, pigs and poultry are found all over the world, but there are many different types, or breeds. The zebu cattle *(below)* feed on poor, coarse grass found in hot countries in Africa and Asia. They provide milk and meat and pull carts and ploughs. Sheep are raised for their meat and wool. Goats graze in highland areas where soils are thin. In many countries, people depend on goats for their meat, milk and skins. Pigs and poultry are usually kept close to the farm buildings where they can be fed regularly.

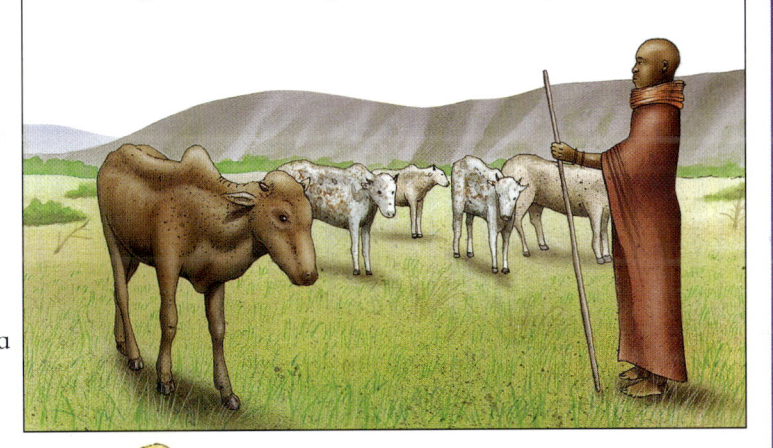

▶ The most important crops are the cereals—wheat, rice, maize, barley, rye and millet. These crops provide many people with their staple diet or basic food. Some root vegetables like potatoes and cassava are also staple foods. Coffee is made from beans, the seeds of a type of small tree grown in plantations.

Wheat, Rice, Coffee, Maize, Cassava

A crop-sprayer applies chemicals that protect the crop from diseases and insect pests.

A combine harvests the crop and separates the grain from the stalks all in one go.

◀ A combine harvester is a huge machine which combines all the jobs of turning a cereal crop into grain. With its wide, front, cutting wheel it gathers and cuts the stalks as it moves through the field. The stalks are dropped from the back and gathered into bales of straw while the grain is emptied into a trailer.

PEOPLE

BUILDINGS AND BRIDGES

THROUGHOUT history, people have made structures for many purposes. Simple buildings provide shelter. Grander buildings, such as castles, temples and pyramids, were built for powerful people, or for religious worship.

Many people work together to construct a building. An architect designs the form of the building while engineers work out how to make it strong and safe. Then builders follow careful plans to construct the building.

St. Peter's basilica

Yakushi pagoda

◄▲ These two buildings are for religious worship. St Peter's basilica in the Vatican City, Rome, is the largest church in the world. Somewhat smaller, this Buddhist pagoda in Japan is cleverly built to withstand frequent earthquakes *(see page 9)*.

Beam bridge

Arch bridge

Cantilever bridge

Suspension bridge

► There are several different kinds of bridge. Beam bridges are supported by columns. Arches give a bridge a very strong structure. Each section of a cantilever bridge is balanced on a central support. Suspension bridges hang from long steel cables that run between tall towers. A cable-stayed bridge uses sets of cables attached to each side of a tower to hold up the bridge.

SEE ALSO: PAGE 78 HOMES AROUND THE WORLD, PAGE 90 RELIGIONS, PAGES 104-121 PAST WORLDS

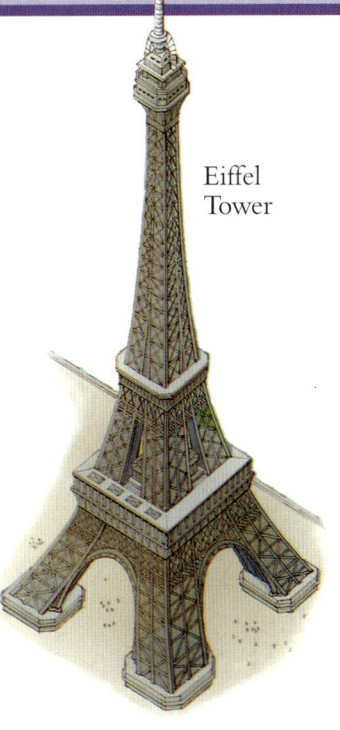

PEOPLE

◀▼ These two structures are famous for the way they were built. The 300-metre-high Eiffel Tower in Paris was built in 1889. It is made of iron held together by 2.5 million rivets (metal pins). Built for the 1972 Olympic Games, the Olympic stadium at Munich, Germany, has a tent-shaped roof made of glass, supported by steel masts and cables. The glass cleans itself when it rains.

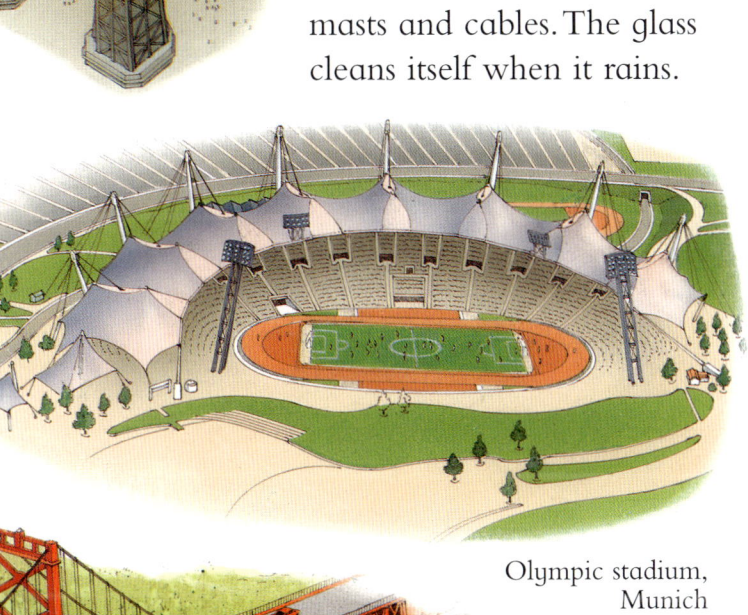

Eiffel Tower

Olympic stadium, Munich

Cable-stayed bridge

SKYSCRAPER

THE TALLEST buildings in the world are called skyscrapers. The John Hancock Center in Chicago, USA, is one of the tallest. Made of steel and glass, it soars to a height of 343 metres. The strong lengths of steel that crisscross the building help it to withstand any kind of weather, especially high winds. Inside the John Hancock Center are 100 floors, containing offices, shops, apartments, a car park and even a swimming pool.

Long steel tubes filled with concrete form the building's foundations, the base that supports its weight on firm rock.

▶ One of the most famous modern buildings in the world, the Sydney Opera House was built during the 1960s. It was designed so that it could be admired from any direction—even from above. Looking like a series of overlapping shells, the white roof is covered with over a million tiles, specially made to fit over the curves of the shells.

Inside the Sydney Opera House are halls for opera, music, theatre and exhibitions, plus restaurants, bars and a library.

PEOPLE

LANGUAGES AND WRITING

THE FIRST language used by early people was probably made up mostly of hand gestures and grunting sounds. Today, there are thousands of different languages spoken in the world. Words are usually given further meaning by movements of the hands or expressions of the face. Some languages have unusual features: the people of Gomera in the Canary Islands still use loud whistles to "speak" to one another across valleys.

Most languages can be written down, using letters or symbols to represent sounds or words. Early writing was in the form of pictures. By working out how to read these pictures, modern scientists can find out fascinating details about life thousands of years ago. Today, most languages use an alphabet, although Chinese and Japanese still use symbols called characters.

Mayan

Ancient Chinese

The earliest writing that we know dates from about 3500 BC. A people called the Sumerians from Mesopotamia (now Iraq) used a reed with a pointed end to draw symbols on slabs of wet clay. In ancient America, Mayan people "wrote" by carving a series of drawings in stone. In ancient China, priests scratched questions on a bone and then held it over a fire. The places where the cracks in the bone crossed the symbols were supposed to give the answers from the gods.

Sumerian

▶ Different languages are spoken not just in different countries, but even within a single country. These may be so different that people living in the same country may not understand one another. There are several spoken versions of Chinese, the commonest being Mandarin. There is only one kind of writing, however, which everyone in China can understand.

China has many different peoples, like this Miao girl, that still keep their own languages.

Hundreds of different languages are spoken in India. This herder boy speaks Gujarati.

Papua New Guinea has more than 800 different languages. Many are spoken only in remote rainforest valleys.

SEE ALSO: PAGE 106 ANCIENT EGYPT, PAGE 110 THE ROMANS, PAGE 112 ANCIENT CHINA, PAGE 114 ANCIENT AMERICA

PEOPLE

"Japan"

"Denmark"

"USA"

Many deaf people learn to read the shapes made by people's lips to work out what they are saying. There is also a special language for the deaf called sign language. Hand movements and different expressions made with the face stand for words or groups of words. Sign language differs from one country to another, but the names of the countries themselves are "signed" in the same way.

Ancient Egyptians used a form of picture writing called hieroglyphics. They were the first to use paper, made from strips of papyrus reed. Young Egyptians practised their writing using a reed pen or a thin brush on pieces of broken pottery.

More people speak Chinese than any other language. English would be the commonest language if all the people who have learnt to speak it were included. Hindi is one of several major languages spoken in India. Spanish is spoken not only in Spain but also in much of Central and South America, where many Spanish people came to live hundreds of years ago.

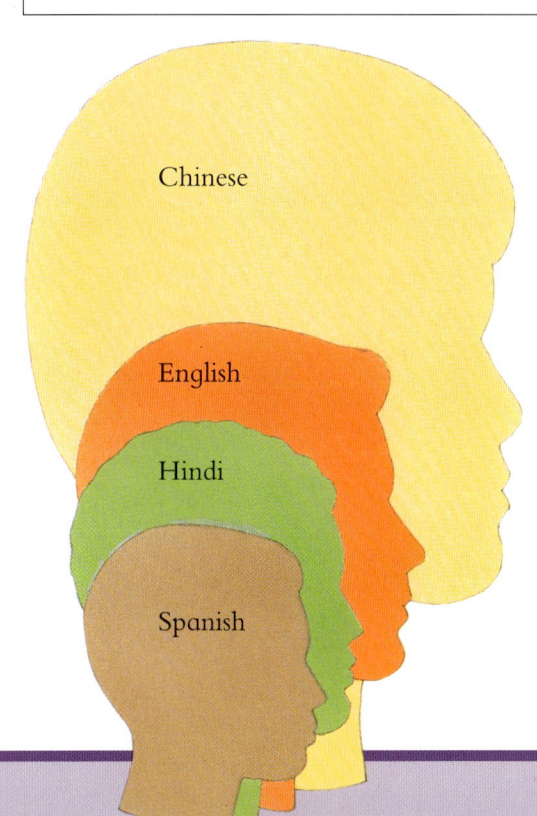

The language of the Khoisan people of southern Africa contains clicks made with the lips and tongue.

HOW IS IT WRITTEN?

ALL the words on the right mean "book" in different languages. Many languages use an alphabet, a collection of letters that can be arranged to make thousands of different words. English and many other languages use the Roman alphabet. Hindi, Greek, Russian and Arabic all have their own alphabets.

Some languages, for example, Spanish, Italian and French, have many similar words. This is because these languages are descended from Latin, the language of the Romans when Spain, Italy and France were all part of the Roman empire.

Book
English

Kőnyv
Hungarian

Nángseŭh
Thai

Kitabu
Swahili

पुस्तक
Hindi

βιβλίο
Greek

книга
Russian

書
Chinese

كِتَاب
Arabic

Chinese

English

Hindi

Spanish

These are the four most commonly spoken first languages (those which are learnt from birth).

Chinese: more than 1 billion speakers

English: 450 million speakers

Hindi: 400 million speakers

Spanish: 350 million speakers

85

MUSICAL INSTRUMENTS

TO MAKE MUSIC, you can either use your voice or play a musical instrument. For some people, playing musical instruments is their job. For others, it is simply fun! A large group of musicians play together in an orchestra. It is divided into sections, each containing similar kinds of instrument. The players read musical symbols that tell them which notes to play and what rhythm to follow.

The piano is a very popular musical instrument. The player presses the keys with his fingers. He can make the sound louder or softer, and the notes longer or shorter, by pressing pedals with his feet.

Piano

A pianist can use all his fingers and thumbs to play notes. A piano is often used to accompany other instruments.

▼ Many people like to listen to music that is played by pop or rock bands. A band usually contains a drummer, singer and guitarists. The sound is made louder by amplifiers. Many bands travel all over the world to play live concerts.

Drums

Electric guitar

Harp

The harp is a stringed instrument, although its strings are plucked with the fingers. A harpist sometimes sweeps her fingers across the strings. The violin and viola are both held under the chin and played with a bow, although sometimes the strings are plucked instead.

Viola

Violin

Cello

Double bass

◀ Stringed instruments are normally played using a bow which is guided backwards and forwards across taut strings. The player changes the notes by pressing with the fingers on different strings. The double bass, the largest of these instruments, makes the deepest sounds. The cello, the next largest, is held between the player's legs. Next comes the viola, and, smallest of all, the violin. There are more violinists in an orchestra than players of any other instrument.

SEE ALSO: PAGE 18 LIGHT AND SOUND

PEOPLE

The percussion section of the orchestra contains instruments that are beaten to make sounds. The timpani (kettledrums) are well known for drum rolls. The huge bass drum is hit with a padded stick to give out thudding sounds. The triangle player can make a tinkling sound, or one clear note.

Timpani

Bass drum

Cymbals are a pair of metal discs. They are crashed together at exciting moments!

Cymbals

Triangle

The horn is a mellow-toned brass instrument. It has two long, coiled tubes between the mouthpiece and bell.

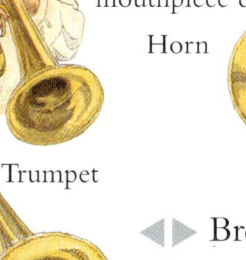

Horn

Trumpet

Trombone

Tuba

Brass and woodwind players use their breath to play their instruments. The trumpet makes a high, thrilling sound. The trombone player slides a tube in and out to get different notes. The tuba plays very low sounds.

Most woodwind instruments, such as the clarinet and oboe, make sounds using a thin piece of cane, called a reed, in the mouthpiece. The flute player blows across a hole in the mouthpiece.

THE CONDUCTOR

ALTHOUGH he does not play an instrument himself, the conductor has a very important part in the orchestra. He must make sure that each group of instruments plays its music at the right time and in the right manner, for the best overall effect.

The conductor waves a stick called a baton to show the orchestra the correct speed and rhythm. He also points to each section as its turn comes to play. The conductor has to know the piece of music very well.

The saxophone is a woodwind instrument made of brass. It has a reed like a clarinet. Rarely used in an orchestra, the saxophone is often heard in jazz music.

Saxophone

Flute

Oboe

Bassoon

Clarinet

87

PEOPLE

Television

TELEVISION (TV) was invented during the 1930s. It first became popular in the 1950s as people bought television sets to have in their homes. Now TV is the most important source of entertainment and information in the world. Programmes are even beamed into homes from satellites thousands of kilometres up in space.

Television works using electronics *(see page 23)*. The broadcasting station transmits (sends out) radio waves which are turned into sounds and pictures by TV sets. Some programmes, especially news and sport, are broadcast live: they are transmitted as they happen. But many TV programmes are recorded on video tape for broadcasting at a later date. We can also play video tapes at home on a videocassette recorder (VCR). This records sounds and pictures and plays them back through the TV set.

As well as the camera and sound crew, the floor manager works in the studio. He makes sure everything runs smoothly.

In the production control room, pictures appear on TV screens in front of the director and her assistants. Responsible for what pictures we see on our screens, the director gives instructions to the people in the studio and the vision and sound controllers.

◀ A satellite is an object that travels about a planet while being held in orbit by gravity *(see page 20)*. Earth has one natural satellite, the Moon, and many artificial satellites. Satellites are used in weather forecasting, for providing telephone links and to help ships and aeroplanes pinpoint their positions. TV programmes are transmitted to satellites by earth stations and picked up by dish aerials.

PEOPLE

THE MOVIES

THE FIRST CINEMA showing of a motion picture, or "movie", took place in Paris on 28th December 1895. On that day, the brothers Louis and Auguste Lumière showed movies using their newly invented film projector, the *Cinématographe*. The audience saw a film in which a gardener was tricked into soaking himself with a hosepipe!

Hundreds of people work together to make a movie. They are brought together by the producer. The director guides the actors and the camera operators. When everyone is ready the clapperboard is held in front of the camera and the director calls "Action!"

Cinema very quickly became popular all over the world. In 1907 the first studios were built at Hollywood, a district of Los Angeles, California. It was an ideal location, close to many kinds of natural scenery. By the 1920s Hollywood was the centre of the world film industry. Favourite actors and actresses became famous film stars. To begin with, the movies had no sound. Titles appeared on screen from time to time to explain the story. *The Jazz Singer,* made in 1927, was the first full-length movie with a soundtrack. Technicolor and cartoon films arrived in the 1930s.

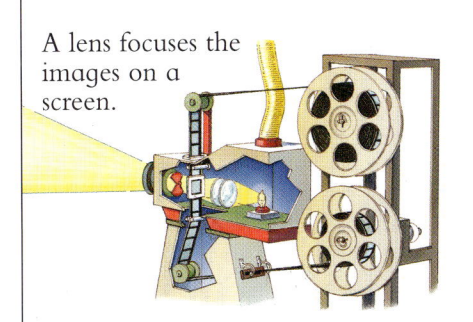

A lens focuses the images on a screen.

A long strip of film containing a series of images, or frames, passes through the projector in front of a light. The film moves at 24 frames per second, so our eyes see continuous moving action.

◀ Many TV programmes are made in a studio. There are usually control rooms attached. A TV camera turns the pictures it "sees" into electric signals, which are sent down a cable to the control room. The microphone does the same for sounds. In the control room, the pictures and sounds are mixed together and recorded or sent to a transmission station.

The operator steers the camera while checking the picture in the viewfinder.

◀ Television signals are transmitted on radio waves. Different channels are carried by waves of different frequency (the number of waves sent out each second). Aerials on people's homes pick up the signals and the TV set turns them back into pictures and sound. Dish aerials can pick up TV signals from a satellite. In some areas, cables in the ground also carry TV signals into homes.

89

SEE ALSO: PAGE 18 LIGHT AND SOUND, PAGE 22 ELECTRICITY, PAGE 102 SPACE TRAVEL

PEOPLE

RELIGIONS

RELIGION means a belief in something that is beyond the world around us (the "physical" world)—usually a god, or gods (a "spiritual" world). Since earliest times people have believed that an unseen power of some kind created their world and have felt the need to worship this creator.

The many different world religions, of which the most important are Christianity, Islam, Hinduism, Buddhism and Judaism (the religion of the Jews), have many things in common. Besides a god or gods, there is the belief that a person has a soul, a kind of inner spirit that never dies. Religious people pray regularly and visit special places, for example, a church, a mosque, synagogue or temple, to worship.

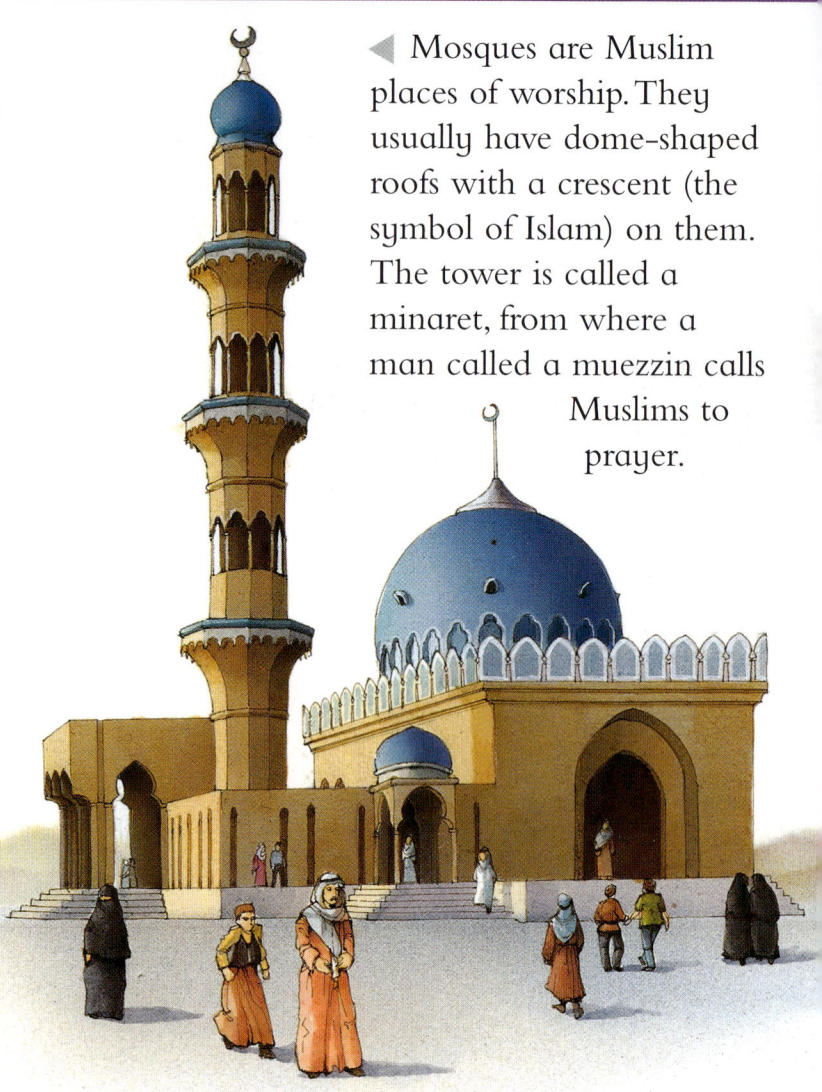

◀ Mosques are Muslim places of worship. They usually have dome-shaped roofs with a crescent (the symbol of Islam) on them. The tower is called a minaret, from where a man called a muezzin calls Muslims to prayer.

Jesus Christ *(above)* lived in Palestine, part of the Roman empire, 2,000 years ago. He taught people love and forgiveness. Jealous Jewish leaders persuaded the Romans to condemn him to death by crucifixion. Jesus had to carry his own cross.

◀ Christians follow the teachings of Jesus, who was named Christ, which means "the anointed one", by his followers. They believe Jesus was the son of God: he had come to Earth to save everyone from wrongdoing by sacrificing his own life. Christians believe that when they die their souls will go to Heaven.

People are welcomed into the faith by baptism *(left)*, a sign of washing away wrongdoing. Babies have water sprinkled on their heads. Some people are immersed completely.

SEE ALSO: PAGE 82 BUILDINGS AND BRIDGES, PAGE 110 THE ROMANS, PAGE 116 GREAT EMPIRES

PEOPLE

Followers of Islam are called Muslims. Like Jews and Christians, they believe in just one god, whom they call Allah. In particular, they follow the teachings of the prophet Muhammad, who was born in Mecca, now in Saudi Arabia, in AD 570. Their holy book, the Qur'an, contains the message of Allah, the Five Pillars of Wisdom.

In places where Islam is strict, women wear clothes that completely cover their bodies.

Muslims always face towards the holy city of Mecca to pray.

Jews believe there is only one god. They trace their history back about 4,000 years, to when Abraham, a member of the Hebrew tribe, heard God's voice telling him that the Hebrews would one day have a land of their own, called the Promised Land. In return, they must obey God's laws. Jews everywhere still follow these laws, written in their holy books, the Torah and the Talmud. Many come to pray at the Western Wall, the only remaining part of their ancient temple in Jerusalem.

This man is a Hasidic Jew. He wears the dress of Poland in the 1700s.

BUDDHISM

The golden stupa in Yangon, Burma (Myanmar).

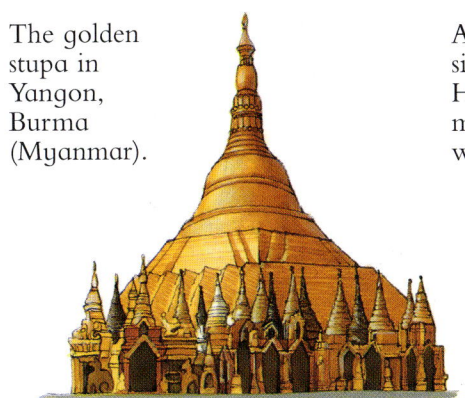

A statue of Buddha sitting in thought. His long ear lobes mean he has great wisdom.

THE NAME Buddha means "the enlightened one". It was given to a man called Siddhartha Gautama who lived in India about 2,500 years ago. He wondered how people could escape suffering. He realized that the answer lay in people controlling their own selfishness. They should lead a life of good deeds and thoughts.

Today, 500 million people, mostly from south-east Asia, follow the teachings of Buddha. Temples called stupas contain what are said to be the remains of Buddha.

Brahma — Vishnu — Shiva

HINDUISM

HINDUS believe in a supreme being called Brahman. They worship Brahman in the shape of other lesser gods, of whom the three most important are Brahma the Creator, Shiva the Destroyer and Vishnu the Preserver. Vishnu appears in many different forms, such as the brave and fun-loving Krishna. Hindus believe that a person's soul does not die, but moves from body to body (sometimes even reappearing as an animal). A life of goodness will lead the soul nearer to Brahman.

91

PEOPLE

Sports

MANY PEOPLE enter sports competitions, either on their own or as part of a team. In some sports, the person who runs fastest or throws furthest is the winner. In others, such as tennis or football, players win by scoring more points or goals. In sports such as diving, gymnastics or ice skating, judges decide who are the best performers.

The most famous competition is the Olympic Games, named after Olympia, the home of the Games in ancient Greece. The modern Games are held once every four years. Men and women try to win gold, silver or bronze medals by gaining first, second or third place in their sport.

◀ Basketball is a fast-moving game for two teams. A net, or "basket" is fixed high at each end of the court. The players try to shoot the ball through the other team's basket. The game was invented in the USA in the 19th century. Early players used fruit-picking baskets. After each score, someone had to climb a ladder to get the ball out of the basket!

▶ Horses are used in many sports, including racing. In showjumping, horses are ridden around a course, leaping over a variety of fences.

SEE ALSO: PAGE 108 ANCIENT GREECE, PAGE 110 THE ROMANS, PAGE 114 ANCIENT AMERICA

PEOPLE

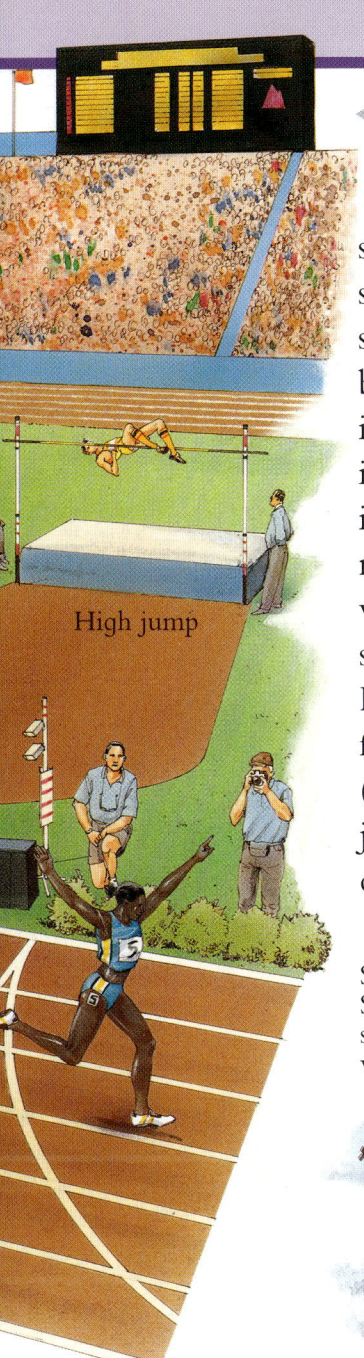

◀ Many kinds of sport take place in an athletics stadium, often at the same time. Shaped like a squashed "O" with straight sides, the running track borders the central field. It is divided by white lines into strips, or "lanes", inside which the athletes run. Races can last a few very exciting seconds, or several testing minutes. Inside the track are areas for throwing and jumping ("field") events such as the javelin, pole vault and long and high jumps.

High jump

Skiing is an exciting sport for all. Skis allow you to slide over the snow smoothly and quickly without sinking.

Kayaks and canoes are long, narrow boats, usually with room for only one person. They are moved along in the water using a long paddle. Some dare to paddle their kayaks or canoes through very rough waters.

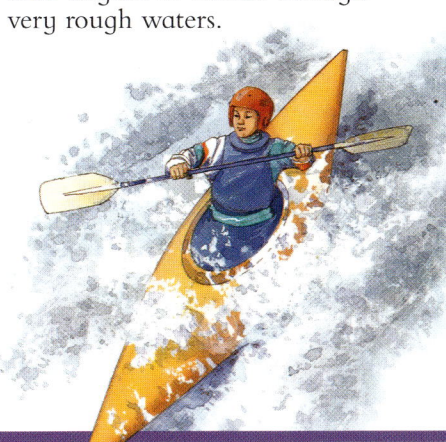

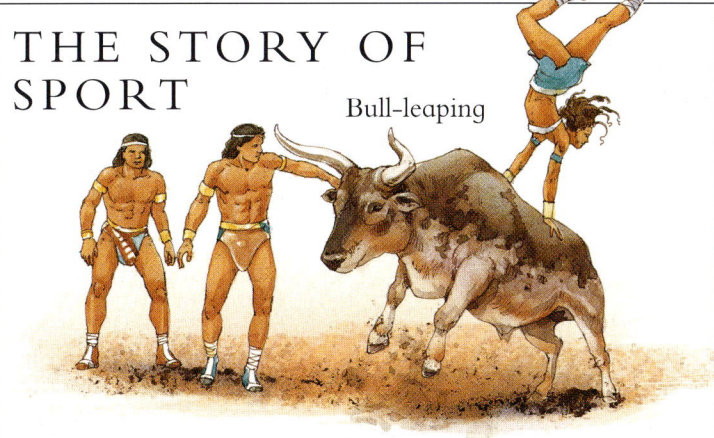

THE STORY OF SPORT

Bull-leaping

SPORTS such as running, swimming and throwing date back to earliest times. Competitions in fighting and horse-riding helped warriors train for battle. A popular sport among the Minoans of ancient Crete was bull-leaping. Daring men and women would grasp the horns of an oncoming bull, then turn a somersault over its back.

Sumo wrestling

Many ancient sports are still popular today. Sumo wrestling, for example, began as a ceremony in Japan to please the gods. The wrestlers fought to the death. New sports, such as beach volleyball, are often developed as variations of well-known ones.

Beach volleyball

93

THE STORY OF TRANSPORT

Ships

THE FIRST BOATS were probably just rafts of logs or reeds tied together. As time went on, people learnt to make boats by hollowing out logs and, later, by fixing planks together. Adding sails made it possible to use the power of the wind. Now big boats, or ships, could make long journeys by sea.

Sailing ships took explorers, such as Christopher Columbus, to all corners of the Earth. Later, metal ships with engines were built. The spinning, curved blades of their propellers drove the ships through the water.

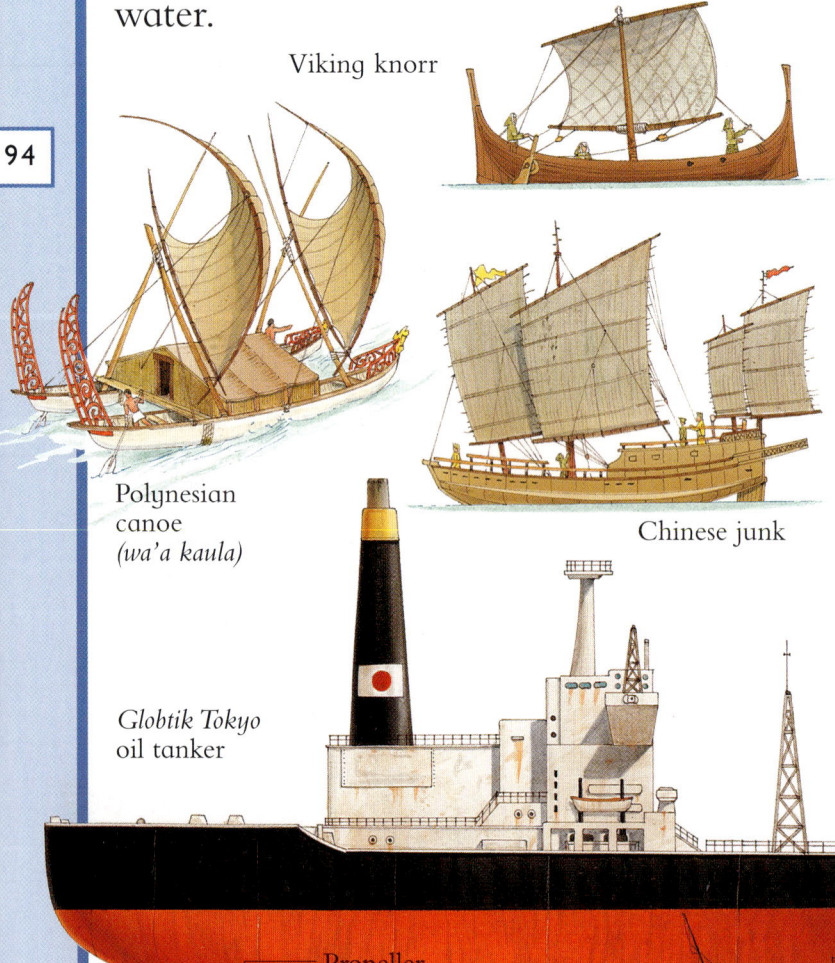

Viking knorr

Polynesian canoe (wa'a kaula)

Chinese junk

Globtik Tokyo oil tanker

◀ The Vikings (see page 120) were the first to cross the Atlantic Ocean about 1,000 years ago. Polynesian islanders also made long journeys across the Pacific Ocean in double canoes. They used the stars to find their way. The Chinese still use traditional sailing boats called junks. They have bamboo canes across the sails to keep them flat.

Propeller

Spanish galleon

SEE ALSO: PAGE 20 FORCES AND MATTER, PAGE 64 OCEANS, PAGE 108 ANCIENT GREECE, PAGE 120 EXPLORERS

THE STORY OF TRANSPORT

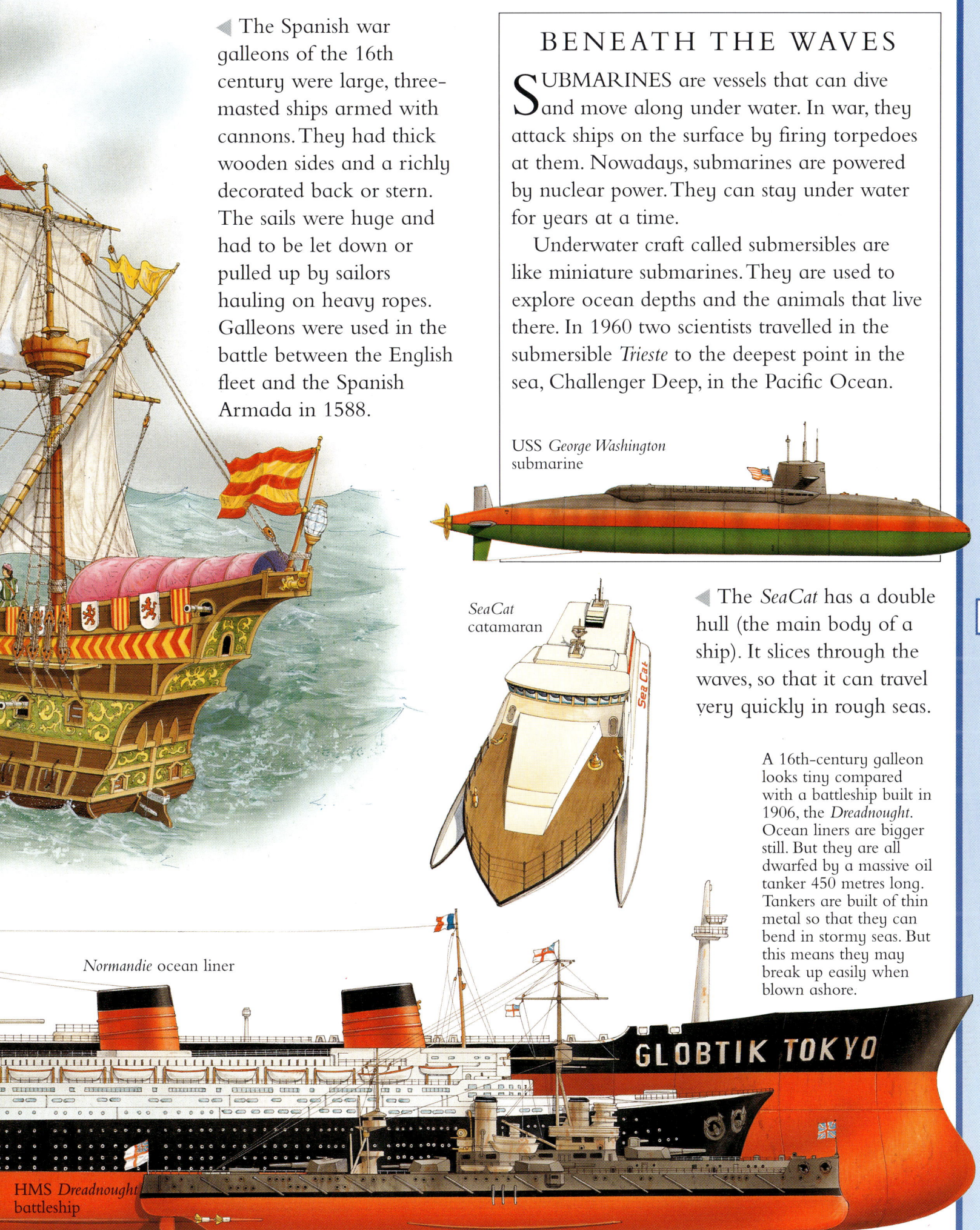

◀ The Spanish war galleons of the 16th century were large, three-masted ships armed with cannons. They had thick wooden sides and a richly decorated back or stern. The sails were huge and had to be let down or pulled up by sailors hauling on heavy ropes. Galleons were used in the battle between the English fleet and the Spanish Armada in 1588.

BENEATH THE WAVES

SUBMARINES are vessels that can dive and move along under water. In war, they attack ships on the surface by firing torpedoes at them. Nowadays, submarines are powered by nuclear power. They can stay under water for years at a time.

Underwater craft called submersibles are like miniature submarines. They are used to explore ocean depths and the animals that live there. In 1960 two scientists travelled in the submersible *Trieste* to the deepest point in the sea, Challenger Deep, in the Pacific Ocean.

USS *George Washington* submarine

SeaCat catamaran

◀ The *SeaCat* has a double hull (the main body of a ship). It slices through the waves, so that it can travel very quickly in rough seas.

A 16th-century galleon looks tiny compared with a battleship built in 1906, the *Dreadnought*. Ocean liners are bigger still. But they are all dwarfed by a massive oil tanker 450 metres long. Tankers are built of thin metal so that they can bend in stormy seas. But this means they may break up easily when blown ashore.

Normandie ocean liner

GLOBTIK TOKYO

HMS *Dreadnought* battleship

95

THE STORY OF TRANSPORT

Trains

BEFORE the invention of trains, long-distance journeys on land could only be made riding on domesticated animals, in a carriage drawn by horses or oxen, or on foot. Trains allowed people to reach their destinations quickly and easily. Heavy goods could also be transported by rail.

The first trains were invented almost 200 years ago and were driven by steam-powered engines, called steam locomotives. Some later steam locomotives were huge machines that billowed out clouds of smoke. Now, in most parts of the world, the age of the steam train is over. Modern trains are pulled by diesel- or electric-powered locomotives. The trains of the future may include "maglev" trains, which hover over magnetic tracks.

The British locomotive *Mallard* was the fastest-ever steam locomotive. It set a speed record of 201 km/h in 1938. In this illustration (and the TGV, *bottom right*), parts of the body are removed so we can see inside.

Trevithick's steam locomotive

George and Robert Stephenson's *Rocket*

A typical train used in the USA in the late 19th century.

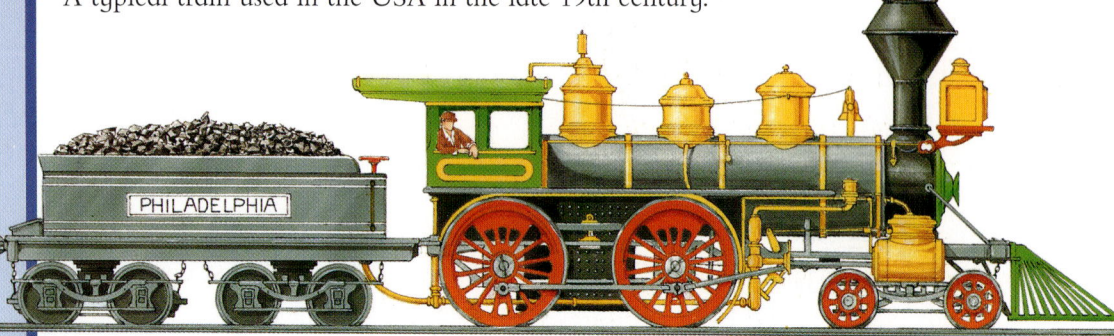

◀▲ The first steam engine or locomotive to run on rails was built in 1804 by a British engineer, Richard Trevithick. Early locomotives were used to carry coal between coalmines in England. In 1829 a competition was held for the best steam locomotive. *Rocket,* built by George Stephenson and his son Robert, won the £500 prize. It moved at 56 km/h and its design was used to make all later steam locomotives. In 1830 the first passenger railway was opened. Soon there were railways and locomotives all over the world.

SEE ALSO: PAGE 20 FORCES AND MATTER, PAGE 22 ELECTRICITY

THE STORY OF TRANSPORT

KEY
1 Furnace
2 Boiler
3 Cylinder
4 Driving wheels
5 Funnel

ABOVE AND BELOW

ELECTRIC TRAINS are very useful in places where smoke or diesel fumes cannot easily escape into the air. Many large cities now have networks of electric trains which run underground, linking up all areas of the city. The first underground trains ran in London in 1863. Originally steam-powered, they are now electric *(above left)*.

Trains usually run on double rails on the ground, but one kind of train, called a monorail, runs on a single rail. The illustration *(above right)* shows the suspension monorail trains of Wuppertal, Germany that run along with the rail above them.

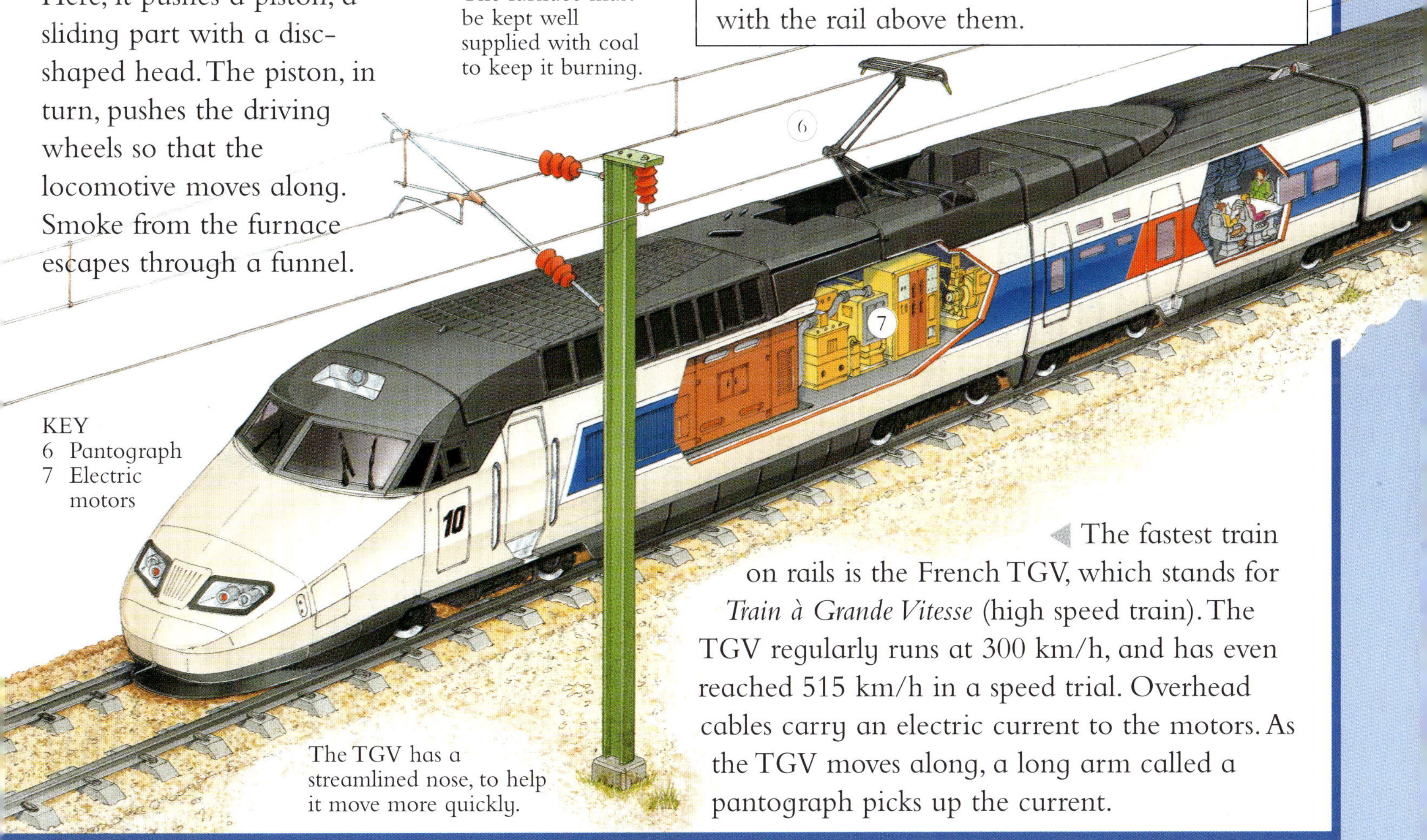

▲ A steam locomotive uses the energy produced when water heats up and becomes steam. Coal is burnt in the furnace, heating water in the tubes inside the boiler. The water turns into steam, which is forced into a cylinder. Here, it pushes a piston, a sliding part with a disc-shaped head. The piston, in turn, pushes the driving wheels so that the locomotive moves along. Smoke from the furnace escapes through a funnel.

The furnace must be kept well supplied with coal to keep it burning.

97

KEY
6 Pantograph
7 Electric motors

◀ The fastest train on rails is the French TGV, which stands for *Train à Grande Vitesse* (high speed train). The TGV regularly runs at 300 km/h, and has even reached 515 km/h in a speed trial. Overhead cables carry an electric current to the motors. As the TGV moves along, a long arm called a pantograph picks up the current.

The TGV has a streamlined nose, to help it move more quickly.

THE STORY OF TRANSPORT

Road transport

EARLY ROADS were used mainly by armies or traders who travelled on foot or on horseback. Roman roads, made from layers of earth, pebbles and stone slabs, were built to last. Later, horsedrawn carriages and bicycles also went by road. The first road vehicle which ran on its own power was built in 1769 by a Frenchman, Nicolas Cugnot. It was driven by steam, but moved so slowly it would have been quicker to walk! Cars did not become a practical way to travel until petrol engines were invented in the 1880s.

Nowadays, people are concerned about the amount of pollution that petrol engines give off into the air. One day, most cars may run on much cleaner sources of power such as electricity or compressed air.

The first petrol-driven car was invented by the German engineer, Karl Benz, in 1885. It had three wheels and its top speed was only 15 km/h.

▶ The first cars were simple vehicles known as "horseless carriages". By the beginning of the 1900s, modern kinds of engine, tyre, gears and steering had been invented. The first car to include them all was the Mercedes, first produced in 1901 by the German company Daimler. The Mercedes was a luxury car that only the very rich could afford.

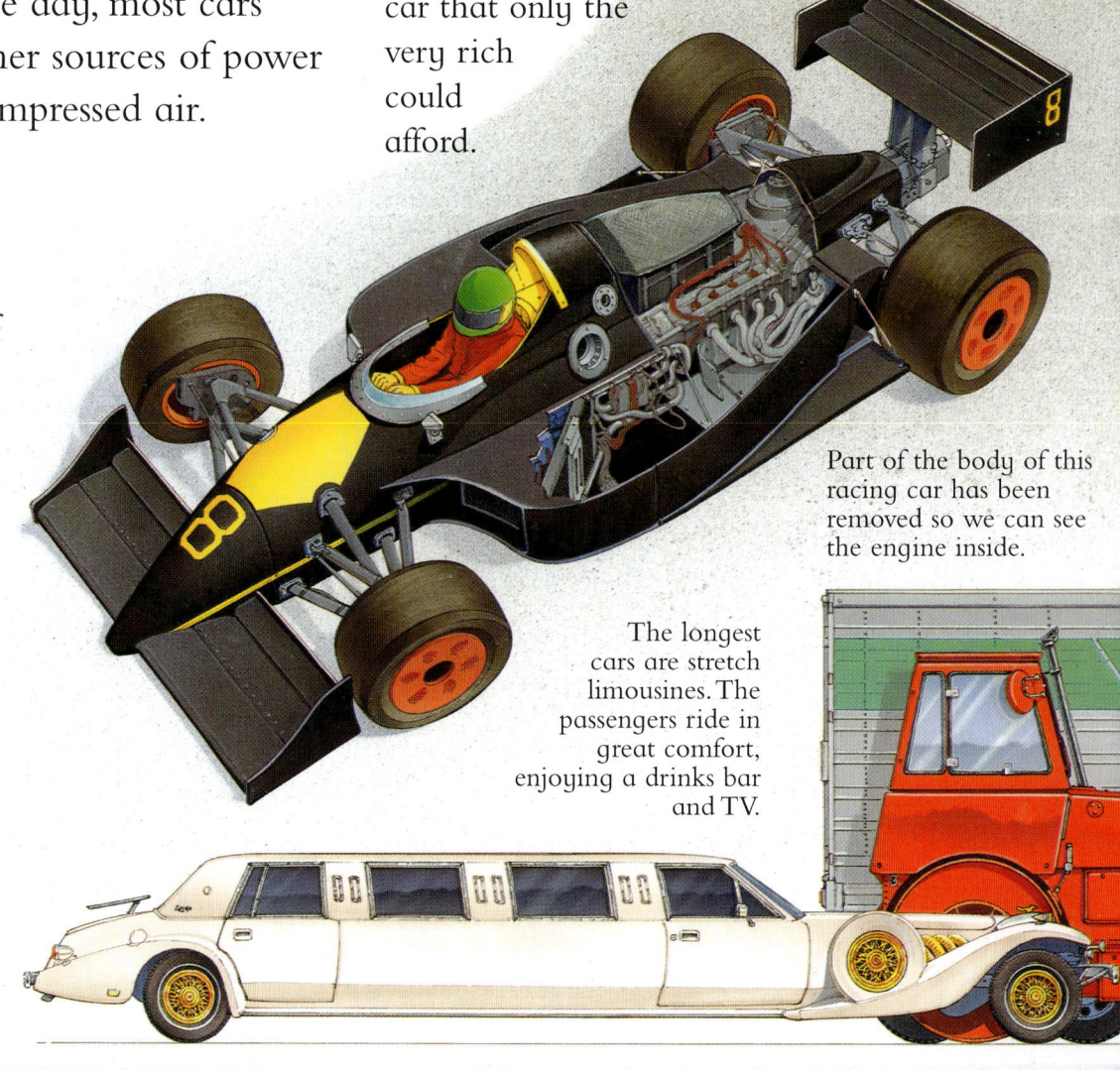

1901 Mercedes

▶ Modern car engines work by drawing fuel (petrol or diesel oil) and air into them. A spark makes the mixture explode inside a small space. The force of the explosion pushes pistons and rods that make the wheels go round. Racing cars are designed to go very fast. They have powerful engines and a low, streamlined shape so that the car can push through the air more easily. Their broad tyres grip the surface of the track as the cars roar around tight corners.

Part of the body of this racing car has been removed so we can see the engine inside.

The longest cars are stretch limousines. The passengers ride in great comfort, enjoying a drinks bar and TV.

SEE ALSO: PAGE 20 FORCES AND MATTER, PAGE 22 ELECTRICITY, PAGE 110 THE ROMANS

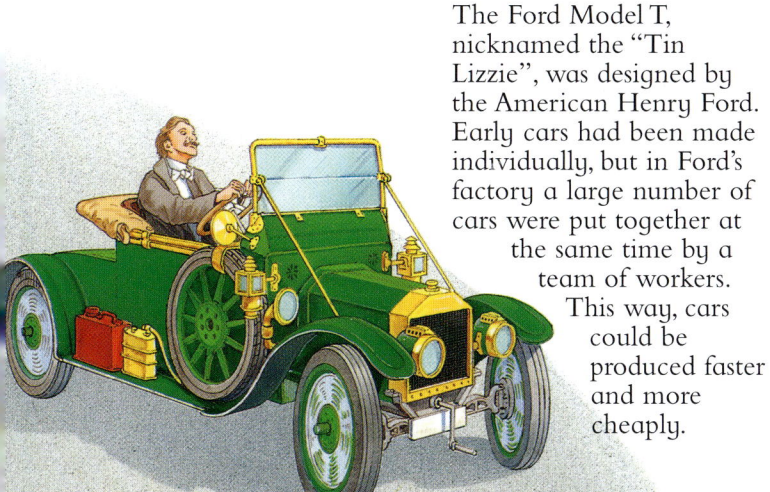

THE STORY OF TRANSPORT

The Ford Model T, nicknamed the "Tin Lizzie", was designed by the American Henry Ford. Early cars had been made individually, but in Ford's factory a large number of cars were put together at the same time by a team of workers. This way, cars could be produced faster and more cheaply.

The Volkswagen "Beetle" (so called because of its beetle-like shape) was first built in Germany in the 1930s.

BICYCLES

THE FIRST bicycles were invented about 200 years ago. They had no pedals. Instead, the riders pushed along the ground with their feet. The first pedal-powered bicycle was built in 1839 by a Scotsman, Kirkpatrick Macmillan. Early bicycles, known as "bone-shakers", had wooden or iron wheels, which gave people a very bumpy ride. They came in some strange shapes, too: the Penny Farthing had a huge front wheel but only a tiny back wheel. Modern bicycles have a light frame, rubber tyres and a chain to drive the wheels.

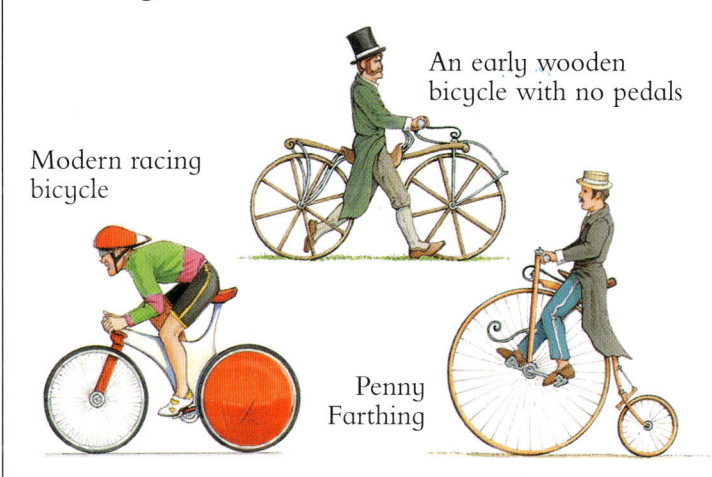

An early wooden bicycle with no pedals

Modern racing bicycle

Penny Farthing

▼ The first motorcycles, built about 100 years ago, were just like bicycles with an engine attached. Modern racing machines are extremely powerful, capable of speeds of more than 250 km/h.

▼ Some road vehicles dwarf even the largest cars. Huge lorries *(below right)* travel across continents carrying goods. There are giant vehicles specially designed for use on building sites. Dumper trucks *(centre)* can lift up their backs and empty out their load. Heavy rollers *(left)* flatten the surface of a new road.

99

THE STORY OF TRANSPORT

Aircraft

PEOPLE have long wished they could fly. The first people to invent a flying machine were the French brothers, Joseph and Étienne Montgolfier. Their hot-air balloon made the first manned flight over Paris in 1783.

About a hundred years ago, many people were trying to build aeroplanes but their machines usually crashed! Then, in 1903, two young American brothers, Wilbur and Orville Wright, tried out their plane on sand dunes at Kitty Hawk, North Carolina. It flew for only 12 seconds before landing just 36 metres away. It was the first ever controlled, powered flight by an aeroplane.

The Fokker Dr. 1 triplane was the favourite plane of German First World War ace Baron Manfred von Richthofen, known as the "Red Baron". It had a machine gun that could fire forwards without hitting the aircraft's own propeller.

▼ The Boeing 747, the world's largest airliner, normally carries up to 420 people. It is the only airliner which has an upper deck. The wingspan of the Jumbo Jet, as it is often called, is wider than the entire distance flown by the Wright brothers' aeroplane on its first flight! Its tail is as high as a six-storey building. In this illustration, parts of the body have been removed so we can see inside.

Tail fin

Crew rest area

Baggage hold

Tailplane

The Wright brothers' plane, *Flyer 1,* was powered by a small petrol engine. The pilot lay on his front on the lower wing to steer the aircraft. His controls allowed him to twist the wings so that *Flyer* could "roll" slightly to the left or right.

The Douglas DC-3 Dakota, which first flew in 1935, was one of the earliest airliners. It could carry 21 passengers.

THE STORY OF TRANSPORT

The British Spitfire warplanes fought German fighters and bombers in the Battle of Britain during the Second World War.

▼ The pilot and co-pilot sit in the flight deck of a Jumbo Jet with hundreds of lights, levers, dials and screens in front of them. For much of a normal flight, the aeroplane flies itself. It has an autopilot that uses computers to control the aircraft's speed and direction and check its position.

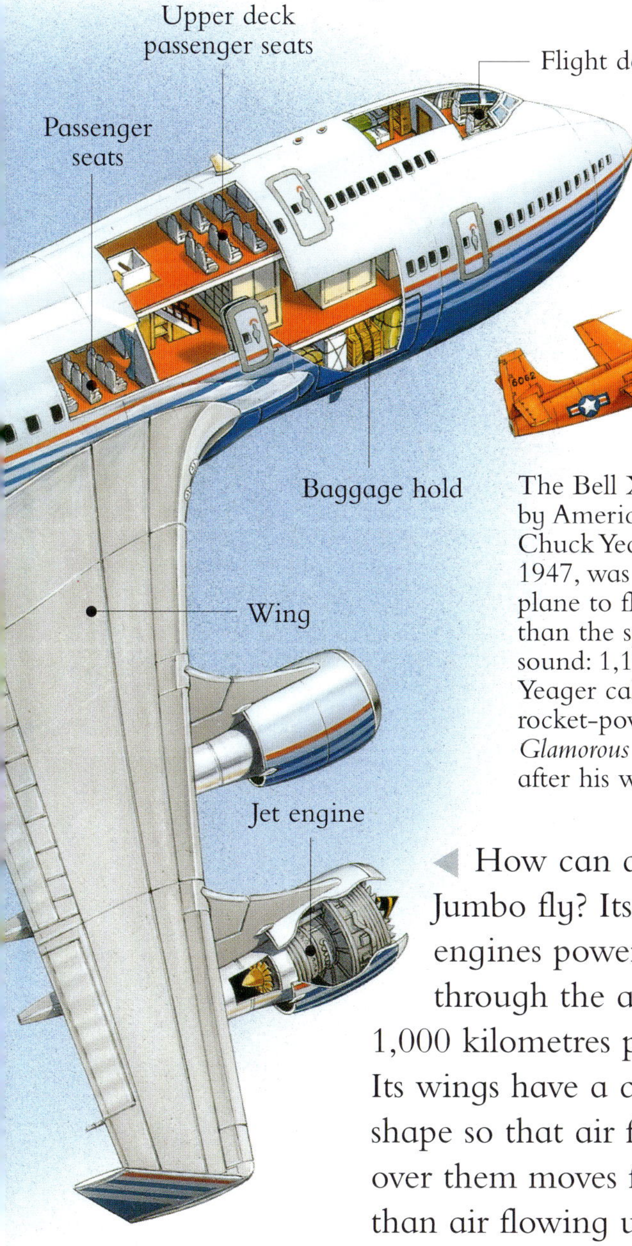

Upper deck passenger seats
Passenger seats
Flight deck
Baggage hold
Wing
Jet engine

The Bell X-1, flown by American pilot Chuck Yeager in 1947, was the first plane to fly faster than the speed of sound: 1,196 km/h. Yeager called his rocket-powered plane *Glamorous Glennis* after his wife.

◀ How can a heavy Jumbo fly? Its four jet engines power it through the air at 1,000 kilometres per hour. Its wings have a curved shape so that air flowing over them moves faster than air flowing under them. This produces a lifting effect. (See this for yourself by blowing over the top of a small piece of paper held in one hand.)

HELICOPTERS

HELICOPTERS can fly backwards or sideways as well as forwards, hover in mid-air and take off or land vertically. They do not need the runway that aeroplanes must have for take-off or landing. Because of this, helicopters are very useful for rescuing people in mountains or out at sea. They can also transport people to and from oil rigs or the tops of skyscrapers in cities.

All helicopters have rotor blades shaped like long, thin wings. They rotate very quickly and drive the aircraft through the air. The tail rotor stops it from spinning round.

101

The French Mirage 2000 is a modern jet fighter. It can fly at more than twice the speed of sound.

▶ In 1986 Americans Dick Rutan and Jeana Yeager in *Voyager* made the first flight around the world without refuelling. Their aircraft had very long wings. The two pilots were squeezed inside a space only a little larger than a telephone booth. It took them nine days to make the flight.

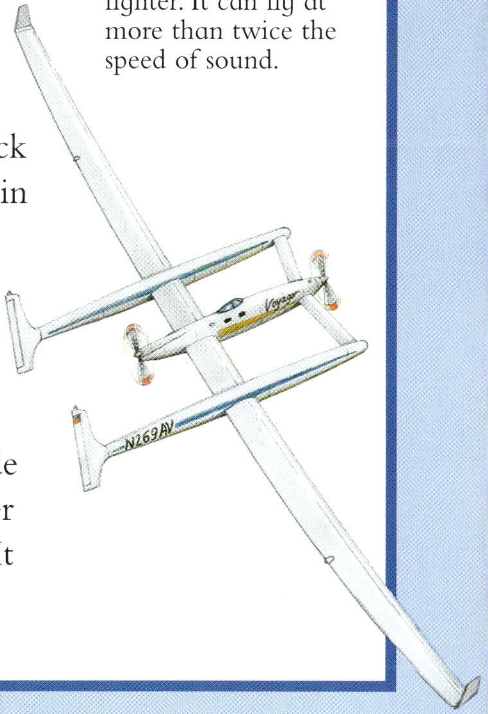

SEE ALSO: PAGE 18 LIGHT AND SOUND

THE STORY OF TRANSPORT

Space Travel

A SPACE vehicle uses powerful rocket engines because it must travel very fast to escape the pull of the Earth's gravity *(see page 20)*. The first spacecraft, a satellite called Sputnik 1, was launched in the Soviet Union* in 1957. It had no people on board. The first living thing to travel in space was a dog called Laika, sent up in a spacecraft later that year. Then, in 1961, a Russian called Yuri Gagarin became the first human in space.

Space travellers, known as astronauts (or cosmonauts in Russia), have since been to the Moon and made many trips into space in the Space Shuttle. A number of space probes, unmanned spacecraft, have travelled to distant parts of the Solar System.

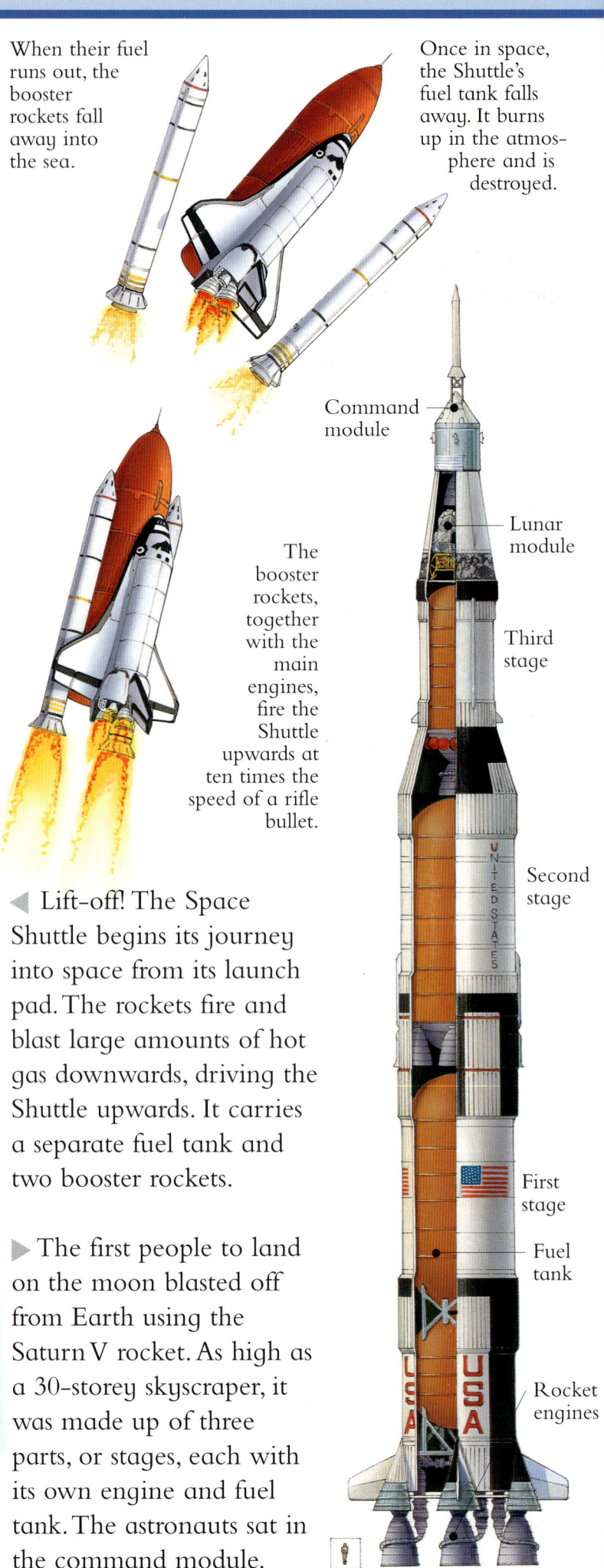

▼ Space probes are spacecraft that explore planets and moons which are too far away for people to visit. As they pass by their targets, the probes send back pictures to Earth. The *Galileo* space probe dropped its own probe down into Jupiter's atmosphere in 1995.

Galileo space probe

When their fuel runs out, the booster rockets fall away into the sea.

Once in space, the Shuttle's fuel tank falls away. It burns up in the atmosphere and is destroyed.

The booster rockets, together with the main engines, fire the Shuttle upwards at ten times the speed of a rifle bullet.

◀ Lift-off! The Space Shuttle begins its journey into space from its launch pad. The rockets fire and blast large amounts of hot gas downwards, driving the Shuttle upwards. It carries a separate fuel tank and two booster rockets.

▶ The first people to land on the moon blasted off from Earth using the Saturn V rocket. As high as a 30-storey skyscraper, it was made up of three parts, or stages, each with its own engine and fuel tank. The astronauts sat in the command module.

Command module
Lunar module
Third stage
Second stage
First stage
Fuel tank
Rocket engines

* Now 15 new countries, one of which is Russia.

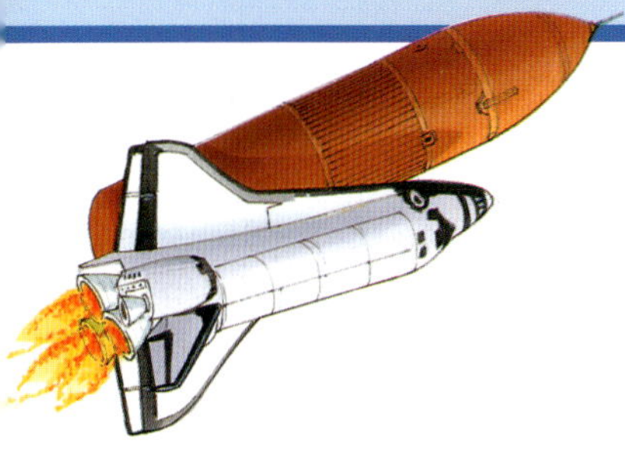

THE STORY OF TRANSPORT

MOON LANDING

▼ The Space Shuttle is a spacecraft which is designed to be used over and over again. It can carry satellites (see page 88) up into orbit. It also takes people up to retrieve or repair these satellites or to carry out experiments.

When an object enters the Earth's atmosphere, it becomes extremely hot. To prevent the Shuttle from burning up into dust on its return to Earth, a special outer layer of tiles protects it from the intense heat.

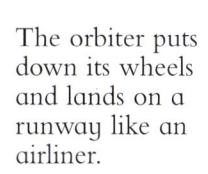

The Shuttle crew perform their "mission". In this case it is to launch a satellite.

Small rockets are fired and the orbiter glides back to Earth.

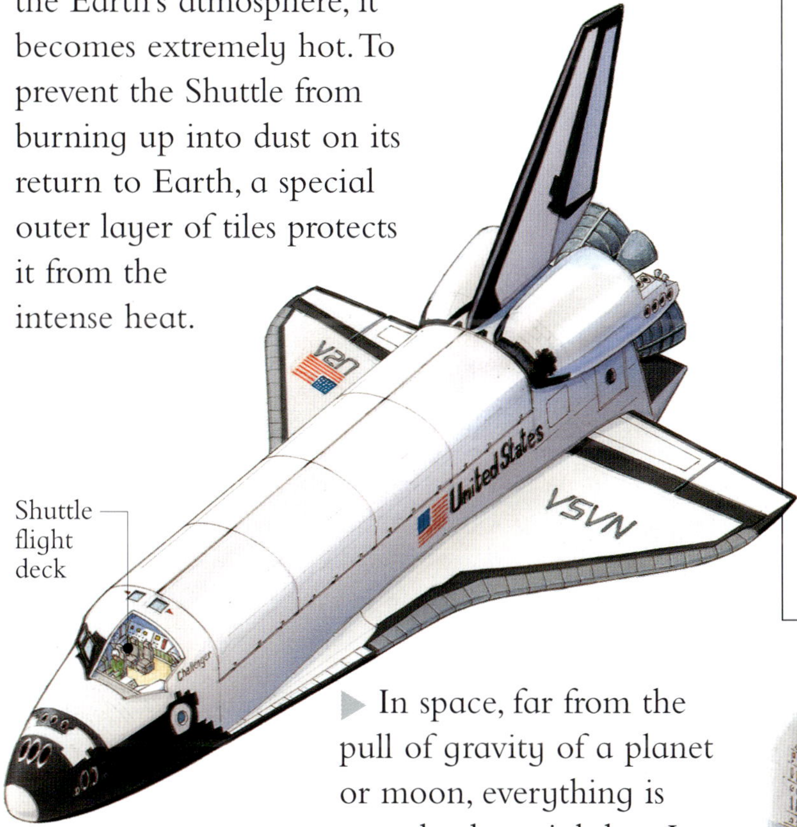

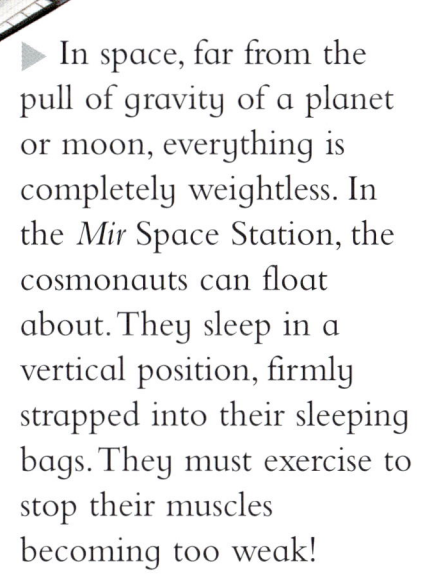

Shuttle flight deck

The orbiter puts down its wheels and lands on a runway like an airliner.

▶ In space, far from the pull of gravity of a planet or moon, everything is completely weightless. In the *Mir* Space Station, the cosmonauts can float about. They sleep in a vertical position, firmly strapped into their sleeping bags. They must exercise to stop their muscles becoming too weak!

IN JULY 1969 US astronaut Neil Armstrong became the first person to set foot on the Moon. He travelled to the Moon with two other astronauts on a mission called Apollo 11. Between 1969 and 1972 eleven other astronauts landed on the Moon. They explored the surface, taking photographs and carrying out experiments. They also brought back rock samples for scientists to study. Later missions used a Lunar Rover to move about on the surface of the Moon. Here, the astronauts are seen in their space suits. These contained breathing and temperature devices, and a radio link with the spacecraft.

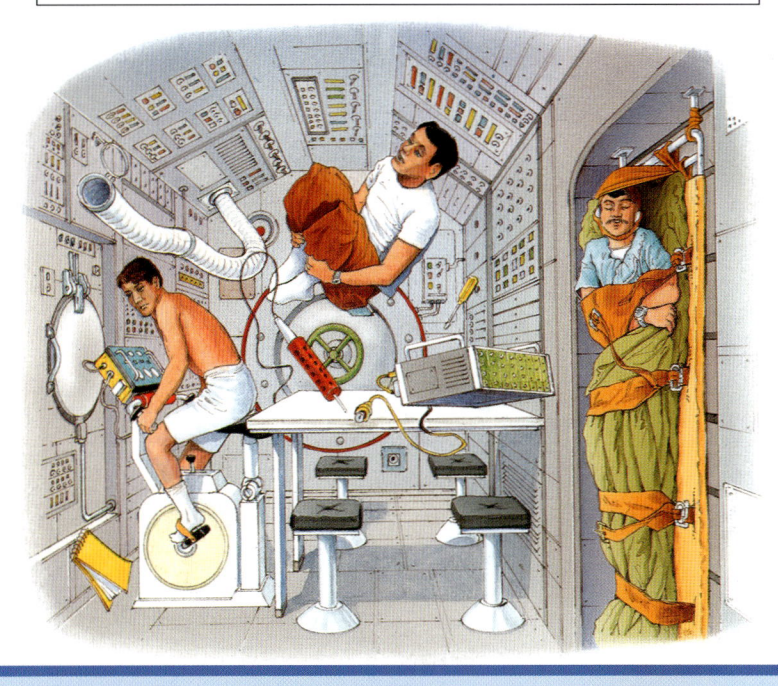

SEE ALSO: PAGE 6 SOLAR SYSTEM, PAGE 8 EARTH AND MOON, PAGE 20 FORCES AND MATTER, PAGE 88 TELEVISION

PAST WORLDS

EARLY PEOPLE

WE KNOW how people lived from the time when writing was first invented, about 5,500 years ago. Before that, the many objects that people left behind—pots, weapons, remains of buildings and so on—tell us much about how they lived. But the story of humans goes back millions of years, to when an ape-like creature first began to walk on two feet.

Scientists are starting to piece together how early humans lived by studying the remains of skeletons. Their discoveries show that, over the years, humans gradually became more and more intelligent, learning how to use tools, live and work together, talk to one another, hunt and build shelters.

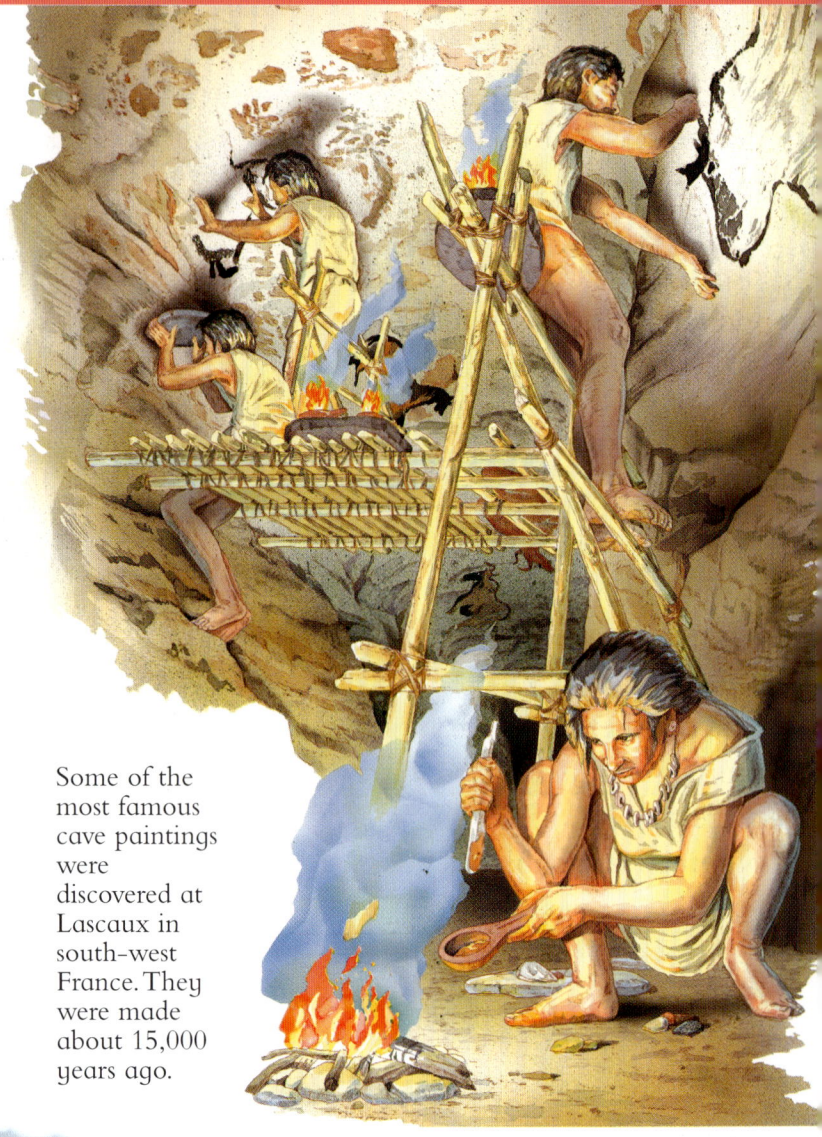

Some of the most famous cave paintings were discovered at Lascaux in south-west France. They were made about 15,000 years ago.

Bringing down a woolly mammoth, a giant prehistoric elephant, was dangerous work. People hunted together in groups.

◀ About 100,000 years ago, the climate in many parts of the world was much colder than it is today. This period, known as the Ice Ages, lasted until about 10,000 years ago. Thick ice covered wide areas of North America, Europe and Asia. People lived during these cold, bleak times by hunting animals like woolly mammoths. They used wooden spears with stone blades. For shelter, people lived in tents made from branches and animal skins, or in caves.

SEE ALSO: PAGE 30 PREHISTORIC LIFE, PAGE 80 FARMING, PAGE 90 RELIGIONS

PAST WORLDS

◀ During the very coldest years of the Ice Ages, people started to paint pictures on cave walls. They worked by the light of lamps and used colours made from powdered rocks or plants. The paintings they made were probably not just for decoration. The bison, deer and mammoths that appear in them were a vital source of food. The paintings may have been meant as offerings to the gods, in the hope that the animals would always be there to be hunted. Cave paintings from this time have been found all over the world, including South America and Australia.

In many places, such as the North American coast, people fished as well as hunted.

Nuts, fruits and berries gathered in summer also provided food in the winter months.

THE FIRST HUMANS

HUMANS were descended from ape-like animals. We have the same ancestor as the chimpanzee. The first kinds of human-like animals that walked upright on two feet were called australopithecines. They lived in Africa more than 4 million years ago. *Homo erectus (below)*, a later kind of early human that lived in both Africa and Asia, was a skilled toolmaker and had learnt how to cook food over fires. Modern humans first appeared on Earth about 125,000 years ago.

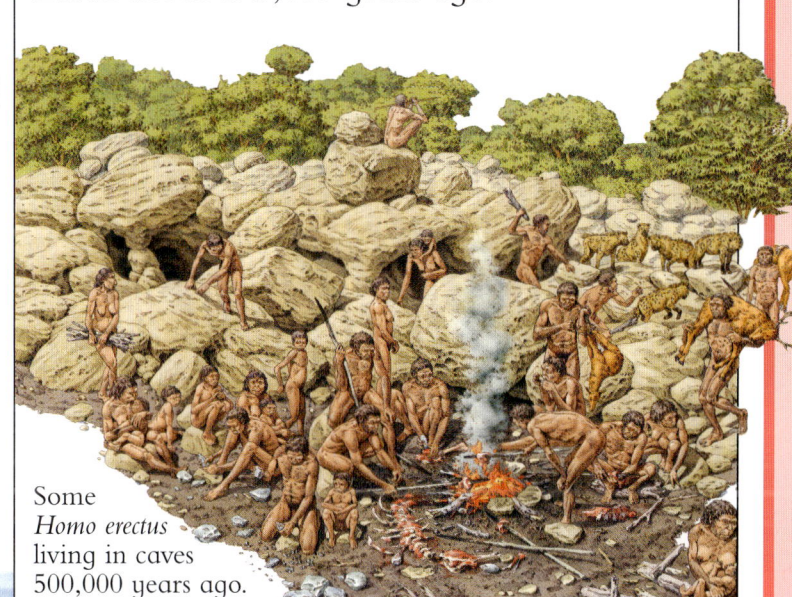

Some *Homo erectus* living in caves 500,000 years ago.

105

A farming village in China about 5,000 years ago. People kept goats and pigs and grew maize.

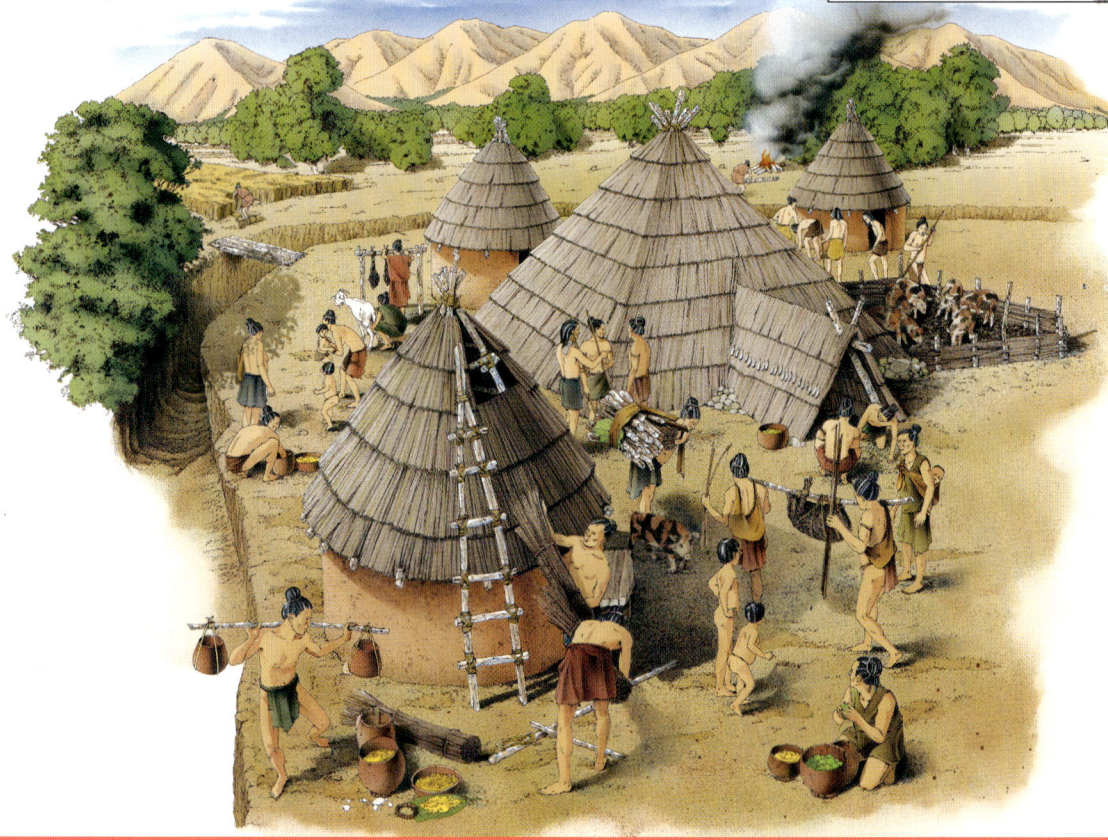

◀ When the Ice Ages came to an end, the climate became warmer. People discovered that they could gather the seeds of some wild plants and plant them in fields. Some grasses produced grain that they could grind into flour from which they could make bread. These people, the first farmers, could now settle in villages close to their fields. They also tamed animals like cattle and pigs and kept them for their milk and meat.

PAST WORLDS

ANCIENT EGYPT

A GREAT KINGDOM grew up on the banks of the River Nile in Egypt 5,000 years ago. It was a time of amazing human achievements. Wonderful monuments such as pyramids and vast temples were built. The people of ancient Egypt invented a kind of picture writing called hieroglyphics.

Surrounded by desert, the Nile valley was fertile because the river watered the soil and crops could be grown easily. The Nile was also the Egyptians' highway. Boats could carry many more goods and people than pack animals could.

To build a pyramid, huge blocks of stone were taken to the site by boat. Workers built massive ramps and dragged the stone blocks up on rollers.

Shaduf

◀ Wealthy Egyptians owned large houses and land. Their sons went to school and eventually served the rulers of Egypt. Ordinary people worked in the fields, herding animals or growing crops. They used a *shaduf*, a weighted pole with a bucket, to raise water for their crops from the river. Some people made pottery, carved wooden goods or produced metalwork. Women wove linen and made bread. The children worked with their parents. The girls often helped with cooking.

PAST WORLDS

The pyramids were built about 4,500 years ago. They were tombs where the pharaohs of Egypt were buried.

These are called hieroglyphs. Each picture stands for a word or sound. They could be written from left to right, right to left, or top to bottom.

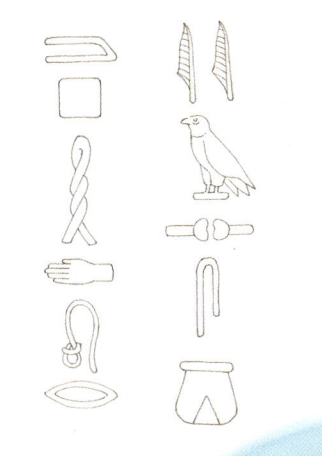

◀ The pharaohs were the kings of ancient Egypt. People believed that they were like gods. The pharaohs had absolute power over everyone, but they also used wealthy advisers called scribes to help them rule the country. When the pharaohs died, they were buried in tombs inside pyramids or beneath temples. Fantastic treasures, pots and even boats were buried in the tombs, too. The Egyptians thought the pharaohs would need them in the next world.

THE MUMMY'S TOMB

THE EGYPTIANS believed that preserving their ruler's body after death was very important. By doing this, his spirit would live on forever. A preserved body is called a mummy. First, the body was cleaned and packed with salt to dry it out. Then it was wrapped up in layers of long linen bandages. Finally, the body was placed in a brightly painted coffin and buried in a tomb.

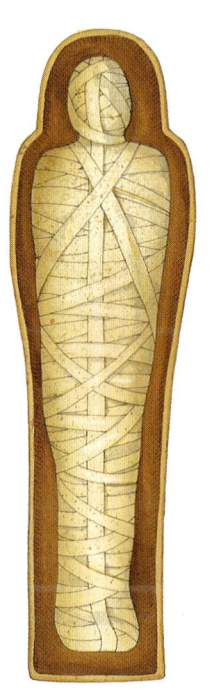

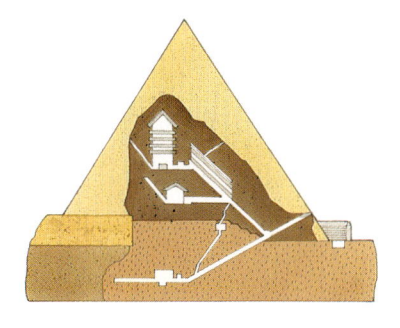

107

This is a view inside a pyramid. Passageways lead to the burial chamber as well as to two empty chambers. Although the entrance was sealed by rock, robbers broke in and stole the pharaoh's treasure.

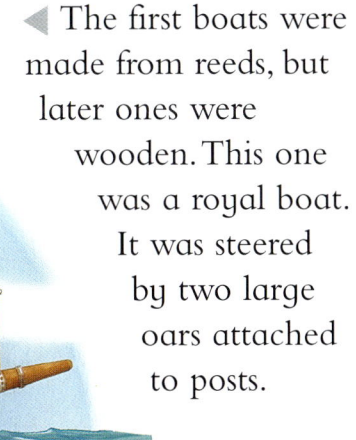

◀ The first boats were made from reeds, but later ones were wooden. This one was a royal boat. It was steered by two large oars attached to posts.

SEE ALSO: PAGE 84 LANGUAGES AND WRITING, PAGE 94 SHIPS, PAGE 104 EARLY PEOPLE

PAST WORLDS

ANCIENT GREECE

ABOUT 2,500 years ago, Greece enjoyed a time of wealth, discovery and invention. It was known as the "Golden Age" of Greece. The country was divided into small states, each normally consisting of a city or town and its surrounding villages. The city-state of Athens was the most powerful of all. It was full of beautiful temples and theatres, and the Athenian people lived well.

The ancient Greeks had many ideas which have passed down to us today. They were the first to use a system of government called democracy, in which ordinary people choose their leaders by voting for them. Greek doctors understood that some illnesses could be cured by medicines made from herbs and plants. The Greeks created an alphabet that is the origin of the one we use today.

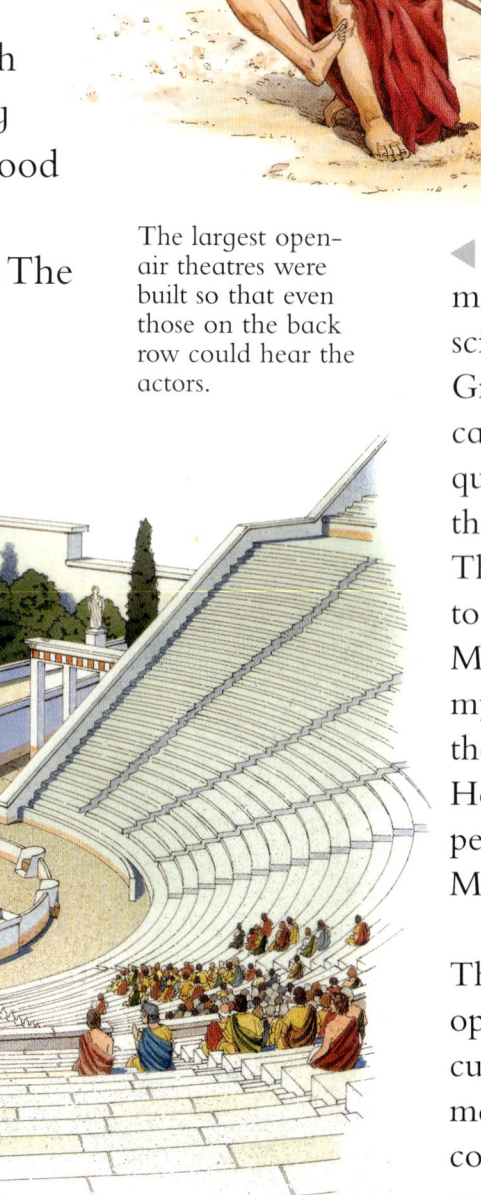

The largest open-air theatres were built so that even those on the back row could hear the actors.

◀ Brilliant writers, mathematicians and scientists lived in ancient Greece. Clever people, called philosophers, asked questions about the world that still puzzle us today. The Greeks loved to listen to music, poetry and songs. Many told stories, or myths, about heroes and the gods, such as Zeus, Hera and Artemis, whom people believed lived on Mount Olympus.

Plays were very popular. The Greeks built huge open-air amphitheatres, cut into hillsides so that as many people as possible could see the play. The actors were always men.

SEE ALSO: PAGE 92 SPORTS, PAGE 94 SHIPS

PAST WORLDS

◀ Health and fitness fanatics, the Greeks held a festival of sport every four years at Olympia. (Today, we have our own version called the Olympic Games.) The Greeks also prized freedom of speech. Political speeches were often made in the city marketplace.

ALEXANDER THE GREAT

ALEXANDER the Great came from Macedonia in northern Greece. His father, King Philip of Macedonia, ruled the whole of Greece. When Philip died, Alexander was only twenty years old. However, he led his powerful army on to conquer a huge area of land stretching from Egypt to northern India, including the mighty Persian empire. By the time he died, Alexander's empire was almost as large as the United States is today.

◀ The men from the city-state of Sparta were fierce warriors. Boys had to leave home to learn to fight when they were only seven years old. Spartan soldiers, called hoplites, wore armour and carried shields and spears.

The Greeks had fleets of warships called triremes. They carried masts for sailing, but they were rowed into battle. Inside, the rowers were positioned on three levels. A trireme had a heavy wooden pole at the front, which was used as a battering ram to smash holes in enemy ships.

PAST WORLDS

THE ROMANS

BEFORE the city of Rome was founded in 753 BC, it was a group of small villages in central Italy. Later, it became a republic: its leaders were chosen by the people. Under Julius Caesar and Augustus, the first emperor, the Romans conquered many countries. But by AD 300 their empire had become too large to control and foreign invasions began.

The Romans built long, straight roads, well-planned towns and elaborate heating and plumbing systems. They had public theatres and baths and enjoyed games that nowadays we think cruel, such as captive men fighting to the death against wild animals—or against each other.

The audience roars with excitement as the chariots hurtle round the track. Many of the charioteers were killed.

◀ Most Roman towns had at least one bath-house. Everyone, rich and poor, went there to bathe, exercise and meet friends. The baths had several rooms, including a room full of hot air and steam from basins of hot water. There was also a warm bath to soak in. The hot air came from a "hypocaust", a system of furnaces under the floor, and travelled up through channels in the walls and roof. To get themselves clean, people had oil rubbed into their skins by slaves. The oil was then scraped off, taking the dirt with it.

A Roman soldier wore armour over a thick woollen tunic.

SEE ALSO: PAGE 84 LANGUAGES AND WRITING, PAGE 90 RELIGIONS, PAGE 92 SPORTS

PAST WORLDS

◀ Chariot racing was a very popular sport. Thousands of people would flock to see this thrilling spectacle. Drawn by teams of four horses, the chariots raced at top speed seven times around a long barrier which ran down the centre of the racetrack.

INSIDE A DOMUS

IF YOU WERE a wealthy Roman living in the town, you would have a large house, called a domus. Roman people liked to be private, so there were very few windows on the outside of the house. Instead, the large hall, or atrium, had a skylight to give the rooms around it light and air. There was a pool under the skylight to catch any rain.

Wealthy people enjoyed a life of luxury. They spent a great deal of time in the dining room lying on couches, while slaves filled the table with a wide selection of exotic food.

The Roman empire stretched from northern Britain to the Middle East. Its 60 million people wore Roman clothes and spoke Latin, the language of the Romans.

◀ The Roman army was divided into legions, each containing about 5,000 men, or legionaries. The Roman empire was vast, and much of a legionary's time was spent marching from place to place. He had to carry his armour, shield, javelin, sword and tools as well as provisions.

▶ The Roman empire was at its greatest in the 2nd century AD. Such a huge empire was difficult to control. There were rebellions and the threat of invaders from beyond its borders.

■ Roman empire in 200 AD

Britannia
Germania
Gaul (France)
Hispania (Spain)
Rome • Italia
Asia minor
Syria
Mediterranean Sea
AFRICA
Aegyptus (Egypt)

111

PAST WORLDS

ANCIENT CHINA

PEOPLE began to farm the fertile lands bordering the Yellow River in northern China 8,000 years ago. Later, the land became a kingdom under rulers of the Shang dynasty. Their rule was overthrown and China became a land of warring kingdoms until 221 BC, when it was united as one empire ruled by the Qin (pronounced "chin") dynasty.

The first emperor, Shi Huangdi, commanded new roads and canals to be built, and everyone had to use the same writing, coins, weights and measures. In 202 BC the Han dynasty came to power and ruled China for 400 years. It was a time of wealth, trading and invention.

◀ When emperor Shi Huangdi died, he was buried in an underground tomb. In 1974 farmers digging a well near the lost tomb discovered life-size heads made from clay. Since then, scientists have uncovered several pits containing about 8,000 clay soldiers, chariots and horses. It is clear that Shi Huangdi wanted an army to defend him at all times—even in his tomb. The soldiers held bronze weapons such as swords, spears and arrows, some of which are still sharp after 2,000 years.

Many of the statues were broken when discovered, and their colours had almost disappeared. Each clay soldier has a different face, probably because the statues were modelled on real people.

SEE ALSO: PAGE 84 LANGUAGES AND WRITING, PAGE 104 EARLY PEOPLE, PAGE 116 GREAT EMPIRES

PAST WORLDS

◀ The Shang people discovered how to make strong tools and weapons from a metal called bronze, a mixture of copper and tin. With their new weapons, the Shang rulers became powerful on the field of battle. They loved to go hunting elephants, rhinoceros and tigers. The king and his attendants shot arrows at their prey from a chariot.

Thousands of people worked in terrible conditions to build the Great Wall. They had to carry food supplies and building stone from many kilometres away.

GREAT INVENTIONS

The Chinese wheelbarrow needed much less effort to push it than modern Western machines.

MANY THINGS we use today were first invented in China. Paper money, printing, kites, wheelbarrows and umbrellas are all Chinese inventions. Methods of planting crops and ploughing fields also came from China, as did rockets, mechanical clocks, magnetic compasses, suspension bridges and a clever device for recording earthquakes called a seismograph *(below)*. Some of these inventions found their way to Europe through reports from travellers. Sometimes Europeans came up with the same idea themselves, but hundreds of years later.

When this seismograph is shaken by an earthquake, one of the dragons drops a ball into the mouth of a toad below. This gives the direction of the quake.

◀▶ Over the centuries, emperors of China built and re-built a huge wall across the north of the country to stop invaders. Today, the Great Wall of China is 6,000 kilometres long. It is the largest object ever made by mankind.

Chinese traders carried their silks on camels for thousands of kilometres to trade it for gold and horses. The route they took across Central Asia became known as the Silk Road.

113

ANCIENT AMERICA

PEOPLE had lived in the Americas for thousands of years before the first European settlers arrived. In the eastern woodlands of North America, they farmed the land and built huge earth burial mounds. To the west, people followed the buffalo herds on the Great Plains, while the Inuit lived in the frozen north. In the deserts of the south-west, the Anasazi people built stone and mud brick houses.

Meanwhile, great empires grew up in Central and South America. Their inhabitants built cities with magnificent stone temples and palaces. They used metal such as gold, silver and copper to make tools, weapons, jewellery and ornaments. Roads, bridges and canals enabled people to travel and trade goods.

▶ Peoples of the North American plains hunted the buffalo that roamed the grasslands in vast herds. The meat provided them with food, while the hides were made into clothing. The women cleaned and stretched the buffalo hides, rubbing them with a paste to make them soft. Warrior chiefs wore spectacular headdresses of feathers and buffalo horns.

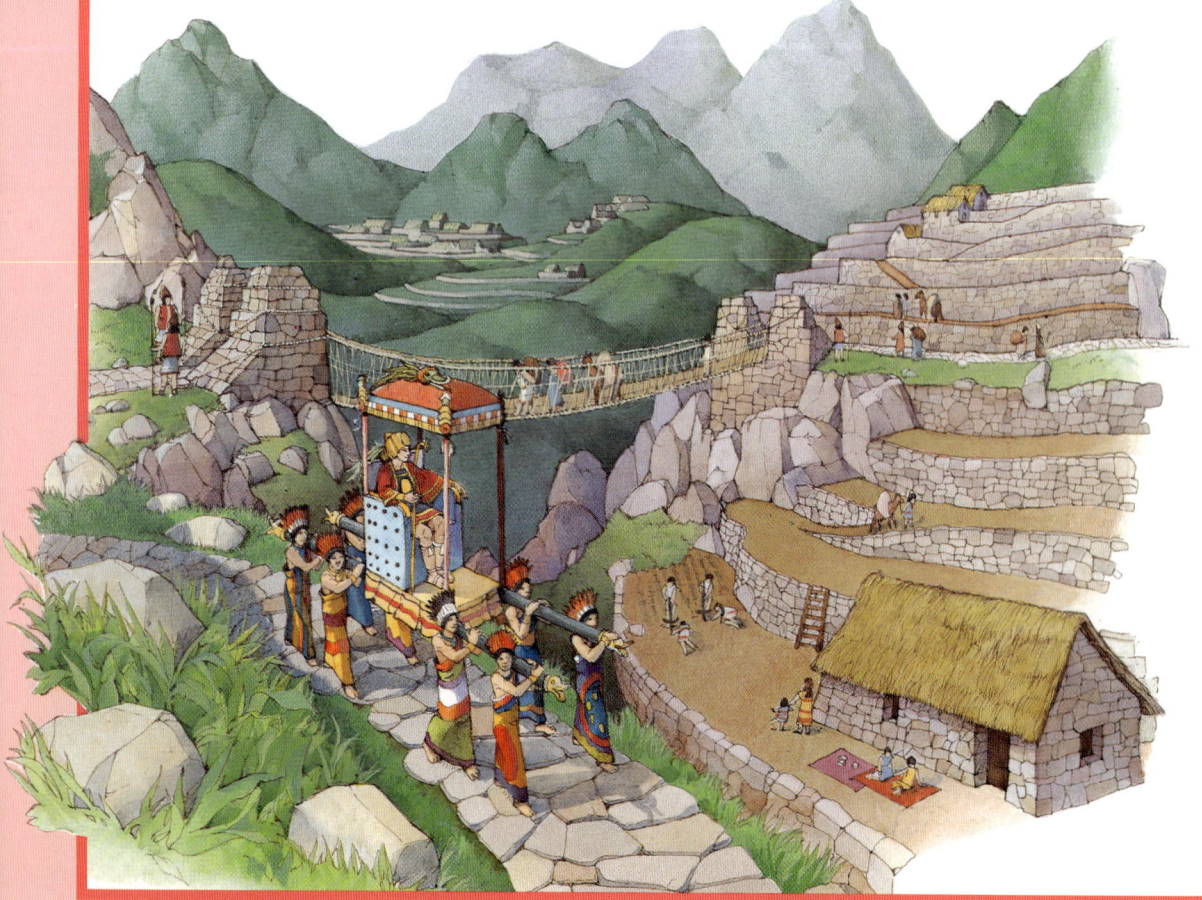

◀ About 500 years ago, the Incas ruled an empire in the Andes Mountains of South America. They built a network of roads across the mountain empire. Bridges made out of twisted vines crossed deep ravines. Messengers and troops walked along the roads, but important people were carried in litters by servants.

The Incas were great craftsmen. They cut and shaped blocks of stone until they fitted together exactly. Many of their sturdy buildings, walls and roads still stand today.

SEE ALSO: PAGE 72 NORTH AMERICA, PAGE 74 SOUTH AMERICA, PAGE 84 LANGUAGES AND WRITING

PAST WORLDS

Plains peoples lived in tents called teepees, made from long wooden poles covered with buffalo hides. They used wooden backrests for support while sitting, and slept under hides on the floor. A warm teepee was often a place to tell stories.

THE MAYA

THE MAYA built magnificent stone cities, temples and palaces in the rainforest of Central America. They invented a number system for counting and used picture writing *(see page 84)* to record important events. They studied the movements of the Sun, Moon, stars and planets, and created a calendar.

The Maya played a ball game on courts in front of their temples. Two teams had to knock a ball through a ring on the court wall using only their forearms, hips or knees. Members of the losing team were condemned to death.

The Aztec Jaguar Knights wore animal skins and wooden helmets carved in the shape of jaguars' heads. They carried the macahuitl, a wooden club edged with sharp stone blades.

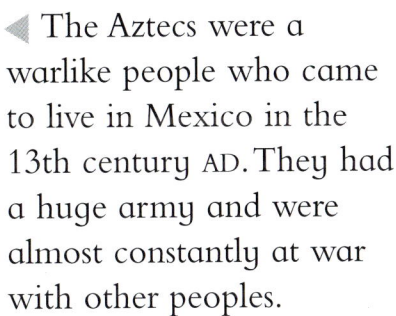

◀ The Aztecs were a warlike people who came to live in Mexico in the 13th century AD. They had a huge army and were almost constantly at war with other peoples.

◀ The Pyramid of the Sun in Teotihuacan, Mexico, was built over a cave where, it was said, the Sun was born. This gigantic pyramid still stands today.

115

PAST WORLDS

GREAT EMPIRES

AN EMPIRE is a region covering many lands and peoples that is under the rule of one nation or person. Often, the language, customs and religion of that ruler would be adopted in all parts of the empire.

Empires need a lot of organization. The Persian empire, which stretched from Egypt to India in ancient times, was divided into provinces, each with its own governor. Such large empires were frequently under attack from surrounding peoples. In 330 BC Alexander the Great (see page 109) overran the Persians and made their lands part of his vast empire.

The Mongols were expert riders and archers. They often took their enemies by surprise with the speed of their fierce attacks. Any cities that tried to defend themselves were burnt down. Mongol riders fired arrows at their enemies while galloping at top speed.

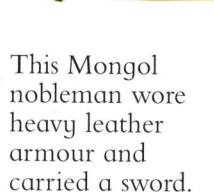

This Mongol nobleman wore heavy leather armour and carried a sword.

Great cities such as Baghdad were market-places for goods such as frankincense (sweet-smelling gum from trees), gold, ivory, pots, plates, carpets and jewellery.

◀ The Arab empire was built up in the 7th and 8th centuries AD. Inspired by Muhammad, the founder of the Islamic religion, the Arabs conquered vast territories. At its height, the empire stretched from Spain, through North Africa and across Asia as far as India. Aboard their ships, known as dhows, the Arabs traded goods around the Mediterranean Sea and between Africa and Asia. Arab scholars made great advances in astronomy, mathematics and medicine.

PAST WORLDS

◀ The Mongols were a nomadic (wandering) people who lived in north-east Asia. In 1206 they joined together under a leader they called Genghis Khan ("ruler of all"). Over the years, they conquered much of Asia and even eastern Europe. The Mongol empire was the greatest land empire the world has ever seen.

AFRICAN EMPIRES

FOR HUNDREDS of years, African peoples mined gold and other metals and traded with China and Arabia. Many, such as the west African empires of Ghana and Mali and the southern African empire of Zimbabwe, grew rich and powerful. An important trade centre, the walled settlement of Great Zimbabwe *(above)* grew up in the 1400s in a land of cattle herders and farmers. The ruler and his followers lived in round, thatched houses protected by high walls. In places, the walls were several metres thick. They were skilfully made by shaping stone blocks so that they fitted together perfectly.

A Mongol archer

◀ More powerful even than the emperor and his rulers (the shoguns), the samurai dominated Japan from the 12th to the 18th centuries. They were rich landowners who had their own private armies. The most important samurai lived in fine castles.

▶ The Moghul empire in India lasted from 1504 to 1858. When his beloved wife Mumtaz Mahal died in 1631, emperor Shah Jahan vowed to build the most beautiful tomb in the world for her. Called the Taj Mahal, it is made of white marble, studded with thousands of jewels.

Samurai warriors wore heavy armour and face masks.

SEE ALSO: PAGE 90 RELIGIONS, PAGE 112 ANCIENT CHINA, PAGE 114 ANCIENT AMERICA

117

MIDDLE AGES

WE CALL the period of European history between about AD 500 and 1500 the Middle Ages. During these years, Europe became a patchwork of kingdoms, frequently warring amongst themselves.

Knights and noblemen fought in wars for their kings. In return, they were given land. Very often, they became more powerful than the kings themselves. They let peasants live and work on their land and made them pay taxes. This was known as the feudal system.

Noblemen's families lived comfortable lives. The boys trained as knights while the girls learnt to read, play music and do fine sewing. But life for poorer families was often a struggle.

Many town-houses were built with a wooden frame filled with brick or stone and plaster.

◀ Once or twice a week, the town market was held. Local farmers brought produce to sell to the townspeople. Travelling merchants sold fine cloth to those who could afford it. Jugglers entertained people with their clever tricks.

▶ To practise their fighting skills, or to decide who should win an argument, knights took part in tournaments. In exciting contests known as jousting, two knights rode towards each other at top speed, each using his lance to try to knock the other off his horse.

PAST WORLDS

Often, a whole town was built inside castle walls. Battlements, the jagged tops to the walls, gave guards some protection.

◁ A nobleman's castle was built to keep out his enemies. It had strong, thick, stone walls and a moat full of water. Soldiers stood guard on the walls looking out for danger. Sometimes, enemies would lay siege to a castle: they would surround it and wait for the people inside to starve. Here, they are attacking the castle with powerful weapons. The castle's soldiers fire arrows from their crossbows on to the enemy below.

The enemy filled in the moat with straw so that they could push their battering rams right up to the castle doors. They used huge catapults to smash holes in the walls, or a tall, wooden tower to climb over them.

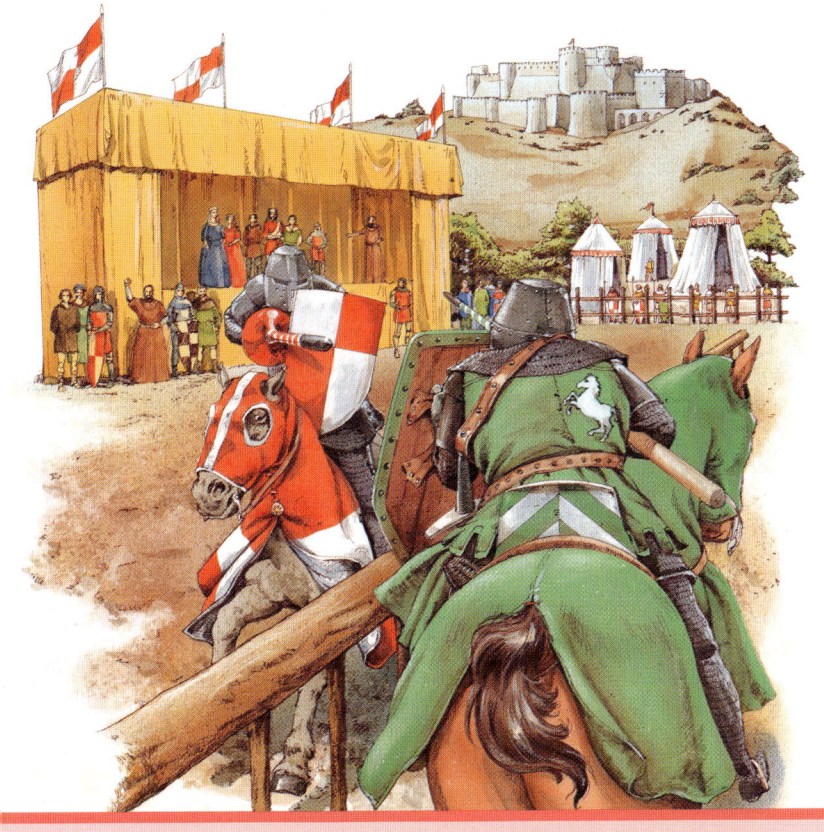

LIFE IN THE COUNTRY

NOBLEMEN divided up the lands given to them by the king into manors. These consisted of three large fields: one each for wheat and barley and a third left unsown (lying fallow) so that the soil could recover its richness. The fields were, in turn, divided into strips. Peasants worked their strips of land and lived in the villages that grew up around a manor house. They grew or made everything they needed to live. Their animals pulled their ploughs and provided meat and clothing. At harvest time, the crops were gathered in and the grain ground into flour using windmills.

◁ Between 1347 and 1349 a terrible disease called the bubonic plague swept Europe and Asia, killing millions of people. Known as the Black Death, it was carried by rats and the fleas that lived on them. No-one then understood the causes of the plague or knew how to cure it. Whole villages disappeared as more and more people died. Carts went round collecting the bodies.

119

SEE ALSO: PAGE 80 FARMING, PAGE 110 THE ROMANS, PAGE 116 GREAT EMPIRES

PAST WORLDS

Explorers

TODAY, we have a detailed knowledge of our world. Satellites *(see page 88)* take pictures of the Earth from space. Cars, trains, ships and aircraft have taken people to most parts of the world. But a few hundred years ago, with only sailing ships, pack animals and their own two feet as means of transport, very few people travelled any distance at all. Those who risked their lives to discover other lands are remembered today as famous explorers.

Early explorers had no maps to guide them and many lands were discovered by accident. More than five hundred years ago, Christopher Columbus sailed west from Spain and reached America. However, he believed he had sailed round the world to the Far East!

Magellan's ships battled through terrible storms off the coast of South America, finally finding a way through into the Pacific Ocean by what is now called Magellan's Strait.

◀ In 1519 Ferdinand Magellan set out from Spain with five ships. His aim was to reach the Spice Islands in the Far East by travelling west around South America. It took just over two years to reach the Spice Islands. Magellan himself was killed by natives in the Philippines. Only one of the ships, the *Vittoria*, returned to Spain, 1,082 days after leaving. Out of a crew of over 200 men, only 18 were left. But they had made the first voyage around the world.

SEE ALSO: PAGE 48 POLAR LANDS, PAGE 94 SHIPS, PAGE 116 GREAT EMPIRES

PAST WORLDS

◀ The Vikings made many expeditions by sea from their homelands in Scandinavia. In about AD 1000 Eric the Red landed on a large island which he named Greenland. Viking settlers lived in this bleak, harsh landscape, grazing their animals and catching fish and seals.

◀ In 1271, at the age of 17, Marco Polo set off from his home in Venice, Italy, with his father and uncle. They travelled across Asia to the palace of Mongol emperor Kublai Khan in China. When Marco's amazing stories were later told in a book, hardly anyone believed them!

POLAR EXPLORERS

THE FIRST person to reach the North Pole was an American, Robert Peary. He had already made seven Arctic expeditions and had lost most of his toes to frostbite. He recorded in his diary that he had reached the Pole in April 1909.

The first person to reach the South Pole was the Norwegian Roald Amundsen *(above)*, in 1911. He was racing against a rival British team led by Robert Scott. Amundsen used husky dogs to pull his sledges quickly. When Scott arrived at the Pole he found Amundsen had already beaten him. On their way back, Scott and his team died in a blizzard.

◀ In France in the early 1820s a prize was offered to the first person to travel to Timbuktu in Africa and return safely. René Caillié took up the challenge. He reached the city after a journey of about 2,400 kilometres, mostly on foot.

◀ Captain James Cook, a British sailor, went in search of the fabled "southern continent" in 1772. Although he did not find it, Cook explored and mapped the east coast of Australia and the islands of the Pacific Ocean.

Cook's ship, the *Endeavour*, carried large supplies of fresh meat and vegetables. These kept the sailors healthy.

121

INDEX

Page numbers in **bold** type refer to main entries.

A

aardvark 41
Abidjan 77
aboriginal peoples 70
Abu Dhabi 68
Accra 77
Aconcagua, Mount 75
acorn 45, 46
actors 89, 108
addax 54
Addis Ababa 77
Adelaide 70
aerials 88-89
aeroplanes *see* aircraft
Afghanistan 69
Africa 52-53, **76-77**, 79, 81, 117, 121
Africa, ancient 117
air 14, 15, 19
aircraft 88, **100-101**, 120
airliners 100-101
Akmola 69
Alabama 73
Alaska 72, 73
Albania 67
albatross, wandering 38
Alberta 73
Aleutian Islands 72
Alexander the Great 109, 116
Alexandria 77
algae 44
Algeria 77
Algiers 77
Allah 91
alligator 36, 61
Allosaurus 30, 31
Almaty 69
alphabet 84-85, 108
Alps 58, 59, 67
altocumulus 14
altostratus 14
Amazon rainforest 40, 56, 74-75
Amazon, River 56, 74-75
America, ancient 84, 105, **114-115**
American Samoa 70
Amman 68
ammonites 11
amphibians 30, **36-37**, 45, 60-61
  birth and growth of 37
amphitheatres 108
amplifiers 86
Amsterdam 67
Amundsen, Roald 121
Amur, River 69
anaconda 56-57
Anasazi people 114
Andaman Islands 69
Andes Mountains 58, 74-75, 114
Andorra 66
anemone, sea 63
angelfish 65
anglerfish 64
Angola 77
animals
  dangerous 34-35, 56-57
  desert 54-55
  domestic 80-81, 92, 96, 105
  grassland 41, 52-53, 76
  mountain 38, 58
  ocean 34-35, 38, 42-43, 64-65, 74
  polar 48, 49
  rainforest 40, 56, 57
  rare 40-41, 57
  river 36-37, 41, 42-43, 60-61
  seashore 62-63
  woodland 50-51
Ankara 68
ant 32, 50
  leafcutter 57
Antananarivo 77
Antarctica 48-49, 74, 121
anteater 41
  giant 41
  tree 56-57
antelope 52, 54
Antigua and Barbuda 73
Apollo 11 103
apples 45
Arab empire 76, 116
Arabia 79
Arabian Sea 68-69
Arabic language 85
arachnids 33
Aral Sea 69
Archaeopteryx 31
archer fish 63
architect 82
Arctic Ocean 48-49, 64, 69
Argentina 75
Arizona 55, 73
Arkansas 73
Armada, Spanish 95
armadillo 57
Armenia 68
Armstrong, Neil 103
army
  Roman 111
  underground clay (China) 112
arteries 25
Ashkhabad 69
Asia 66, **68-69**, 81, 91, 117, 121
Asmera 77
asteroids 6
astronauts 102-103
astronomers 5, 16
astronomy 5, 16, 115, 116
Asunción 75
Athens 67, 108
athletics 93
Atlanta 73
Atlantic Ocean 64, 66, 73, 74-75, 77, 94
Atlas Mountains 77
atmosphere 8, 103
atoms 21, 22
atrium 111
Auckland 70
Augustus 110
Australia 13, 65, 70, 121
australopithecines 105
Austria 67
autopilot 101
autumn 13, 51
aye-aye 57
Ayers Rock *see* Uluru
Azerbaijan 68
Aztecs 115

B

babies 19, 28-29
baboon 40
Babylon 16
bacteria 31
badger 51
Baffin Bay 73
Baffin Island 73
Baghdad 68, 116
Bahamas 73
Bahrain 68
Baikal, Lake 69
Baja California 73
Bajau people, Philippines 79
Baku 68
Balearic Islands 66
baler shell 65
Balkhash, Lake 69
ball game, Maya 115
balloon, hot-air 100
Baltic Sea 67
Bamako 76
Bangkok 69
Bangladesh 69
Bangui 77
Banjul 76
Banks Island 73
baobab 47
baptism 90
Barbados 73
Barcelona 66
Barents Sea 67
barley 81, 119
barnacle 42
barracuda 64-65
basalt 10
basketball 92
bassoon 87
bat 31, 42-43
  horseshoe 43
baths, Roman 110
baton 87
batteries 22
battering rams 119
Battle of Britain 101
battleships 95
beaches 62
bear
  brown 51
  polar 49
beaver 43
Bedouin 79
bees 32
beetle 50
  great diving 60
  head-stander 54
  rhinoceros 33
"Beetle", Volkswagen 99
Beijing 69
Beirut 68
Belarus 67
Belém 75
Belgium 67
Belgrade 67
Belize 73
Bell X-1 101
Belmopan 73
Belo Horizonte 75
Benin 77
Benz, Karl 98
Bering Sea 69, 72
Berlin 67
Bern 67
Bhutan 69
biceps 29
bicycles 98-99
bird of paradise 38
birds 30-31, **38-39**, 48-49, 51, 53, 54, 56-58, 60-63, 65, 71
  beaks 38
  eggs 39
  feet and claws 39
  largest 39
  migration 38
  nests 39, 62
  of prey 38
  smallest 39
  songs 38
Birmingham 66
birth 29
Bishkek 69
Bissau 76
Black Death 119
Black Sea 67, 68
blackbird 51
bladder 25
blenny 62
blood 24-25
  vessels 25, 28
boa constrictor 37
boats 66, 79, 93, 94-95, 78, 106-107
body 37
  human 24-28
Boeing 747 100
Bogotá 75
Bolivia 75
Bombay *see* Mumbai
bones 26, 28-29
Bonn 67
Borneo 69
Bosnia & Herzegovina 67
Boston 73
Botswana 77
Brahma the Creator 91
Brahman 91
brain **26-27**, 28-29
Brasília 75
Bratislava 67
Brazil 75, 79
Brazzaville 77
breathing 25
Bridge of Sighs 66
bridges 66, **82-83**, 114
  arch 82
  beam 82
  cable-stayed 82
  cantilever 82
  suspension 82, 113
Brisbane 70
British Columbia 73
broadcasting 88-89
bronze 113
Brunei 69
Brussels 67
Bucharest 67
Budapest 67
Buddha 91
Buddhism 82, 90-91
Buenos Aires 75
buffalo 114-115
bug, thorn 57
builders 82
buildings 67, 68, 72, 76, 78-79, **82-83**, 90-91, 106-111, 114-115, 117, 118
  African 117
  ancient Egyptian 106-107
  ancient Greek 108
  ancient American 114-115
  homes 78-79, 111, 114, 119
  religious 67, 76, 82,

INDEX

90-91, 117
Roman 110-111
skyscrapers 72, 83
Bujumbura 77
Bulgaria 67
bull-leaping 93
bunting, snow 39
Burkina Faso 77
Burma 69
Burundi 77
butterfly 33, 57
   birdwing 57
   morpho 56-57
   swallowtail 33
butterflyfish 65

C

Cabinda 77
cacti 54
Caesar, Julius 110
Caillié, René 121
Cairo 77
calabash 76
calculator 23
Calcutta 68-69
calendars 17, 115
Calgary 73
California 73
Cambodia 69
camel 55
camera 88-89
Cameroon 77
camouflage in animals 36
Canada 48, 72-73
canals 66
Canary Islands 76, 84
Canberra 70
canine teeth 28
cannons 95
canoes 93, 94
Cape Horn 74-75
Cape of Good Hope 77
Cape Town 77
capybara 56-57
Caracas 75
carbohydrates 24
carbon dioxide 25, 44
Caribbean Sea 72-73
caribou 49
Caroline Islands 70
Carpathian Mountains 67
carriages 98
cars 20, 98-99, 120
cartoons 89
Casablanca 77
Caspian Sea 68-69
cassava 81
castles 82, 119
catamarans 95
catapults 119
caterpillars 33
cattle 81, 105
   zebu 81
Caucasus Mountains 66-67
cave paintings 104-105
caves 11, 104-105, 115
Cayenne 75
cayman 57
cello 86
cells 29
centipedes 30, 33
Central African Republic 77
Central America 115
centrifugal force 21
centripetal force 21
cereals 80-81
Chad 77
Chad, Lake 77
Challenger Deep 64, 95
chameleon 36
   flap-necked 36
chariot racing 111
Chatham Island 70
cheetah 52-53
chemicals 18
Chennai 69
cherry 45
chestnut, sweet 45
Chicago 73
Chile 75
China 68-69, 84, 94, 121
   ancient 84, 105, **112-113**
   inventions 17
Chinese language 84-85
Chisinau 67
Chongqing 69
Christianity 90
Christians 90
Christmas Island 71
chrysalis 33
churches 82, 90
cinema 89
Cinématographe 89
cirrocumulus 14
cirrostratus 14
cirrus 14
clam, giant 65
clarinet 87
cliffs 62
climate **12-13**, 50, 64, 76, 104-105
clocks 16-17, 113
   pendulum 17
clouds 14-15, 21
clownfish 65
coal 10-11, 97
   mining 11, 96
cobra, king 37
coconut 47
   palm 47
coffee 81
cold-blooded animals 36, 37, 54
Colombia 75
Colombo 69
Colorado 73
Colorado River 55, 73

colours 18
Columbus, Christopher 94, 120
combine harvester 80-81
comets 6-7
Comoros 77
compass 20, 113
Compsognathus 30-31
computers 19, 23
Conakry 76
concerts 86
condensation 15, 54
condor, Andean 38
conductor 87
cones 46-47
Congo 77
Congo, River 77
Congo-Brazzaville 77
conifers 46-47
Connecticut 73
constellations 4-5
   Great Bear 5
   Orion 4
   The Plough 5
continents 9
Cook Islands 71
Cook, James 121
Cook, Mount 70
Copenhagen 67
Copernicus 5
copper 113, 114
coral 65
   daisy 65
   gorgonian 65
Corsica 67
cosmonauts 102-103
Costa Rica 73
Côte d'Ivoire 77, 78
cottonmouth 61
counting 115
crab 35, 62-63
   fiddler 63
   hermit 62
crampons 59
craters
   of Moon 9
   volcanoes 8
crayfish 60
Crete 67
   ancient 93
cricket, bush 57
Croatia 67
crocodile 36, 63
   Nile 36
   saltwater 63
crop-spraying 80-81
crops 12-13, 14, 76, 80-81, 106, 113, 119
crossbill 51
crossbows 119
crustaceans 35, 42
Cuba 73
cucumber 45
Cugnot, Nicolas 98
cumulonimbus 14
cumulus 14
curlew 62-63

currents, ocean 64
cymbals 87
Cyprus 67
Czech Republic 67

D

Daimler 98
Dakar 76
Damascus 68
dams 43, 61
damselfish 64-65
damselfly 60
Danube, River 67
Dar es Salaam 77
Darling, River 70
Darwin 70
Dead Sea 68
deafness 85
deer, roe 51
Delaware 73
delta 61
democracy 108
Denmark 67
density 21
Denver 73
desert
   Gobi 54, 69
   Kalahari 77
   Sahara 54-55, 76-77
deserts 13, **54-55**, 76, 106, 114
   animals of 54-55
Detroit 73
dew 15
Dhaka 69
dhows 116
diesel trains 96-97
digestion **24-25**
dinosaurs 11, 30-31, 36
Diplodocus 30
director 88-89
diving 92
Djibouti 77
Dnieper, River 67
doctors 108
Dodoma 77
Doge's Palace 66
dolphin 31, 42-43, 65
   common 42
Dominica 73
Dominican Republic 73
domus, Roman 111
Don, River 67
Donetsk 67
dormouse 51
double bass 86
Douglas DC-3 Dakota 100
Douglas fir 47
dragonfly 30, 56-57, 60
Dreadnought battleship 95
drink 24
drum, bass 87

drums 86
Dublin 66
dumper trucks 99
dunes 55
Dushanbe 69

E

eagle
   golden 58
   harpy 57
ear 26
eardrum 26
Earth 4, 6, **8-9**, 16-17, 20-21, 58, 63, 64, 88, 102-103, 120
   birth of 8
   interior of 8-9
   life on 6, 8, 31
   orbit of 12
   plates 9, 10, 58
   position in Solar System 6
earthquakes 9, 78, 82, 113
earthworm 50
Easter Island 71
echoes 19
Ecuador 75
eel
   electric 56
   gulper 64
   moray 34, 65
Efe pygmies 79
eggs 32, 39, 41, 48
egret 63
Egypt 76-77
   ancient 16-17, 85, **106-107**
Eiffel Tower 83
El Salvador 73
Elbe, River 67
Elbrus 66-67
electric trains 96-97
electricity 15, 18, 21, **22-23**, 61, 88-89, 96-97, 98
   current 22, 97
   mains 23
   static 22
electronics 23, 88
electrons 22
elements 10, 21
elephant 41, 52, 76
   African 41
   Asian 41
elk 51
Ellesmere Island 73
embryo 29
emperors 112-113, 117, 121
   Chinese 112-113
   Japanese 117
   Mongol 121
   Roman 110
empires **116-117**
   African 117

123

INDEX

ancient American 114-115
Arab 76, 116
Chinese 112
Greek 109, 116
Moghul 117
Mongol 117
Persian 109, 116
Roman 85, 90, 110-111
enamel 28
Endeavour 121
energy 4, 18, 21, 22, 24, 97
engineers 82, 96, 98
engines
  diesel 98
  jet 101
  petrol 98, 100
  rocket 101, 102
  steam 96-97, 98
England 66
English language 85
epiglottis 25
Equator 12-13, 56
Equatorial Guinea 77
equinox 12-13
Eric the Red 121
Erie, Lake 73
Eritrea 77
erosion 60
Estonia 67
Ethiopia 77
Europe **66-67**, 118-119
Everest, Mount 59, 68-69
Everglades 61
evolution 30-31, 105
explorers 94-95, **120-121**
extinction 30-31, 40-41, 57, 61
eyes 19, 27
Eyre, Lake 70

F

Faeroe Islands 66
Falkland Islands 75
Far East 120
farming 12-13, 76, **80-81**, 105, 106, 112-113, 118-119
  arable 80-81
  fruit 80
  livestock 80-81
fats 24
feather star 65
feathers 38
femur 28
ferns 44
feudal system 118
fibre 24
fields 80-81, 119
Fiji 70
film
  projector 89

stars 89
studio 89
films 89
Finland 67
fire 18, 105
fireworks 18
fish 30, **34-35**, 56-57, 60, 62-63, 64-65
  birth of 34
  breathing 34-35
  characteristics of 34
  dangerous 34, 57
  deep-sea 18, 64
  light-producing 18, 64
fishing 65, 72, 105
Five Pillars of Wisdom 91
flamingo 38, 61
fleas 33, 119
floor manager 88
Florida 73
flowers 44-45
flute 87
Flyer 1 100
flying fish 35
focus 19
foetus 29
fog 15
Fokker Dr. 1 triplane 100
food 24-25
foot 28
football 92
forces **20-21**
Ford, Henry 99
Ford Model T 99
forest
  boreal 50
  mangrove 63
forests *see* woodland
fossils 10-11
foundations 83
fox 51
  kit 54
France 66-67, 85, 97, 104, 121
Freetown 76
French Guiana 75
French Polynesia 71
friction 20
frigate bird 39
frog 37, 60
  spawn 37
  tree 56-57, 61
frost 15
fruits 45, 46-47, 80
fuel 11
fungi 45

G

Gabon 77
Gaborone 77
Gagarin, Yuri 102
Galapagos Islands 37, 74

galaxies 4-5
Galileo 5
Galileo space probe 102
gall bladder 24
galleon, Spanish 94-95
Gambia, The 76
Ganges, River 69
gases 21
gazelle, Thomson's 52
gecko, common 36
Genghis Khan 117
Georgetown 75
Georgia (Asia) 68
Georgia (USA) 73
Germany 67, 97
geysers 71
Ghana 77, 117
giant sequoia 47
Gibraltar 66
Gila monster 54
Gilbert Islands 70
gills 34-35
giraffe 41, 52-53, 76
glaciers 48, 59, 60
Glamorous Glennis 101
Glasgow 66
Globtik Tokyo oil tanker 94
glow worms 18
goat 81, 105
Gobi desert 69
gods 90-91, 93, 105, 108
gold 114, 117
Gomera, Canary Islands 84
gondolas 66
gorges 60
  on Venus 6
goshawk 51
government 108
Grand Canyon 55, 73
grasshoppers 32-33
grasslands **52-53**, 76, 114
  animals of 41, 52-53, 76
gravity 20, 63, 88, 102-103
Great Barrier Reef 65, 70
Great Bear Lake 73
Great Plains 114
Great Slave Lake 73
Great Wall of China 113
Great Zimbabwe 117
Greece 67
  ancient 5, 92, **108-109**
Greek language 85, 108
Greenland 48, 72-73, 121
Grenada 73
Guadalajara 73
Guadeloupe 73

Guatemala 73
Guinea 76
Guinea-Bissau 76
guitar, electric 86
Gujarati language 84
Gulf of Guinea 77
Gulf of Mexico 72-73
gums 28
gymnastics 92

H

Hague, The 67
Haida people 72
hail 14
Haiti 73
Hamburg 67
Han dynasty 112
hand 28
Hanoi 69
Harare 77
harp 86
harrow 80
harvest 13, 80-81, 119
Havana 73
Hawaii 16-17
Hawaiian Islands 71
hawkmoth 33
hazel 45
hearing 26-27
heart 25, 29
heat 21, 22
Heaven 90
Hebrews 91
hedgehog 51
helicopters 101
Helsinki 67
hemisphere
  northern 12-13
  southern 12-13
hen 81
heron 60
hibernation 12, 51
hieroglyphics 85, 106-107
high jump 93
Hillary, Edmund 59
Himalayas 58-59, 68-69
Hindi language 85
Hinduism 90-91
hippopotamus 43
hips 28
Ho Chi Minh City 69
hoatzin 56-57
Hollywood 89
homes **78-79**, 111, 114-115
Homo erectus 105
Honduras 73
honeybees 32
hoplites 109
horn 87
horse 54, 92, 96
Horsehead Nebula 4
horse racing 92
Houston 73

Huang, River 69
Hubble Space Telescope 5
Hudson Bay 73
humans 30, 40
  early 80, 84, 104-105
hummingbird 39, 57
Hungarian language 85
Hungary 67
hunting 104-105, 113
Huron, Lake 73
hurricanes 15
hyena 52-53
hypocaust 110

I

Ibadan 77
ibex, Himalayan 58
ibis, scarlet 38
ice 14-15, 21, 48, 59, 104
  cap 48
  crystals 14-15
  pack 48
  polar 48
  skating 92
Ice Ages 104-105
icebergs 48
Iceland 66
ichthyosaur 11
Idaho 73
iguana
  marine 74
  tree 57
Illinois 73
Incas 74, 114
incisors 28
India 68-69, 84, 91, 117
Indian Ocean 64, 68-69, 77
Indiana 73
Indians, South American 74-75
Indonesia 68-69
Indus, River 69
inertia 20
insects 60, **32-33**, 44, 50, 53, 54, 57, 60
  birth of 32
  carrying disease 38
  characteristics of 32
  colonies 32
  killers 33
  largest 33
instruments 86-87
Internet 23
intestines 24
Inuit people 48, 72, 114
inventions, Chinese 113
invertebrates 35
Io 7
Iowa 73
Iran 68-69

124

INDEX

Iraq 68, 84
Ireland 66
iris 27
Irkutsk 69
Irtysh, River 69
Islam 76, 90-91, 116
Islamabad 69
islands 64
Israel 68
Istanbul 67
Isthmus of Panama 74-75
Italy 67, 85, 110-111, 121

J

jacana 39, 57
jaguar 56-57
Jaguar Knights, Aztec 115
Jakarta 68-69
Jamaica 73
Japan 69, 82
    ancient 93, 117
Japanese language 84
Java 69
javelin 92-93
jay 45, 51
jazz 87
Jazz Singer, The 89
jellyfish 35
Jerusalem 68, 91
Jesus Christ 74, 90
jet fighter planes 101
jewellery 114
Jews 90-91
    Hasidic 91
Johannesburg 77
John Hancock Center 83
joints 28
jousting 118
Judaism 90-91
Jumbo Jet 100-101
jumping events 93
junks 94
Jupiter 5, 6-7, 102
    moons of 5, 7

K

K2 59
Kabul 69
Kalahari desert 77
Kamchatka peninsula 69
Kampala 77
kangaroo 41
    red 41
Kansas 73
Karachi 69
Kathmandu 69
kayaks 93
Kayapo Indians 75
Kazakhstan 69

Kentucky 73
Kenya 77
kettledrum *see* timpani
Khartoum 77
Khoisan people, Africa 85
kidneys 25
Kiev 67
Kigali 77
Kilimanjaro 53, 59, 77
kingfish 65
kingfisher 60
Kingston 73
kinkajou 57
Kinshasa 77
Kiribati 70
kite, Everglade 61
kites 113
Kitty Hawk 100
kiwi 71
knee 28
knights 118
koala 41
Kombai people 78
Komodo dragon 36
Korea
    North 69
    South 69
Kremlin 67
krill 42
Krishna 91
Kuala Lumpur 69
Kublai Khan 121
Kuwait 68
Kyrgyzstan 69

L

La Paz 75
Ladoga, Lake 67
lagoons 66
Lagos 77
Lahore 69
Laika 102
lakes 60-61
language 16, **84-85**, 111, 116
Laos 69
larvae 32-33
larynx 25
Lascaux 104
Latin 85, 111
Latvia 67
lava 8-9
Lebanon 68
legionaries, Roman 111
Lena, River 69
lens 19, 27, 89
leopard, snow 58
Lesotho 77
levees 61
Liberia 76
Libreville 77
Libya 77
Liechtenstein 66-67
ligaments 28

light **18-19**, 21, 22, 27
lightning 15, 22-23
lightning conductor 23
Lilongwe 77
Lima 75
limestone 11
limousines 98
limpets 62-63
Limpopo, River 77
Line Islands 71
liners, ocean 95
lion 52-53, 76
lionfish 65
lipas 79
liquids 19, 21
Lisbon 66
Lithuania 67
liver 24-25
"living stones" 55
lizard 36, 54
    anole 56-57
Ljubljana 67
lobster 35
    spiny 64-65
locust 33
Loire, River 66-67
Lomé 77
London 66
long jump 93
lorries 99
Los Angeles 73, 89
Louisiana 73
Luanda 77
Lubumbashi 77
Lumière, Louis and Auguste 89
Lunar Rover 103
lungs 25
Lusaka 77
Luxembourg 67
lynx 51

M

macahuitl 115
macaw 38
    scarlet 57
Macedonia 67, 109
Mackenzie, River 73
Macmillan, Kirkpatrick 99
Madagascar 77
Madeira, River 75
Madras *see* Chennai
Madrid 66
Magellan, Ferdinand 120
Magellan's Strait 75, 120
maglev trains 96
magnets 20
magnetism 20, 96, 113
magnifying glass 19
maidenhair tree 47
Maine 73
maize 81, 105
Malabo 77

Malawi 77
Malaysia 69
Maldives 69
Mali 76-77, 117
mallard 39
Mallard locomotive 96
Malta 67
mammals 30-31, **40-43**
    birth of 40
    characteristics of 40
    land 31, 40-41, 49, 50-58, 60-61, 63, 71, 76, 80-81, 92
    of the air 43
    skulls 41
    teeth 41
    water 42-43, 48-49, 61
mammoth, woolly 104-105
Managua 73
manatee 42
    West Indian 42
Manaus 75
Mandarin Chinese 84
mandrill 40
Manhattan 72
Manila 69
Manitoba 73
manors 119
Maoris 71
maple 45, 47
maps 120
Maputo 77
Marianas Trench 64
markets 76, 116, 118
Marquesas Islands 71
Mars 6
Marseille 67
Marshall Islands 70
marsupials 41, 71
Martinique 73
Maryland 73
Maseru 77
Massachusetts 73
mathematicians 108
mathematics 116
matter **20-21**
Matterhorn 59
Mauritania 76
Maya 84, 115
mayfly 60
Mbabane 77
McKinley, Mount 73
meanders 61
Mecca 68, 91
medicine 116
Mediterranean Sea 66-67, 68, 116
Mekong, River 69
Melbourne 70
Mercedes 98
Mercury 6
mermaid's purse 63
Mesopotamia 84
meteorites 7, 9

meteors 6-7
Mexico 72-73, 115
Mexico City 73
Miami 73
Miao people 84
Michigan 73
Michigan, Lake 73
microphone 23, 89
Middle Ages **118-119**
Middle East, ancient 16
Midnight Sun, Land of the 16
migration 13, 38, 42, 49
Milan 67
Milky Way Galaxy 4-5
millet 81
millipede 33, 50
Mimas 7
minerals 10, 11, 24
Minnesota 73
Minoans 93
Minsk 67
Mir Space Station 103
Mirage 2000 101
Miranda 7
mirrors 19
Mississippi 73
Mississippi, River 73
Missouri 73
Missouri, River 73
mite 50
moat 119
Mogadishu 77
Moldova 67
mole 50
molecules 21
Monaco 66-67
money 113
Mongolia 69, 78
Mongols 116-117, 121
monkey 56
    howler 57
    proboscis 63
    spider 57
    squirrel 57
monorail 97
monotremes 41
Monrovia 76
monsoon 68
Mont-St-Michel 66
Montana 73
Montevideo 75
Montgolfier, Joseph and Étienne 100
Montréal 73
Moon 5, **8-9**, 63, 88, 115
    exploration of 102-103
    phases of 9
moons 6-7, 9, 102
moorhen 60
moraines 59
Morocco 77
Moscow 67
mosques 76, 90
mosquito 33

125

INDEX

moth 33
    Io 56-57
motorcycles 99
mountain ash *see* rowan
mountaineers 59
mountains 13, 53, **58-59**
    animals of 38, 58
movement 27, 29
movies 89
Mozambique 77
mudskipper 63
Muhammad 91, 116
Mumbai 69
mummy, Egyptian 107
Mumtaz Mahal 117
Munich 67
Murray, River 70
Muscat 69
muscles 24, 27, 29
mushrooms 45
music 19, 86-87
musical instruments 19, **86-87**
musicians 86-87
Muslims 76, 90-91
mussels 62-63
Myanmar *see* Burma
myths 108

N

Nairobi 77
Namibia 77
narwhal 49
Nasser, Lake 77
Nauru 70
Ndjamena 77
Nebraska 73
nebulas 4
Negro, River 75
Nepal 69
Neptune 6-7
    moons of 7
nerves 26-27
nests 39, 62
Netherlands 67
nets
    drift 65
    purse seine 65
    trawl 65
Nevada 73
New Brunswick 73
New Caledonia 70
New Delhi 69
New Hampshire 73
New Jersey 73
New Mexico 73
New Orleans 73
New South Wales 70
New York 16, 72-73
New Zealand 70-71
Newfoundland 73
newt 37
    great crested 60
Newton, Isaac 18, 20
Niamey 77

Nicaragua 73
Nicosia 67
Niger 77
Niger, River 77
Nigeria 77
Nile, River 76-77, 106
Nile valley 106
nimbostratus 14
Niue 70
Nizhniy Novgorod 67
nomads 78-79, 117
Normandie ocean liner 95
Normandy 66
North America **72-73**, 114-115
North Carolina 73
North Dakota 73
North Island (New Zealand) 70-71
North Pole 48, 121
North Sea 66-67
Northern Ireland 66
Northern Territory (Australia) 70
Northwest Territories (Canada) 73
Norway 67
Nouakchott 76
Nova Scotia 73
Novaya Zemlya 69
Novosibirsk 69
nuclear power 95
numbers 115
Nunavut 73
nutrients 24-25, 44
nuts 45, 51
Nyasa, Lake 77
nymphs 32

O

oak 46
oases 55
Ob, River 69
oboe 87
Oceania **70-71**
oceans 9, 15, 34-35, 48, 62-63, **64-65**
    animals of 34-35, 38, 42-43, 64-65, 74
    floor 64, 95
octopus 35
Odesa 67
oesophagus 24
Ohio 73
oil tanker 94-95
Oklahoma 73
Olympia 92, 109
Olympic Games 83, 92, 109
Olympus, Mount 108
Oman 68
Ontario 73
Ontario, Lake 73
Orange, River 77

oranges 45
orbit 6-7, 12, 88, 103
orca *see* whale, killer
orchestra 86-87
Oregon 73
organs 27, 28
Orinoco, River 75
Orion 4
Osaka 68-69
Oslo 67
osprey 39
ostrich 38-39
Ottawa 73
otter 60
    sea 43
Ouagadougou 77
owl 51
    burrowing 52
    tawny 51
ox, musk 49
oxen 96
oxygen 25, 44, 46
oystercatcher 63

P

Pacific Ocean 64, 68-69, 70-71, 73, 75, 94-95, 120-121
paddies 81
pagodas 82
Pakistan 69
Palestine 90
palm tree 47
pampas 52
Panama 72-73
pancreas 24
panda, giant 40
pantograph 97
paper 85
Papua New Guinea 70, 84
papyrus 85
Paraguay 75
Paramaribo 75
Paraná, River 75
Paris 16-17, 66, 83
parrotfish 65
particles 22
Patagonia 75
Peary, Robert 121
peas 45
pendulum 17
penguin 38
    Adélie 48
    Emperor 48
Pennsylvania 73
Penny Farthing 99
people, early 80, 84, 104-105
perch 60
percussion 87
periscopes 19
Persian empire 109
Persian Gulf 68
Perth 70
Peru 75

pharaohs 107
Philadelphia 73
Philip of Macedonia 109
Philippines 69
philosophers 108
Phnom Penh 69
Phoenix Islands 70
photosynthesis 44
piano 86
picture writing 84-85, 106, 115
pig 81, 105
pika 58
pilots 100-101
piranha 56-57
pirarucu 56
piston 97, 98
Pitcairn Island 71
plague, bubonic 119
Plains peoples, North America 114-115
planets 4-5, 6-7, 20-21, 102, 115
    coldest 7
    gravity 20
    largest 7
    orbits 6-7
    smallest 7
plankton 44, 49
plants **44-45**, 46-47, 50, 54-56, 60, 62, 80
    feeding 44
    parasites 45
    reproduction 44
platypus, duck-billed 41
plays 108
ploughing 80, 113
plough 80
Pluto 6-7
Poland 67, 91
polar lands 13, **48-49**, 72
    animals of 48, 49
pole vault 92-93
Pole Star 5
Poles 16
poles, magnetic 20
pollen 44
pollination 44
pollution 98
Polo, Marco 121
Polynesia 71, 94
polyps 65
Pompeii 59
pop music 86
Port Moresby 70
Port-au-Prince 73
Porto-Novo 77
Portugal 66
Portuguese man-o'-war 35
potatoes 81
pouches 41
poultry 81
power stations 23
Prague 67

prairie dog 52
prairies 52
prawn 63
praying mantis 32-33
prehistoric life **30-31**
Pretoria 77
Prince Edward Island 73
printing 113
prisms 18
producer 89
production control room 88
programmes, television 88-89
Promised Land 91
propellers 94, 100-101
proteins 24
protons 22
pseudoscorpion 50
pterosaurs 31
Puerto Rico 73
puffin 62
pupil 27
pygmies 79
Pyongyang 69
Pyramid of the Sun 115
pyramids 82, 106-107, 115
Pyrenees 66
python, Indian 37

Q

Qatar 68
Qin dynasty 112
Québec 73
Quechua 74
Queensland 70
Quito 75
Qur'an 91

R

Rabat 77
rabbit 51
    swamp 61
racing cars 98
racoon 61
radio 88-89
Rafflesia 45
rafts 94
railways 96-97
rain 14-15, 68
rainbow 18
rainforest 40, 45, **56-57**, 74-76, 79, 84, 115
    Amazonian 40
    animals of 40, 56-57
    peoples of 56
rat 41, 119
    kangaroo 54
rat-tail fish 64
rattlesnake 52
ray 34

INDEX

eagle 65
Recife 75
rectum 24
"Red Baron" 100
Red Sea 68, 77
reed warbler 60
reefs 65
reflection 19
reflex 27
reindeer 49, 51
religions 76, 82, **90-91**, 106-107, 116
reptiles 30-31, **36-37**, 54, 56-57, 61, 63, 65, 74
    birth of 36
    characteristics of 36
reservoirs 61
retina 27
Reykjavik 66
Rhine, River 67
rhinoceros 41
    black 41
    Javan 57
Rhode Island 73
Rhône, River 67
rhythm 86
ribs 28
rice 81
Richthofen, Manfred von 100
Riga 67
Rio de Janeiro 74-75, 79
Rio Grande, River 73
rivers 15, 55, 56, **60-61**
    animals of 36-37, 41-43, 60-61
Riyadh 68
roadrunner 54
road transport **98-99**
roads 98-99, 114
    Roman 98, 110
rock music 86
rock pools 63
Rocket, Stephenson's 96
rockets 19, 102-103, 113
rocks **10-11**, 60-61, 62
    igneous 10
    metamorphic 10
    sedimentary 10-11, 55
Rocky Mountains 58, 72-73
rollers, heavy 99
Romania 67
Romans 59, 85, 90, 98, **110-111**
    emperors 110
Rome 67
    ancient 59, 85, 90, 98, 110-111
Rotorua 71
rowan 47
running 93
Russia 51, 67, 69, 102-3

Russian language 85
Rutan, Dick 101
Rwanda 77
rye 81

S

saguaro cactus 54
Sahara Desert 77
sailors 95
sails 94-95
St. Basil's Cathedral 67
St. Lawrence, River 73
St. Louis 73
St. Lucia 73
St. Peter's basilica 82
St. Petersburg 67
St. Vincent 73
Sakhalin Island 69
salamander, blue 37
saliva 24
salmon 34
Samoa 70
Samara 67
sampans 78
samurai 117
San Francisco 73
San José 73
San Marino 67
San Salvador 73
sand 55, 62-63
Santiago 75
Santo Domingo 73
San'a 68
São Paulo 75
Sarajevo 67
Sardinia 67
Saskatchewan 73
satellites 14, 88-89, 102-103, 120
Saturn 6-7
    moons of 7
Saturn V rocket 102
Saudi Arabia 68, 91
savannah 52-53
saxophone 87
Scandinavia 16, 121
schichi-go-san 68
scientists 48, 108
scorpion 33, 54
Scotland 66
Scott, Robert 121
scribes 107
sea *see* ocean
sea anemone 64-65
sea cow *see* manatee
sea lions 42
sea slug 65
sea spider 64
sea urchin 64-65
SeaCat catamaran 95
seagull 62
seahorse 34, 64-65
seal 42, 49
    leopard 42, 48
    northern fur 42
seashore 10, **62-63**

animals of 62-63
seasons **12-13**, 51
Seattle 73
seaweed 44, 62
seed drill 80
seeds 44-45, 46-47, 80-81
seismograph 113
Senegal 76
senses 26
Seoul 68-69
shadows 18
shaduf 106
Shah Jahan 117
Shang dynasty 112-113
Shanghai 69
shantytowns 74, 79
Shanxi province, China 78
shark 34
    hammerhead 64-65
    tiger 34-35
sheep 81
shellfish 48
Shi Huangdi 112
shield bug 33
ships 21, 88, **94-95**, 109, 116, 120-121
Shiva the Destroyer 91
shoguns 117
shooting stars 7
showjumping 92
shrimp 35
Siberia 68-69
Sicily 67
Siddhartha Gautama 91
sidewinder 54
siege 119
Sierra Leone 76
sight 19, 26-27
sign language 85
silicon chips 23
Silk Road 113
silver 114
Singapore 69
singing 19, 86
Sirius 4
skeleton **28-29**
skiing 93
skin 27
Skopje 67
skyscrapers 72, 83
sloth 40, 56-57
    three-toed 40
Slovakia 67
Slovenia 67
slug 50
smell 26-27
snail 50, 60
    pond 60
snake 36-37
    tree 56-57
snow 14-15, 48, 59
snowflakes 15
Society Islands 71
Sofia 67
soil 11, 50-51, 119

Solar System **6-7**
    exploration of 102-103
soldiers
    in Middle Ages 119
    Roman 110
    Spartan 109
solids 19, 21
Solomon Islands 70
solstice, summer 12-13
Somalia 77
sound **18-19**, 26, 88-89
    speed of 101
South Africa 77
South America 56, **74-75**, 85, 114-115, 120
South Australia 70
South Carolina 73
South China Sea 69
South Dakota 73
South Island (New Zealand) 70
South Pole 48, 121
Soviet Union 102
space 4-5, 6-7, 102-103, 120
    probes 102
    stations 103
    suits 103
    travel **102-103**
Space Shuttle 102-103
Spain 66, 85, 94-95, 120
Spanish language 85
Sparta 109
spears 104
spectrum 18
speech 25, 27
sperm 29
Spice Islands 120
spider 33, 50, 57
    bird-eating 57
    webs 33
spinal cord 26-27
spine 26, 28
Spitfire 101
sponge, red 65
spoonbill 61
spores 44-45
sports **92-93**, 109, 110-111, 115, 118
spring 12
springs 60
springtail 50
Sputnik 1 102
squirrel 45
    grey 51
    ground *see* prairie dog
    red 51
Sri Lanka 69
stadium 93
    Munich Olympic 83
stalactites 11
stalagmites 11
starfish 35, 62-65
    crown-of-thorns 64

stars **4-5**, 6, 94, 115
    birth of 4
    brightest 4
    gravity 20
    how to find 5
    Pole Star 5
    Sirius 4
    studying 5
    Sun 4-5, 6-7
statues 112
steam engine, first 96
steam
    power 96-97, 98
    trains 96-97
Stegosaurus 31
Stephenson, George and Robert 96
steppes 52
stickleback 60
stingray 34
stoat 51
Stockholm 67
stomach 24
stonefish 34-35
Stonehenge 17
stork, marabou 53
storms 15
stratocumulus 14
stratus 14
streams 56, 60
studios 88-89
stupas 91
submarines 95
submersibles 95
Sucre 75
Sudan 76-77
Sugar Loaf mountain 74
Sulawesi 69
Sumatra 69
Sumerians 84
summer 13, 16
Sumo wrestling 93
Sun 4-5, 6-7, 8-9, 12-13, 15, 16-17, 18, 21, 63, 115
    distance from Earth 4
    size of 6
sundial 17
sunflower 45
sunlight 18
sunspots 6
Superior, Lake 73
Suriname 75
Swahili language 85
Swaziland 77
sweat 27
Sweden 67
sweet chestnut 47
swift 38
swimming 93
Switzerland 67
Sydney 70
Sydney Opera House 83
synagogues 90
Syria 68

127

INDEX

T

tadpoles 37
Tagus, River 66
taiga 51
Taipei 69
Taiwan 69
Taj Mahal 117
Tajikistan 69
Tallinn 67
Talmud 91
tamarind, golden 57
Tanganyika, Lake 77
Tanzania 77
tapir 56-57
tarpon 61
Tashkent 69
Tasman Sea 70
Tasmania 70
taste 26-27
taste buds 26
Tbilisi 68
teepees 115
teeth 24, 28, 41
Tegucigalpa 73
Tehran 68
telephones 23, 88
telescopes 5
television **88-89**
temperate climate 12-13
temples 82, 90-91, 106, 108, 115
Tennessee 73
tennis 92
tents 78-79, 104, 115
Tenzing Norgay 59
Teotihuacan 115
termite 32, 53
    soldier 53
tern, Arctic 49
terraces 81
Texas 73
TGV 97
Thai language 85
Thailand 69
theatres 108
throwing sports 93
thrush, song 51
thunder 15, 22
thunderclouds 15
thunderstorms 22
Tibet 69
tides 63
    neap 63
    spring 63
tiger 40
Timbuktu 77, 121
time **16-17**
Timor 69
timpani 87
tin 113
"Tin Lizzie" 99
Tiranë 67
tit, great 51
Titicaca, Lake 75
toad 37
fire-bellied 37
spawn 60
Suriname 56-57
toadstool 45, 51
    fly agaric 45
Togo 77
Tokelau Islands 70
Tokyo 16-17, 68-69
tombs 107, 117
Tonga 70
tongue 24, 26-27
tools 104-105, 113, 114
Torah 91
tornadoes 15
Toronto 73
torpedoes 95
tortoise 36-37
    Galapagos giant 37, 74
totem poles 72
toucan 57
touch 26-27
tournaments 118
trachea 25
trade
    ancient China 113
    Arab 76, 116
    in Middle Ages 118
trains **96-97**, 120
transformers, electrical 23
transmission station 89
trees 12-13, 45, **46-47**, 50-51, 56-57, 80
    coniferous 46, 50-51
    deciduous 12, 46, 50-51
    evergreen 46
    growth of 47
    leaves 47
    structure of 46
    uses of 46, 57
trenches, ocean 64
Trevithick, Richard 96
triangle 87
triceps 29
Trieste submersible 95
Trinidad and Tobago 73
tripodfish 64
Tripoli 77
triremes 109
Triton 7
trombones 87
Tropic of Cancer 12
Tropic of Capricorn 13
trumpets 19, 87
Tuamotu Archipelago 71
Tuareg people 55
tuba 87
tundra 49, 72
Tunis 77
Tunisia 77
Turkana, Lake 77
Turkey 67-68
Turkmenistan 69
turtle 36-37, 65
    marine 64-65
    river 57
Tuvalu 70
tyres 98-99

U

Uganda 77
Ukraine 67
Ulan Bator 69
ultrasound 19
Uluru 70
umbilical cord 29
umbrellas 113
underground trains 97
United Arab Emirates 68
United Kingdom 66
United States of America 72-73
Universe 4-5
Ural mountains 66-67, 69
Uranus 6-7
    moons of 7
urine 25
Uruguay 75
Utah 73
Uzbekistan 69

V

valleys 60
valves 25
Vancouver 73
Vanuatu 70
vaporetto 66
Vatican City 66-67, 82
veins 25
Venezuela 75
Venice 66-67, 121
Venus 6
Venus fly trap 45
Vermont 73
Vesuvius 59
Viangchan 69
vibrations 19, 26
Victoria 70
Victoria Falls 77
Victoria Island 73
Victoria, Lake 76-77
video 88-89
videocassette recorder 88-89
Vienna 67
Vietnam 69
Vikings 94, 121
Vilnius 67
vine, jungle 45
viola 86
violin 86
viperfish 64
Virginia 73
Vishnu the Preserver 91
vitamins 24
Vittoria 120
Vladivostok 69
voice 86
volcanoes 8-9, 59, 64, 71
    on Jupiter 7
    on Venus 6
vole 51
    water 60
Volga, River 66-67
Volgograd 67
Volkswagen 99
volleyball, beach 93
Volta, River 77
Voyager 101
vulture 38

W

wa'a kaula 94
Wales 66
Wallis and Futuna 70
walnut 45
walrus 48-49
warplanes 100-101
warriors
    Aztec 115
    Mongol 116-117
    North American plains 114
    Samurai 117
    Spartan 109
Warsaw 67
warships 95
    Greek 109
warthog 52
Washington 73
wasp 32
water 14-15, 21, 44, 60-65, 97
    cycle 14, 60
water boatman 60
water scorpion 60
waterfalls 60
waves 63
    radio 88-89
    sound 19
weapons 113-114
weather 12-13, **14-15**, 64, 88
    forecasting 14
Wellington 70
West Virginia 73
Western Australia 70
Western Sahara 76
Western Wall, Jerusalem 91
wetlands 61
whale 31, 42, 49
    blue 49
    grey 42
    humpback 49
    killer 49
wheat 81, 119
wheelbarrows 113
whelks 62
wildebeest 52-53
Windhoek 77
windmills 119
windpipe *see* trachea
winds 15, 94
wings, aircraft 101
Winnipeg 73
Winnipeg, Lake 73
winter 12, 16
Wisconsin 73
Wodaabe 77
wolf 49
    grey 41
womb 29
wombat 41
woodlands **50-51**
    animals of 50-51
    coniferous 51
    deciduous 51
woodlouse 50
woodpecker 39
    Gila 54
    green 51
woodwind 87
World Trade Center 72
worms 60
worship 90-91
Wright, Wilbur and Orville 100
writing **84-85**, 104
    earliest 84
Wuhan 69
Wuppertal 97
Wyoming 73

XY

Xianggang (Hong Kong) 69
yak 58
Yakushi pagoda, Japan 82
Yangon 69, 91
Yangtse, River 68-69
Yaoundé 77
Yeager, Chuck 101
Yeager, Jeana 101
Yellow River 112
Yemen 68
Yenisei, River 69
Yerevan 68
Yucatán Peninsula 73
Yugoslavia 67
Yukon 73
yurts 78

Z

Zagreb 67
Zambezi, River 77
Zambia 77
zebra 41, 52-53
Zeus 108
Zimbabwe 77, 117
zoos 57

128